I0134747

HOLDING THE FORT

By: Robert L. Kelly

I was an inmate in America's largest prison. I fought the battle of recidivism by becoming a GED instructor, and created a unique class which taught a group of bad men how to become millionaire, Wall Street Traders.

It is the true story of how I shared my Christian faith in one of America's most dangerous places, and became branded "The White Devil," by radical Islamists inside Fort Dix.

I also nearly died in the process.

A **PUBLICATION**
JACKASS BANKER™

HOLDING THE FORT

By: Robert L. Kelly

Library of Congress Control Number: 2017949231
All Rights Reserved. Printed in the U.S.A.
© 2017 Robert L. Kelly

Jack Assbanker and the neon-striped zebra are trademarks of Jackass Banker, LLC. Reproduction, or translation, of any part of this work beyond what is permitted by the 1976 United States Copyright Act without the express written permission of the copyright owner, is unlawful. Requests for permission, or further information, should be addressed to the publisher at (or, via email at jackassbanker@gmail.com):

Jack Assbanker™ Publications
412 N. Main Street, Ste. 100
Buffalo, WY 82834

A   PUBLICATION
JACKASS BANKER™

ACKNOWLEDGEMENTS

This book is written to all the very good men I met in prison. While there were many bad apples at Fort Dix, I found the life, servitude, brotherhood, humility and grace among the men who society has left behind, a life-changer. I am forever grateful to those who helped shape and mold my life there. Society considers us now, all "bad" men---but I, for one, know different.

To the men who knew I was there for them at any time of the night or day, and especially to the men who saved my life and violated Bureau of Prison regulations to do so, I am eternally grateful.

In this regard, I expressly and particularly want to thank Larry Chin and Al Cipoletti. They, along with Pablo Cruz, Darnell Duckett (aka,"Oz") and Joe Kerns saved me on October 7, 2015 and in the days which followed. The bravery of Larry and Al, especially, needs to be called out and applauded. It is the spirit of taking care of your brother first, before yourself, which puts these men directly in the spirit and mind-set of Jesus Christ, whether these men know it, or not.

To the men in ESL ("English as a Second Language") and Spanish GED, who went from disdaining me and my efforts to teach them, to understanding my true desire to help them find a better path in life, I say "Muchas Gracias!" To Ricky Lopez, Pablo Cruz, Rosado, Sr. Perez, Caballo, Jose, Sr. Roman, "Don" Rafael and many, many others, you will always be remembered by me.

To Mr. Brown, Mr. Gray, Troy (the "$85 million man"), "DJ" Spence, Larry, Taylor, Chet, Dillon Edwards, Mr. Love, and the one and only "I'm tired, Joe"---Jeffrey Eugene, and everyone who spent many great hours learning math, science, English, and social studies, please know I will cherish the memories of our discussions, always.

They hold a special place in my heart and I wish you all the best life can bring!

The world can learn from our camaraderie, as we found a way for Christians, Muslims, Jews, Buddhists and even men of no faith to find a way to share a good laugh together---despite our striking differences in background and experience.

Perhaps our time in class helped all of us take our minds off of the isolation and loneliness which prison drapes over every man...and indeed, every one of us missed our families, and loved ones. As I look back on the experience, this was the tie which bound us all together. To be sure, these men were all pillars of strength to me while I was imprisoned.

Thanks, guys.

To the men who were brave enough to take my "Trade Like a Turtle" class, thank you for putting up with me and my demanding ways in the classroom! To change one's life and make it on Wall Street (either publicly, or privately), you have to be smart, tough and fast---not unlike the way in which many men in prison have been brought up on the "street."

Each of the students in the Turtle class seemed to grasp they were learning something extremely special, and looked to me for guidance---both intellectually, and psychologically. To a man, they came to understand the importance of my insistence on learning the math, sticking to a game plan and insisting on excellence, above all. They learned they were being provided the tools they needed to have a chance to find real success in the future (and legal, to boot), with some very powerful, newly honed skills.

I was honored to have had the opportunity to teach men whom society thinks are "bad." Most people in prison never even had a chance out of the gates in life, and many others got caught in the promulgation of strangulating regulations in the post-Madoff era.

This, combined with the politicized and plundering prosecution of non-banking, white-collar America during the Obama years (and particularly of "little guys" who were not part of big corporations and didn't have the resources to defend themselves), resulted in the most overcrowded and horrific prison conditions in the modern history of our county.

All of us sent off to prison are deemed "felons," or as the politically correct now call us, "ex-offenders." Regardless of the new identity change and branding, society has burned a Scarlet letter across our chests, and disenfranchised us, truly casting us off as, "deplorables."

As this book will show you, this is a bit of problem, because this branding and disenfranchisement is being applied to *between* 40-60 million American citizens who have been arrested and hauled off to jail, at some point in their lives.

Finally, as I close this acknowledgement, I want to remember my "spacemate," Mike MacCaull (thanks for always having my back, Mike), as well as, Willie Caraballo, Sean Contee, Dave Connolly, Shawn Lee, Leo Reyes, John Barnes, Alberto Vilar, Michael Winans, Rohan Wijetihaka and all the guys in my aisle.

Thank you for accepting me and being great brothers.

To my great friend, Phil Hamilton, leader of the Catholic Church at Fort Dix, and all the men attending Catholic and Christian services, you especially are always, always remembered and are never, ever forgotten. Thank you for being an anchor of hope in my life, and always being faithful to our Lord and Savior, Jesus Christ.

I wish everyone God's blessings with the swift return to your families and loved ones, for those of you who are not yet released from prison.

This book is dedicated to those men I had to leave behind and to:

The men who are still left, <u>Holding the Fort</u>.

About The Federal Reserve Trilogy:

Mr. Kelly's warnings relating to the approaching credit crisis in 2007 and 2008 helped some people avoid devastating losses in their portfolios, because they took action *before* the crisis erupted. As everyone knows, ultimately, there was a complete stock-market meltdown and difficulty! In a "Déjà vu, all-over again" moment, Mr. Kelly is sounding the alarm bells EVEN LOUDER, yet another time.

The Federal Reserve Trilogy issues an urgent warning to all people and documents the causes, the motivations and the outcome of a devastating economic firestorm, called "D'Apocalypse™." It is swiftly approaching and set to strike nations all over the world. The trilogy unveils the secret plans of the bankers and global elite to collapse the financial system and seize control of the world's monetary policy and money supply systems. Mr. Kelly sleuths out the facts, figures, history, charts and patterns, revealing their master strategy, while compellingly providing nations, corporations and all wealth classes, specific recommendations to avoid disaster during this upcoming grab for power. The end result of D'Apocalypse™ will be social devastation and a severe economic meltdown, purposely caused by the bankers and the elite. It will rain ruin on hundreds of millions of people—with the onset of a dangerous and real global war, the likely result!

There are very few people, or organizations, with the ability to analyze and distill sets of complex information into understandable, tactical and easy-to-implement action plans. Mr. Kelly amply demonstrates these abilities, with the writing of The Federal Reserve Trilogy.

The $30 Trillion Heist—Scene Of The Crime?, and The $30 Trillion Heist—Follow The Money!, spell out how the banks, the Federal Reserve and the elite heisted nearly $30 Trillion from U.S. taxpayers—without the knowledge, or consent of Congress. Importantly, the books uncover what they are doing with this heist money. D'Apocalypse™ Now! unveils the logical conclusion and aftermath of the great heist. Reading it will help families, hedge funds, companies, and nations, avoid the worst of this purposely engineered, financial catastrophe.

Fortunes will be made and lost during the Great D'Apocalypse™ and The Federal Reserve Trilogy empowers you to assess the facts and compelling evidence, allowing you to make powerful and intelligent decisions during the course of the next several years. It is a set of books you will want to have in digital format because of their robust links, marvelous images, graphics and artwork. You may also want a hard copy for backup, just in case the lights go out and things really get bad!

A Jack Assbanker™ Publication

TABLE OF CONTENTS

Acknowledgements i

Introduction 1

Chapter 1 5

The Chips Were Down 5

Chapter 2 7

Fort Dix & Prison 7

Chapter 3 23

Pre-Entry 23

Chapter 4 37

The Guards 37

Chapter 5 41

The Camp 41

Chapter 6 51

Classes Start & Chaos Reigns 51

Chapter 7 75

Beluga Caviar 75

Chapter 8 91

Some Guys Just Grow Up Tough 91

Chapter 9 109

Teaching Men To Fish 109

Chapter 10 121

December 2014 –Eureka! 121

Chapter 11 127

The Black Cracker 127

Chapter 12 143

How to Trade Like a Turtle 143

Chapter 13 153

A Sea of Faces 153

Chapter 14 161

The Eleven Disciples 161

Chapter 15 169

The Wheat's Killing Me, Bob! 169

Chapter 16 179

The Interview 179

Chapter 17   **185**
   Results of Turtle Trading   185
Chapter 18   **213**
   The Final Wheat Lesson   213
Chapter 19   **219**
   Battle Scars With The BOP   219
Chapter 20   **259**
   Radical Islam Branded me The "White Devil"   259
Chapter 21   **291**
   The Day I Nearly Died   291
Chapter 22   **315**
   "Ace" Hit With The Bricks   315
Chapter 23   **323**
   The Stone Wall Of Silence   323
   May The Road Rise Up To Meet You   332
Author's Personal Note   **333**
   Invitation to Make a Commitment   333

Holding the Fort is a work of non-fiction. Names, characters, places, and incidents are the product of the author's memory and notes from his experience in America's largest prison, Fort Dix Federal Correctional Institution, thirty miles east and outside of Philadelphia, Pennsylvania. In a few cases, the author has changed the names of certain individuals to protect their identity; however the story of Holding the Fort is based on actual facts and circumstances during Mr. Kelly's prison experience.

The fog of battle, especially in a prison, takes a toll on a person, and you will see from these pages, Mr. Kelly fought a war. No one's memory is 100% perfect, but Mr. Kelly took extensive notes in prison and this story is a realistic portrayal of prison life and the significant problems related to recidivism.

Other works by Robert L. Kelly include The Federal Reserve Trilogy and the Colt Jackson Thriller and Adventure Stories. The three books about The Federal Reserve Trilogy comprise a breakthrough in investigative journalism on the subject of The Federal Reserve System and the great credit crisis.

The trilogy's first two books are The $30 Trillion Heist---Scene Of The Crime? and The $30 Trillion Heist---Follow The Money! while the third book is D'Apocalypse™ Now!---The Doomsday Cycle, prognosticates our economic future, as a result of the great $30 Trillion heist. Mr. Kelly's uncanny market forecasts in D'Apocalypse Now! in the equity, precious metals and currency markets (written in 2013 and published in February of 2014), are stunning and eerily accurate.

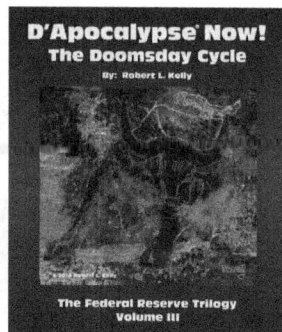

Everyone should be interested in reading about how the Fed, the big banks and the uber elite secretly heisted, without the consent of Congress, nearly $30 Trillion in taxpayer money to bail themselves out from losses they incurred during the credit crisis.

D'Apocalypse Now!--The Doomsday Cycle accurately and specifically predicted the Dow would rise (when the Dow was sitting at about 15,500) to between 22,000 and 30,000 (it already reached nearly 22,000 during 2017, the publication year of this book). It also predicted a collapsing Euro and accurately predicted the drop in the price of gold to the $1100/ounce area, all of which came true. These forecasts were written when the Euro was at $1.36 (i.e., the Euro hit a temporary low of $1.03 in early 2017) and gold was close to $2,000 an ounce when the book was written! Mr. Kelly has also forecasts a huge price movement in gold UPWARD, after certain price projections are hit. This forecast of gold's big move is not yet fulfilled, and reading it now, puts the reader in an interesting position to take advantage of the coming meteoric rise in this precious metal.

Important predictions are left to be fulfilled, but the odds of being correct for the predictions which came true approach 1000-1 (depending on the probability tree used). As a result, D'Apocalypse Now!--The Doomsday Cycle rivals virtually any pundit on television, or in the media. Few people in the world can say they have achieved the kind of prediction-rate success found in this book. Most pundits are always bearish, or always bullish. Mr. Kelly's objective approach to market fluidity helps readers avoid the countless pundits who are always bearish, or always bullish. This is especially true for the cadre of Gold Bugs in the world. These people couldn't trade their way out of a paper bag.

Blood Moon Over D'Apocalypse and Black Storm: Curse on the Caliphate bring to life the figure of Commander "Colt Jackson." Colt is a Christian action hero, armed with some of the world's most advanced technologies, and is an elite member of the Navy SEALS. He fights against treason, and threats against America---both on the home front, and abroad.

He also is entangled between two amazingly, beautiful and intelligent women. Together with his SEAL team, the support of the intelligence agencies and the President himself, he confronts some of the most daunting and challenging threats to our nation. Mr. Kelly has been praised as the next "Tom Clancy," along with letters of thanks from the Chairman of the Joint Chiefs of Staff. Mr. Kelly's devotion to realism, action and detail in his writings make for page-turning excitement.

"Blood Moon" makes it possible for the common man to understand how treason can percolate to the highest levels of finance in the United States, while "Black Storm" is a sweeping epic where Commander Jackson is fighting ISIL, and he must fend off a North Korean nuclear EMP attack against the United States. Both of these books are action-packed page turners, and you won't be able to put them down once you start reading.

© 2014 Robert L. Kelly

"FEDERAL RESERVE   TOP SECRET,"

"And I sincerely believe, with you, that banking establishments are more dangerous than standing armies; and that the principle of spending money to be paid by posterity, under the name of funding, is but swindling futurity on a large scale. I salute you with constant friendship and respect."
---THOMAS JEFFERSON

(Source: The Works of Thomas Jefferson in Twelve Volumes. Federal Edition. Collected and Edited by Paul Leicester Ford. Thomas Jefferson to John Taylor, Monticello, May 28, 1816 and retrieved from:
http://memory.loc.gov/cgi-bin/query/r?ammem/mtj:@field(DOCID+@lit(tj110172))).

The cartoon above was adapted from an Abraham Lincoln-era cartoon titled, "The 'Ins' and the 'Outs,'" created by Frank Leslie's Budget of Fun, published originally in 1861. It may be retrieved at: http://www.abrahamlincolnsclassroom.org/Cartoon_Corner/index3.asp?ID=357&TypeID=4)).

INTRODUCTION

On September 23, 2014, Robert Kelly was sentenced to serve a prison term of twenty-seven months in a Bureau of Prisons facility in the Northeast region of the United States. During his time incarcerated, he became one of the BOP's leading GED teachers, and also taught a group of inmates how to trade on Wall Street---with the group earning millions of dollars on an annualized basis.

He stood strong in his Christian faith and was branded the "White Devil," by elements of radical Islam and men inside the prison. He also nearly died during his prison term---an outcome hardly ordained, or envisioned, by the judge who sentenced him.

As part of his plea agreement, he must say he was guilty, and he cannot enter into any kind of a collateral attack on his sentence, or verdict he received from the government. He also can never appeal his verdict with any court.

Most people don't realize these kinds of restrictions and conditions are placed, integrally, in most plea agreements; however, it sheds light on *why* there aren't more outcries of injustice from the 40,000,000+ convicted felons and ex-offenders we have in America today.

Millions of these people entered into plea bargain agreements---and the restrictions within them create FEAR.

1

The last thing any convicted felon wants is to go back to the hellhole called a Federal Correctional Institution ("FCI") in the United States, for potentially violating conditions of his, or her, release!

In 2013, the circumstances leading up to Mr. Kelly's arrest and his decision to enter into a plea bargain agreement were written about in the introduction of his first book, <u>The Thirty Trillion Heist---The Federal Reserve, Scene of the Crime?</u> the first book in <u>The Federal Reserve Trilogy</u> (as published in February 2014). That introduction was written *before* his plea bargain and sentencing, which took place later in 2014.

While writing <u>The Federal Reserve Trilogy</u>, Mr. Kelly was determined to fight his indictment via a trial and plea of "not guilty." Time, and counsel, changed his mind, as history now shows. The decision by Mr. Kelly to take a plea deal and plead "guilty," came down to a business decision about his life---and ultimately as a Christian, he asked himself, *"Could I have done MORE to disclose information---even though I had hired some of the best attorneys and accountants to make <u>sure</u> related-party transactions were properly made?"*

Mr. Kelly's case was a disclosure case regarding a decade-old software company he privately built and owned, which provided software services to a different company he was running, as its CEO.

In any event, the answer for Mr. Kelly was, *"Yes, I could have."* This is one of the reasons he told the court through his allocution he failed to tell his investors about the *profits* he received from his privately-owned software company. The existence of the related-party contracts and the dollar amounts involved in those international transactions, were previously disclosed to the penny *many* times at the Companies House in England (i.e., the "Companies House" is the U.K.'s version of the SEC's "Edgar" public reporting system), where the company and/or its predecessors had been operating, since 2004. It was also where the contracts were entered into, between the two different companies Mr. Kelly would ultimately run.

Other interesting aspects of the case are the *period* during which Mr. Kelly was accused of wrongdoing, and *when*, exactly, he was arrested and prosecuted. The government's charges were for events during the *time period* at the height of the financial crisis (up to and around, 2007-2008) and Mr. Kelly was arrested and sentenced at the height and zenith of the Obama Administration's attack on non-banker, white-collar executives, and particularly the "little guys," who didn't have the resources to fight blistering government attacks. As history has demonstrated, this marks a period in which before and after, the federal government didn't put a *single* banker in jail, despite the criminal guilty pleas entered into by many banks and financial institutions around the world.

Many believe Mr. Kelly was so upset over being charged with a crime, he became propelled and compelled to write The Federal Reserve Trilogy. These three books detail like no others, the wrong doings of the banks, the elite and the Federal Reserve during, and after, the financial crisis.

"Holding the Fort." is dedicated to a story about change---change for the better by Mr. Kelly and many men he "rode the river with" in prison, and the changes still required in the Bureau of Prisons to successfully reduce recidivism.

This story is indeed about "Holding the Fort" when the chips are down. It is about doing the very best you can, under the most trying circumstances life can throw at you.

Mr. Kelly's many challenges, and small victories, are hoped to be an inspiration for those trying to do the right thing in life, under difficult circumstances. Holding the Fort honorably commemorates the many men Mr. Kelly met in prison---many of whom were 100% innocent. These men have had years of their lives stolen from them.

On the fateful day of September 23, 2014, Mr. Kelly, with his eyes watering, peered up from the intimidating and cavernous, Southern District of Manhattan federal courtroom, awaiting his judgement from his judge.

"Robert Kelly, this court sentences you to serve a term of twenty-seven months and you are to report to the Bureau of Prisons on November 3, 2014."

Down came the gavel and...

"BAM!"

---So ordered Judge Crotty, of the Southern District of Manhattan, and the federal court system, on September 23, 2014.

Mr. Kelly's 27-month saga would now begin.

This is his incredible and true story.

CHAPTER 1

THE CHIPS WERE DOWN

It was at this moment, I knew my world would continue upside down for at least the next two years. The last six years, since the credit crisis, had been a financial and legal hurricane for me. I dreaded to even think about what these next steps of the future might bring.

The most difficult part of the ordeal, up to this time, was worrying about what would happen to my significant other, and my family. I had been able to successfully compartmentalize the looming disaster ripping through my life, and had managed to remain focused---writing several books, while I was awaiting a trial.

Ultimately, I decided to enter into a plea-agreement, to avoid the sentencing dangers a trial can bring---particularly in the Southern District of New York.

As the CEO of a company, I had been accused of securities and wire fraud, and was facing two counts---each with a term of potentially, 20-year sentencing periods. With the Southern District's federal court system boasting a 98% conviction rate, along with a history of harsh sentences if you go all the way to trial, *and lose*, I decided to do a deal and throw myself on the mercy of the court.

I was also financially exhausted and ready for everything to just "be over."

The chips were really down for me, as I had just been crushed by the ruthless and awesome might of the United States Government, with all of its formidable power.

CHAPTER 2

FORT DIX & PRISON

After my sentencing, I would learn from the Bureau of Prisons ("BOP"), I was being ordered to enter the hallowed walls of Fort Dix Federal Correctional Institution on Monday, the third of November, 2014. This, of course, was a great unknown to me, at the time.

Fort Dix imprisons over 4,000 inmates and is located about thirty miles outside Philadelphia, PA---heading due east. Fort Dix is the single, largest Federal Correctional Institution ("FCI") within the BOP and its location, regionally speaking, guarantees its supply of prisoners comes primarily from the Northeast region of the United States.

Mostly, this means inmates originate from the inner cities from some of our nation's toughest places: New York City, Philadelphia, Baltimore, Washington D.C., and Boston. Inmates from these areas easily make up the majority of this prison population. Like most prisons, it's rough and tough.

Fort Dix also maintains a large Hispanic population of inmates and is one of the main destinations for thousands of Puerto Ricans unlucky enough to be caught in the jaws of the U.S. Justice system. Puerto Rico does not have an FCI on its island, and about a third of the inmates at Fort Dix hail from there, or some other Hispanic location.

Fort Dix actually has three *different* prisons on its grounds. I was ordered to be interned at its "Camp." When you speak to people on the outside of prison walls, prison "Camps" have an image of being soft and cushy. In fact, before I was incarcerated, one person was naïve enough to ask if there was a swimming pool and tennis courts there, and then went on to provide the unsolicited and insincere advice to my loved ones, "Don't worry...he'll be back home in six months."

This person was, and still is, absolutely clueless when it comes to anything related to the BOP and life in America's prison systems.

It is astonishing most Americans ignore the reality of the ugly underbelly of prison life. Prisons and jails make a direct and powerful impact on *at least* 40,000,000 American lives, and unfortunately, most prisoners *return* to prison, because they commit other crimes and contribute significantly to the escalating violence across our country.

Lawyer: 68 Million Americans Have Criminal Records – More Than Population of France

(CNSNews.com) – "A trial lawyer who testified last month before the House Committee on the Judiciary Over-Criminalization Task Force said the U.S. is "in danger of becoming a nation of criminals," estimating that over 68 million Americans have criminal records – more than the population of France." (source: "Lawyer: 68 Million Americans Have Criminal Records-More Than Population of France," by Melanie Arter, 7/15/14, CNS News, http://www.cnsnews.com/news/article/melanie-hunter/lawyer-68-million-americans-have-criminal-records-more-population-france).

There were only 138,884,643 "Voting Eligible Population Ballots" for the 2016 Presidential election (60 percent of the voter eligible population). 40,000,000 prisoners amount to 30% of the voting public, but also represents, about 15% of the entire population of the United States. Most Americans don't realize the United States has 5% of the world's population, but holds 25% of the world's *prison population!*

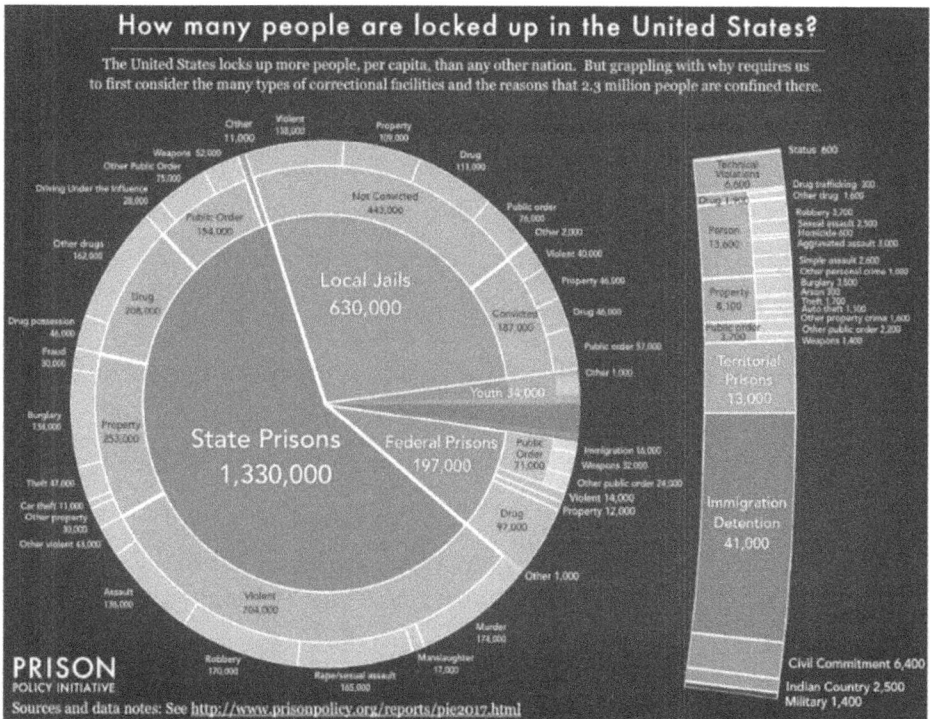

How many people are locked up in the United States?

The United States locks up more people, per capita, than any other nation. But grappling with why requires us to first consider the many types of correctional facilities and the reasons that 2.3 million people are confined there.

PRISON
POLICY INITIATIVE

Sources and data notes: See http://www.prisonpolicy.org/reports/pie2017.html

In 2017, 2.3 million people were locked up in the U.S and every year, 641,000 people walk out of prison gates, while people go to jail over 11 million times---each year! (Source: "The Importance of Successful Reentry to Jail Population Growth," Mr. Alan Beck, Bureau of Prisons Allen J. Beck, Chief Corrections Statistics Program, Bureau of Justice Statistics, June 27, 2006).

Prisoners, and ex-prisoners, as a whole, have been banished from mainstream society. As a result, they tend to alienate themselves from it, and as a group, they could become a powerful voting bloc, which would vote against the powers-that-be. This is one of the key reasons felons have been disenfranchised, generally, of their voting rights. Most politicians are not too eager to empower a group of strong, angry men and women, who would vote against them.

Once again, the issue becomes one of sheer numbers. How long will it take 40,000,000⁺ people to demand a fair shake, now they have paid the price for their crimes---if they were, indeed, truly guilty, in the first place? Should they be doomed forever, scrambling to survive at the bottom of Maslow's hierarchy of needs, which is the case, today?

The result of disenfranchisement and recidivism (i.e., **the tendency of a convicted criminal to reoffend)** is a growing pestilence of hatred and rebellion among the ranks of felons, all the arrested, and everyone tracked in various law enforcement and FBI databases. Society risks a catastrophic eruption if something isn't changed in the system, because for now, anyone who is incarcerated---is branded.

They are branded with "F" for felon, "EO" for ex-offender, "I" for inmate, "P" for prisoner, and let's not forget a big "C" for convict! Somewhere along the line, it might be wise to begin calling these people who did their time, simply, "citizens." "Improved citizens" sounds a whole lot better than the Scarlett Letters currently branded on their chests.

During my time in prison, I witnessed anger, rage, and danger on a daily basis. There were also plenty of fights and a deep frustration among this unseen, yet powerful and forgotten force, in the U.S. population.

Most Americans live their lives, go to work, and then head home at night. Everyone is pretty busy, and the old saying "out-of-sight, out-of-mind" certainly applies to most people in our country, especially with respect to our prison populations. This is a huge mistake, as evidenced by the continuing and rapid growth in crime and violence, particularly in our cities.

The U.S. Government has not made it easy to figure out how many convicted felons are prowling the streets these days. But, some smart people at Princeton believe the number is over 25% of the adult population!

Figure 5 – U.S. Felons and Estimated Ex-felons as Percent of U.S. Adult Population, 1968-2010

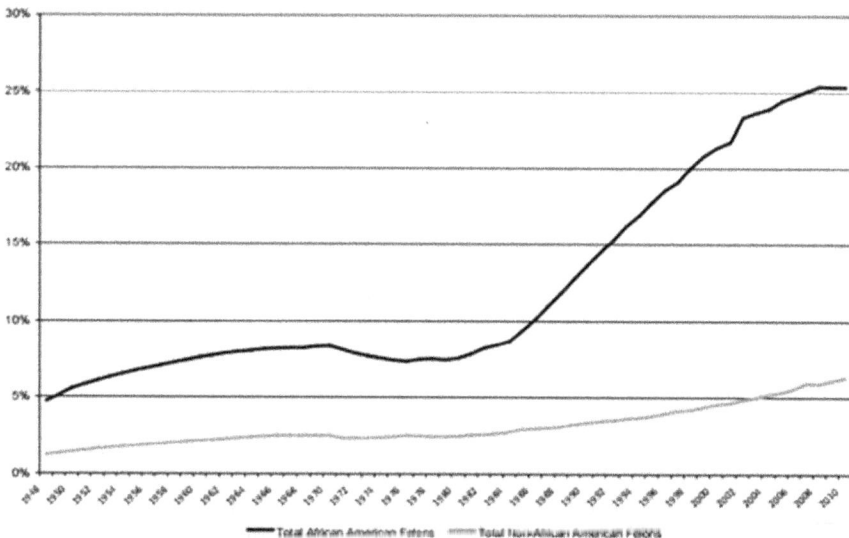

Total African American Felons   Total Non-African American Felons

(Source: "GROWTH IN THE U.S. EX-FELON AND EX-PRISONER POPULATION, 1948 TO 2010," Princeton University, by Sarah Shannon, Christopher Uggen, Melissa Thompson, Jason Schnittker, and Michael Massoglia, http://paa2011.princeton.edu/papers/111687).

As I prepared to enter Fort Dix, I would discover the troubling truth of what lies within the belly of this beast. After my experience and quite frankly, I can say, I have become highly critical of the system.

This book may not do me any favors, I know, but there are millions of men and women who need help and the best way to try and effect change is to talk about the problems and bring the issues to the forefront---peacefully.

What I didn't fully appreciate, prior to entry into the prison system, was because of pressure on BOP budgets, prisons are far more dangerous than even what they used to be. This is directly caused by the BOP's ballooning pension and salary obligations to BOP employees (including millions upon millions paid out in bonuses to executives), wasteful spending within the BOP across the board, and the union's control over the BOP's civil servants. This includes the guards and administration officials. Union control and regulation makes it nearly impossible to fire bad employees.

The results are incompetence, laziness, utter stupidity and tyrannical behavior among many of the personnel within the BOP. The combined impact of these administrative policies, and issues present in most prisons across the United States, has caused prisons to become decidedly more dangerous than even what most people believe. With a known propensity for violence and trouble, there is also a failure to rehabilitate inmates for successful reentry to society. Obviously and because of union and regulation protection, there is widespread indifference among multiple levels of staff nestled in the BOP. These people are merely putting in their time, doing as little as possible, and waiting to collect their sweet pensions. "To hell with the inmates," is a battle cry which, most prisoners might tell you, exists among BOP officials and employees.

Simply speaking, the BOP has cut many corners in the care of inmates, but has been *very* busy taking care of its own pay and benefits. This has been to the detriment of the inmate populations in America, and while men and women may be under incarceration, they aren't stupid.

Inmates and prisoners *know* they are living in deplorable conditions. When they see and read about *millions* of dollars being paid in bonuses and sweet retirement plans for a bureaucracy which has robbed Peter to pay Paul, with "Peter" being the inmates and "Paul" being the administration and Wardens of the BOP---this causes extreme resentment among incarcerated individuals.

Importantly, the resentment among the inmate and prisoner populations doesn't leave when the prisoner walks out the prison gates, either. It many cases, it carries on as a powerful fuel for hatred against authority. If our country wants to stop the violence and stop recidivism, we need to stop the corruption and ineptitude in the system and put the money back to work for the men being incarcerated.

This was and is the intention of Congress. It was *not* the intent of Congress to pay in $7.47 Billion to the BOP to allow the administration and employees, of a governmental entity, to provide themselves with great retirement plans and the good life, at the expense of those incarcerated!

I lived at Fort Dix over the course of two years, and I saw first-hand, how the administration of the BOP made a tremendous *show* of touting the importance of "rehabilitation" and "good treatment" of inmates. They would say, "Rehabilitation starts the first day you walk into prison," and they make a point of prominently posting weekly nutritional information about the "healthy" meals supposedly being served to the prisoners in the chow hall.

The reality, however, of the conditions related to the health, living environment and opportunities for prisoners to become truly rehabilitated, was something entirely different.

Ask any felon who is *not* in prison any longer (and not subject to the threat of being returned) what he, or she, thinks of "rehabilitation" and the living conditions in prisons across the U.S. You will first hear a deep laugh because of the ridiculousness of the question, and second, you will likely receive a response like this: "Rehabilitation programs are non-existent and the food sucks!"

If you then tell this felon you read a government web site extoling the high nutritional standards within prison, this person will tell you they lived with diarrhea during their internment and ate food which most Americans wouldn't even feed their dog. I can attest to this first hand, because I had diarrhea for nearly two years because of the horrific food they served.

Some meals, of course, were exceptions. One of the favorite tricks of the BOP was to serve "good food" when "guests" came to "spot check" the living conditions of the men. Once the guests or auditors left, you could always be sure the food immediately went back to the same old slop, the very next day.

Today's prisons are run without a good focus on rehabilitation and the conditions are terrible, on many levels. This only breeds more discontent among those who are trapped inside the walls meant to contain them, and this means ultimately, bigger trouble ahead for society at large.

Unfortunately, this subject is largely greeted with yawns and the problem is ignored. When the subject is brought up, the typical response is, "Well, they shouldn't have committed a crime in the first place!" Using this kind of short-sighted thinking ignores the grievous risk of a brewing powder keg of discontent, among some 40,000,000$^+$ Americans.

Recidivism gets worse each passing year. Men and women leave prison and can't find work, because they are not rehabilitated and don't have employable skills---while society ignores and rejects them. This combination of continuing factors is like pouring gasoline on a smoldering fire---something bad is going to happen.

You can see signs of the fuse on this powder keg, already lit. Things are erupting in America, particularly among people who don't have much of anything in life. This is especially true among those who have previously been charged with crimes. The signs are everywhere, as can be seen in the rapid increase in violence, murders, drug distribution, and vicious protests erupting across our cities, states and nation.

When people are frustrated, and there is no work because people are not trained, or educated, and shut-out by society, most people will ultimately turn to fighting and violence to take care of themselves and their families---even if they break the law.

In the post-Madoff world, which I am a part of, I entered prison in its most over-populated condition in history. This was due to the massive numbers of prosecutions which had been effected, against a backdrop of historically stressed budgets and corner-cutting which occurred during the management of the BOP the last few decades.

For sure, I knew there would be no swimming pool. I knew there would be no tennis court. In fact, today, white collar offenders are inter-mingled directly with drug dealers, violent offenders, robbers, thieves, and a host of other criminals in prison, most of whom are very familiar with violence and the ways of the street.

It didn't used to be this way, but today the reason for this heterogeneous mixture of people has occurred purely for *budgetary* reasons by the BOP, with little, to no concern, for the safety or health of the men and women in captivity.

It costs the BOP a lot *less* to house and feed men and women in "minimum" security camps, than at higher-level security prisons. In Fort Dix's case, it would use its two higher-level security prisons as a "feeder system" for the Camp. This would keep costs down for this large prison facility, and "on budget," earning the Warden praise in Washington D.C., where the BOP is headquartered. I was in the library when the Warden came through in 2015. You could hear him bragging how the Fort Dix Camp spent the *least* amount of money per prisoner in the entire prison system!

Unfortunately, the implementation of this "low-budget" policy played the very dangerous game of allowing men with highly different backgrounds (e.g. violent vs. non-violent, street vs. non-street, etc.), with many different religions, bunk together in highly over-crowded conditions. In prison, this is a recipe, *pre-ordained* to create trouble.

I found dangers at every turn in Fort Dix. Many men were within a second of losing it and turning to violence---fist-a-cuffs, and worse---if there was a disagreement of any kind. With testosterone flying off of every wall and ceiling in its cramped quarters, For Dix experienced problems nearly every single day. It is common knowledge similar problems existed across the entire scope of the BOP prison system.

Without heat during the winter in 2014-2015, and no air conditioning during the summer, Fort Dix would become a petri dish of friction during my time there, as very bad conditions prevailed for over 4,000 inmates across this FCI.

Because of the huge costs of administering the prison system, threats to society at large, and the dangers of doing nothing, the need for a reduction in recidivism and a revamping of the BOP is critical in helping to fix a severely broken prison system.

While recidivism is discussed periodically by elected representatives in government, the employees of the BOP, and on-air media personalities of TV, they all wind up only paying lip service to the matter. The situation is little changed over decades, while the problem of crime and violence has only gotten much worse. Huge percentages of men and women wind up back inside the walls of federal, state, or local prisons, once they are released---the very definition of "recidivism."

Using a Bureau of Justice study, inmates released from state prisons have a five-year recidivism rate of 76.6%, and a 44.7% re-arrest rate after five years, for federal prisoners. (Source: "Report Documents U.S. Recidivism Rates for Federal Prisoners," by Christopher Zoukis, The Huffington Post, 3/25/16).

This problem creates a multi-billion dollar drain on taxpayers each year. In 2016, The Department of Justice requested a total budget of $28.654 Billion, with $7.47 Billion allotted to the BOP! In easily measurable monetary terms, this equals $1,000 per person in New York City and about $50 for every one of the United States' 138,884,643 "Voting Eligible Population Ballots."

There is also the additional huge and hidden cost, of growing criminality and violence across the United States. This affects the safety of our children, and even impacts our ability to take a walk at night, while creating widespread fear from the obvious:

> 40,000,000$^+$ angry people are walking the streets, and have been disenfranchised by our government and the entirety of the population of the United States of America.

With no voting rights available for most "ex-offenders" to effect peaceful change, what are their options to voice discontent? If you look at the total number of people who have records for arrest, the numbers are mind-blowing. In an excerpt from a *Wall Street Journal* article, you can read:

"America has a rap sheet. Over the past 20 years, authorities have made more than a quarter of a billion arrests, the Federal Bureau of Investigation estimates. As a result, the FBI currently has 77.7 million individuals on file in its master criminal database—or nearly one out of every three American adults." (Source: "The Wall Street Journal," by Gary Fields and John R. Emshwiller, Aug. 18, 2014, "As Arrest Records Rise, Americans Find Consequences Can Last a Lifetime" https://www.wsj.com/articles/as-arrest-records-rise-americans-find-consequences-can-last-a-lifetime-1408415402).

Put in another illustrative way, America has as many criminals, as it has college graduates:

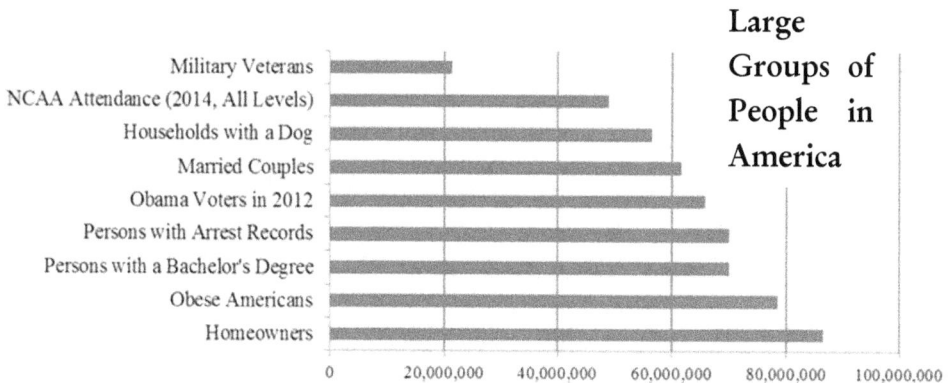

"As of July 1, 2015, more than 70 million people have records indexed by the III (Interstate Identification Index). America now houses roughly the same number of people with criminal records as it does four-year college graduates. Nearly half of black males and almost 40 percent of white males are arrested by the age 23..."

"..If all arrested Americans were a nation, they would be the world's 18th largest. Larger than Canada. Larger than France. More than three times the size of

Australia...Holding hands, Americans with arrest records could circle the earth three times." (Source of preceding two paragraphs and "Large Groups of People in America" chart: "Just Facts: As Many Americans Have Criminal Records As College Diplomas," by Matthew Friedman, November 17, 2015 https://www.brennancenter.org/blog/just-facts-many-americans have-criminal-records-college-diplomas).

If the real number of people actually arrested and charged with a crime is "only" 60,000,000, vis-à-vis the FBI's 77.7 million people, this represents about 20% of the 2016 U.S. population estimate by the Census Bureau---which was 323,127,513 people. (Source: https://www.census.gov/search-results.html?q=population+1900&search.x=0&search.y=0&search=submit&page=1&stateGeo=none&searchtype=web&cssp=SERP).

Today, we are witnessing a rapid rise in violence across America, and it is occurring while we are in a supposed economic "recovery," with the Dow at all-time highs.

Can you imagine how things will get *really dicey* and even *more dangerous*, when America slips into an economic slump (which may be actually recognized by the media)? When people don't have anything, they get desperate to provide for their families. With most of these 60,000,000 people having next to nothing, with no hope for advancement and little prospect for a job, they collectively represent a potentially real threat to society.

Many men and women in prison have grown up around drugs, guns and violence and will not think twice about using these skills to take care of their own. While they may even know what they are doing is wrong, society has sent them back to the "'hood" with no training, no rehabilitation and no hope. When the U.S. economy worsens even more, this is a powder keg waiting to go off. Men and women returned to society with no training, and no ability to get work, are destined to remain at the bottom of Maslow's hierarchy. This smoldering threat is a cache of TNT sitting under the entire nation---ready to explode.

Even though I became familiar with some of these issues and statistics before I went into prison, I knew I was going to live it, "live." I wondered, literally, *"Would I survive it? How would I cope with it? What can I do about it?"* Fortunately, I was able to find peace with these questions before I entered prison, because I had a powerful weapon working for me. It was and is, extremely real, as you will see through my experiences. It became more powerful than any gun, knife, shiv, or belaying pin, ever would be.

You see, I had faith. It wasn't the candy-coated, "make sure we go to church-group and hang out with our friends" kind of faith. It was and is a powerful, gritty faith, which has always protected me, and always guided my steps---even though I constantly fall short of the glory of God. It is this faith in Jesus Christ which gave me power and determination to *know* I could deal with the avalanche of uncertainty heading my way.

Many life-altering events had shattered my world up to my internment on November 3, 2014. They included:

1) The market collapse at the height of the credit crisis in 2008;
2) The destruction of approximately $80 million in personal wealth from stock holdings in my company;
3) An FBI investigation when they came knocking on my door on June 10, 2010;
4) An SEC investigation in the fall of the same year;
5) My arrest on October 2, 2012;
6) My sentencing to 27-months in a federal prison on September 23, 2014; and
7) The near-complete rejection and abandonment of me by my own family, early on in the process.

Despite this hurricane of change and challenge, as I headed into dangerous new territory in the largest prison institution in the United States, I knew God had my back.

As I prepared to meet my fate, I realized this "27-month" prison term would be followed by 3-years of probation---with travel restricted primarily to the island of Manhattan. The entire ordeal would last until October 17, 2019, the last day of probation, and would take 11-years out of my life.

Despite this, I knew God put me at Fort Dix to make a difference. I had firm conviction of this by the Holy Spirit, Himself. But, when I arrived at Fort Dix on the bright, sunny day of November 3, 2014, I didn't have *any idea* how I should go about trying to make that difference.

After all, I had heard prison could be a hellacious place...and it was filled with criminals---now all, just like me.

CHAPTER 3

PRE-ENTRY

On the morning of November 3, 2014, I was rushing around the apartment in New York City, by myself, trying to take care of last minute details, before I went to prison. When you are sent away for a couple of years, you have to think about *everything*.

If you want to keep your phone number, you have to make sure you can pay the bills, if you have email accounts, you have to leave auto-messages, if you want to send online Christmas cards in the future, you have to set them up in advance, if you have bank accounts, you have to make sure they don't go dormant (or else they will be closed), and if you have loved ones, you have to make sure you have all their names, addresses, birth dates, etc. because you can't readily deduce, or easily take care of any of these things in prison. There are no computers for online use, and there is very limited communication capability if you do your time within regulations---and don't use one of the hundreds of cell phones brought in illegally!

I also had to leave behind some instructions, and I had about two-dozen other things to take care of. But, one of the most important things I needed to do, was to make sure the person who had stood by my side the entire time of my ordeal, had love notes left for her---and I left them all over the place!

I hid love notes in every nook and cranny I could think of in the apartment, hoping she would ultimately discover them over time, while I was away. I wanted her to know she was loved and appreciated---and even if I couldn't be there in person, I was there in spirit.

Leaving for prison is toughest on family and loved ones. Sure, a man's freedom is taken away, it is an awful experience, and can be quite dangerous, but it is hardest on those you are forced to leave behind.

I had to report to Fort Dix by 2 p.m. this day, but I had been warned if you didn't make it to the prison by noon, you wouldn't be processed until the next day. This would mean you would spend the night in the "hole."

I decided I probably didn't want to find out what the "hole" was (on the first day, anyway!), and I knew I had to leave early. After I hid all the notes, I departed. My apartment building, near Lincoln Center, was located near the subway, and I hopped on the 1 Train, heading south to Penn Station.

From Penn Station, I boarded the 8:13 a.m. New Jersey Transit train to Trenton, NJ. This train would arrive at the Trenton Transit Terminal at 9:45 a.m., which would leave me plenty of time to get to Fort Dix, or at least, so I figured.

From Trenton, according to my Google map directions, it seemed rather straight forward, though a bit of a drive. I arrived at Trenton on time, with enough cash to pay for a cab.

When the train stopped in the station, I exited its sliding door and I went up the stairs, then turned left and headed out to hail a taxi.

However, just before exiting the station, I spotted a bank of pay phones on my right. I exhaled and knew I had to call my son and my brother, before I went to prison for two years. My significant other was working and her phone would be off, but I would also leave her a message, for sure.

On each call, I'm not ashamed to say, I cried. It is hard to explain, but the feelings I felt, and the tears which dropped, weren't out of fear---God knows I've been through plenty of hardships in my lifetime to deal with just about anything, including hardcore thugs, tough guys, etc.

But, the feelings I felt when I phoned John and Ryan on this day, were 100% about my family and loved ones. I would miss them tremendously. I've always missed my family, but due to circumstances of merely trying to provide for them during my adult years, I was forced to build a business in New York--- while they all remained in other states. I never stopped loving them, though, with all my heart.

Now, I wouldn't be able to see any of them for the next couple of years. As I realized this, my heart wouldn't allow my eyes to NOT cry.

My eyes overflowed like a waterfall, which can only be described as a downpour of pure love. I knew I would miss them and everyone else while I was in prison, but I was ready to go about God's work. I knew this would be yet another new, mysterious, and upcoming chapter in my life.

I had no idea what to expect.

After I hung up the phone and finished all my calls, I thought about what I was facing and the conditions surrounding my decision to enter into a plea agreement.

I now dreaded this decision, knowing I was about to begin a 27-month sentence in a federal prison. When I was finished with the sentence, the federal government still wouldn't be finished with me, as I would be released into the waiting arms of probation. Probation would control my life for yet another three years after my release.

During the probationary period, I wouldn't be able to travel, without permission, outside of New York City's Southern District. I also had to pay back $2,100,000 in restitution---and I had *no idea* where this money would come from, as the years had destroyed me financially.

As I stood by the phone bank in the train station, I reflected on my "plea allocution." In my plea allocution (what you say to the judge during your guilty plea), I plead guilty to not disclosing the *profits* I made from my privately held software company, Rymatics Software Ltd, to the investors in WWEBNET, Inc. (another company I was also running).

I didn't disclose the profits because at the time, I didn't believe a person had to disclose the *profits* he made from a private company, he 100% owned. Apparently, neither did my lawyers, or accountants, because I had the company and its related-party transactions, audited and legally reviewed starting from when WWEBNET's predecessor was founded in 2004 in England (WWEBNET acquired via merger, Direct Choice TV

Communications Ltd.---the original U.K. company and predecessor entity to WWEBNET. Direct Choice had originally contracted with Rymatics, my private software company, for software services and development).

Direct Choice, as a private company, had no *legal* requirement to obtain an audit, either. I insisted on it as CEO, however, because of the related-party transactions in the company---I insisted on their disclosure.

I thought to myself, as I stood next to the phone bank staring off into oblivion, *"This is the ironic part of my whole story."* 100% of every penny of all the related-party transactions *were* disclosed and published publicly, as is the normal legal requirement for any executive running any company in America.

However, even if you think you have done enough disclosure, the courts and aggressive prosecutors may indeed, have a different view. You are free to roll the dice in a full-blown trial, but the records of the courts are very clear: if you don't take a plea deal and go to war with the U.S. Department of Justice--- and *lose*, a 27-month sentence would likely mushroom to 10-15 YEARS behind bars.

For me, at the age of 58 when sentenced, this would have amounted to a death sentence from a professional perspective, with absolutely no chance of earning an income in the future. It certainly would also have ended all hope I ever had of trying to help my family and loved ones.

The fact of the matter is 100% of the related-party transactions *were* disclosed. In England, the predecessor company, Direct

Choice TV Communications, Ltd. <u>publicly filed</u> its audited financial reports (audited by the top-20 international accounting firm, Saffrey Champness, based in the U.K.) through the Companies House. The "Companies House" is the U.K.'s version of the SEC's Edgar public reporting system. Additionally, in the U.S. when we filed our registration statement to go public on the American Stock Exchange, we filed our "Form 10," and our attorneys also made sure the related-party disclosures were made there, as well.

Finally, as I continued to stare off into space past the phone booths in Trenton Station, I thought remorsefully, *"The reason there were related-party transactions in the first place was because the original founders of Direct Choice, Simon Luel and his associates, loved the software my 100% privately-owned company, Rymatics, had been building. They asked me to be their CEO!"*

Furthermore, under my direction, Rymatics had been making an investment in this software for years, since 1999.

So...what was the "Rymatics Software?" The Rymatics software was potentially extremely valuable because it allowed the digital delivery of film and music to digital devices---without the need for a set-top box. We had working software delivering digital media to computers, *years* before Netflix would get around to it. My goal had been to try and get the $15-$20 million we needed to license a library of films from Hollywood (which in 2005-2008 was possible for this amount of money).

As I said, we had Netflix beaten by years. We even had actual contracts with Universal Music in the U.K., as well as Venevision in Miami, and Comarex out of Mexico City.

When Simon and his associates saw the software back in 2003, they entered into a contract with Rymatics to provide the software for their company's exclusive use and ownership--- along with the support services required to run it. This totaled, initially, $55,000 per month and increased to approximately $95,000 per month by the time the credit crisis and other events crippled WWEBNET and Direct Choice TV.

Very soon after signing the initial contract with Direct Choice, and as I indicated, Simon and his associates asked me to become CEO of Direct Choice TV and its original parent company, Dolny Ltd. I accepted and worked very hard for Simon and the shareholders, particularly.

Simon is a man for whom I have great respect. He has remained a true friend and is the epitome of the definition of "loyal."

He was the *sole* shareholder who sent me a letter indicating he would be happy to testify on my behalf during a trial (i.e., that all related-party transactions were disclosed and not done by me in secret), if I went the route of fighting the U.S. Department of Justice in a full-blown trial.

Also of interest for the historical record, frequently, Direct Choice TV *could not pay* Rymatics its monthly fees due under contract. Because I owned all of Rymatics, I was also its CEO. In this capacity, I could have foreclosed on Direct Choice and taken back *everything*, *including* the software---if I hadn't put the shareholders best interests *before* mine. Importantly, Direct Choice became the 100%-owned operating subsidiary of WWEBNET via unanimous shareholder vote in September 2005. If Rymatics had chosen to foreclose on WWEBNET, this meant WWEBNET shareholders would have been wiped out because of WWEBNET's lengthy contract breaches (which happened with great frequency).

At one point, the balance owed, pursuant to the contract with Rymatics, was over $1,000,000! Rymatics floated Direct Choice TV, while the U.S. investors promised they would get our $15-$20,000,000 for the film library and roll-out of the software. This was the financing which the company referred to in its business plans.

At the height of the financial crisis in December of 2008, we ran out of money and I had to tell one of our salesmen he needed to look for a job. I didn't fire him on the spot, but gave him a "heads up" to start looking. This person had been working in a sales capacity, as a consultant to the company for years, but had not brought in a penny of revenue. The timing of this news for him wasn't good, either, because he and his girlfriend were expecting a baby. This would be his third baby by three separate women, as well.

I truly felt badly for him, which is why I didn't fire him outright. I had been loyal to him, but this loyalty proved to be sorely misplaced, because this person went out to anyone and everyone he could find, after I told him he was being let go, and told them I was stealing money. The rest, as they say, is history.

Things escalated to the FBI, the SEC and since it seemed no bankers were being put into jail, the Justice Department under the Obama Administration, started bearing its teeth upon, and going after, little guys like me.

Ultimately, I decided to cop a plea, after anguishing hours with my attorneys, family and loved ones. Together, they showed me how high the risks were if I went to trial in Manhattan and lost. You can imagine how a jury in New York might, or might not, sympathize with a white-collar CEO, in the aftermath of the financial crisis and in the post-Bernie Madoff era.

This was all water under the bridge at the Trenton Station, as I continued to stand paralyzed near the bank of phones, reflecting on these thoughts. I realized nearly fifteen minutes had gone by. I vowed again, to myself, right in front of those phones that even through the tribulation of prison, I would make the best of things and never lose my faith in Jesus Christ. I knew there was a plan and I also knew many Christians had been sent to prison before me.

Abruptly shaken from my thoughts realizing the clock was ticking and I had to get to Fort Dix by noon, I stumbled, half-blindly, out the back door of the Trenton Transit Center. With my adrenaline pumping, I could see to the left of the exit door, a small row of taxis lined up. I fell into the back seat of a beat up, yellow cab and said to the driver, "Fort Dix, please. Can you tell me how much it will cost to get there?"

The Middle Eastern driver replied, "About $50."

I said "That will be fine. Thank you very much."

The bearded driver, with the thick, black hair, drove off.

I only had a limited amount of cash in my possession. The years of litigation and working for WWEBNET from 2008-2012 without any pay (i.e., I worked for free), had made me flat

31

broke. The only reason I had $50 was because my little brother, Scott, and his wife Alison, wired me $500, and they also helped me out during my first few months at Fort Dix.

The remaining cash, after the upcoming taxi trip from hell I was about to take, would go into my commissary account, which is an account inmates use to purchase food and other essentials while imprisoned.

As the cab left the station, I pulled out the Google map directions I had printed previously, and asked the driver if he wanted to use them. He said not to worry, he had GPS and he would get me there. I relaxed, as best I could and once again, thought about all the events which led up to my present circumstances---as I've just recounted for you, in my reflections of that day.

I didn't feel sorry for myself. I just knew, hoped and prayed I would use my time wisely and see if there was something interesting I could do to grow as a person, while imprisoned.

I sort of day-dreamed during the taxi ride, but started noticing the fare was getting quite high. I asked the driver, "Where is Fort Dix?"

He pointed to his GPS and said, in broken English, "I following GPS!"

I looked around and could see we were in a rural area of New Jersey. I knew we should be about thirty miles outside of Philadelphia and Southeast of Princeton. From the landscape and road signs, however, I had no idea where we were in relation to Fort Dix.

I started getting really nervous as the meter hit $100---I knew I would need every last penny I had to make it inside prison. Everything I had read warned me prison is a disaster from a humanitarian perspective (e.g., food, medical, etc.) and you need to have money to survive the experience.

After another ten minutes of driving in farmland, I started losing it. I noticed the taxi driver was driving in a huge CIRCLE, completely wasting money. The meter was now over $120, because the cab had been driven in a big loop several times. I felt myself panicking, because I had to report to prison by noon...or else, spend a night in the gulag.

I kept thinking, *"I do NOT want to go to the hole!"*

I shouted to the driver, "I want to find this street on the Google map! Turn off of this loop you have us on, you are ripping me off!"

I had previously gone to "Street View" on Google maps to see the actual "street view" of the area and had checked out the route to the prison. I believed I could identify the prison's surrounding countryside---if we got close enough and I could spot recognizable intersections, and/or other landmarks.

What I didn't realize was because the Fort Dix prison is actually on the grounds of the Fort Dix *military* base (now called, "Joint Base McGuire-Dix-Lakehurst"---a brilliant, governmental effort to simplify a name, no doubt), the military *protects* the base by making sure commercial GPS systems *don't work* in the base area (i.e., No need to make this sensitive military facility an easy target!). As a result, GPS systems are effectively turned

"OFF" and the signals are juiced to send drivers in an infinite loop---well away from the main base.

As I considered what was happening, I realized the taxi driver, being familiar with Fort Dix as a destination, must have known this, which is why he asked if he could use his GPS map in the first place. I only realized it, because I put "2 and 2" together and figured out the GPS was just running in a loop. Around an important military base, it made sense.

I started really getting ticked off. Fort Dix is important and frequently visited by commercial taxi drivers from Trenton. They take people there every day, either to the military base, or to the prison. Trenton Taxi drivers must have known, *very well*, GPS systems didn't work in, or around, the military base.

This low-life had just ripped me off!

The meter was still running and it was approaching twelve noon---and I could feel my pulse quicken. The Fort Dix web site, and other literature I had read, warned sternly if you didn't arrive by noon, you would be a "guest" in the hole. I'd seen enough TV to know I didn't want to wind up there. I bore into the landscape around me, searching for a clue to find Fort Dix.

Finally we found something familiar---the grounds of the military base and a parking lot. I told the driver, "Pull in and STOP!" I had seen a soldier, and wanted to get to him, before he either vanished onto the base, or road off in a vehicle. I shouted out the window, "Excuse me, sir! Do you know where the Fort Dix Prison is located?"

The man had close-cropped, brown hair and wore his uniform crisply. He looked up, helpfully, but answered, "I'm sorry sir. I do not."

I was disappointed, and let out a long sigh, but then, at this moment, another vehicle approached the lot and stopped alongside my cab.

It was a black Suburban, and a man rolled down his window on the passenger side. His wife was driving and she shouted at *me*, "Excuse me! Do you know where the Fort Dix prison is?"

I had previously gotten out of the cab, after the soldier responded, to see if anyone else was around who might help. I walked over to their Suburban and sized them up. The couple looked normal, but the man appeared pretty shell-shocked and forlorn.

I immediately went to his side of the car and asked, "Are you visiting someone...or, are you self-reporting to prison? My name is Robert Kelly and I'm trying to find the prison myself, because I'm self-reporting."

He answered, "I'm Bob Schaeffer, and yes, I'm also self-reporting. We can't find it, anywhere. My wife and I saw a Burger King up the road and I think we'll go there to ask for directions. Maybe someone will know."

I said, "OK, Bob, nice to meet you. I think I'm going to go this other way." We parted company, and we went in opposite directions. I wondered who would find the prison first.

After leaving the soldier and parking lot, and after another 10 minutes of turns, I finally identified a landmark. The area around the prison was countryside and farmland---with no signs. "Follow that road!" I screamed. The taxi driver turned down the road. I then knew we were on the right path to Fort Dix, and I wondered if Bob and his wife would find it.

As we approached the guard gate, you could see the American flag proudly flying in front of the Warden's building. I had never seen, in person, Old Glory flying *inside* a prison, before.

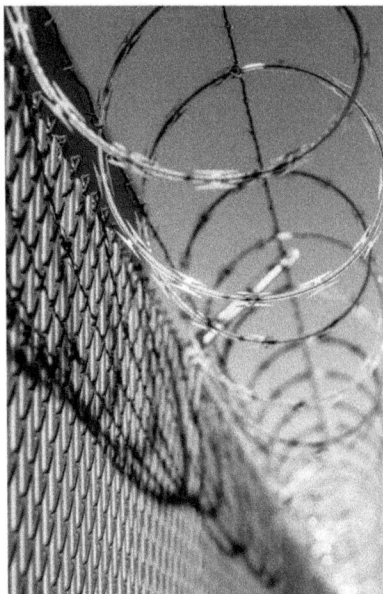

The prison and Old Glory were surrounded by chained-link fence, with the fencing capped off with shiny, extremely sharp, circular spheres of barbed, razor-sharp wire. As I turned to get one last glimpse of freedom down the old country road behind me, I saw a black speck of a vehicle, a half-mile away, swiftly approaching the prison. I could see Bob Schaeffer didn't want to spend the night in the hole, either!

Fort Dix Administration Building---Warden's offices. 36
Source: U.S. Government Bureau of Prisons.

CHAPTER 4

THE GUARDS

I walked into "R&D" at Fort Dix. The only "R&D" I had known previously were R&D centers at technology companies. I found out quickly, it means "Receiving and Discharge" in prison. I was there to be received, and turn myself in.

Shortly after my arrival, Bob Schaeffer showed up. I would learn later, he received a short, six-month sentence for some irregularities in his reporting on his business. It turns out Bob had also recently broken his leg and he limped badly. He tipped his head in my direction, and I did the same in his. I think we were both relieved to have met each other previously.

We were now being interned, and receiving our introduction to the "guards." Guards are trained to treat you like pond scum and can be vicious, as they bark commands and orders at you:

"STRIP NAKED! TAKE EVERYTHING OFF!! EVERYTHING!! FOLLOW THAT LINE!! HURRY UP!! EYES STRAIGHT AHEAD!!!" "SHUT UP!" "SILENCE!!!"

Some guys got scared of this tactic, but I just went through the motions, somewhat numb to what was happening. As an inmate you can only bring a few items with you---the rest they send home. I was allowed to bring my driver's license, social security card and the balance of money from my trip, which now only totaled about $300. This would get credited to my commissary account in a few days. I also brought my medical records and glasses. I had two pairs. I remember Heidi had really put her foot down and insisted I get another pair, in case one got broken, accidentally or *otherwise*, during the next two years. I knew we sure couldn't afford them, but she was tough and insistent, and there was to be no avoiding the expense.

There is no substitute for a faithful woman---one who will stand with you through hell, or high water, and Heidi is the best. She visited me nearly every single Saturday, while I was imprisoned. She had to wake at 4:30 am, to make the Fort Dix gate-opening time by 8:30 a.m. This was the only way to make sure she could get in on visiting day. Fort Dix regularly closed their gates to visitors and you had a much better chance of getting in, if you arrived early. This protocol was in place only because the Captain of the guards would frequently make it difficult for family and loved ones to visit---particularly on the weekends. He would order the visitor's gate closed early, or would never even open it, at all. Many men had families turned away at the gate with no explanation, and no forewarning many times, even if their families had traveled from very far away.

If this wasn't bad enough, Fort Dix frequently made visitors wait in their cars, outside the guard gate, for HOURS. Fort Dix is also in a rural, isolated area. These artificially induced "waits," as ordered by the Captain, or other guard on duty, forced men, women and *children* to pea (or worse) in the woods. The BOP wouldn't even provide a port-a-potty--- despite the fact its leadership was the one regularly and arbitrarily, causing the delays. This is the sort of callous attitude which seems to exist in the BOP toward inmates and their loved ones. It is one of many things which must change, if the system and the rate of recidivism are to improve.

Antagonizing inmates, who are already under an entity's complete and powerful control, does not breed good will for those men's return trip to society. In fact, the plain, cruel behavior of power-hungry Captains and their Lieutenants, contributes greatly to the rate of recidivism in America, today.

On this point, history begs us to listen. When you torture and abuse prisoners---psychologically, or otherwise, you don't make many friends---particularly regarding matters of family. Thousands of families deal with these issues, every day.

Heidi is a real saint and wonderful human being. I owe her my life and love her very much. I know to a man, all prisoners feel the same way about loved ones who sacrificed for them, too.

As my shakedown and check-in ended, I left R&D. I was prodded to enter the largest prison in the United States. Indelibly inked in my mind, are the images of razor wire and prisoners in orange uniforms. Inmate's clothed in bright orange, were tightly controlled behind the fencing around me.

Fort Dix was, and still is, overcrowded. With over 4,500 prisoners, it is the single largest prison in America, run by a single warden. Other "prisons" may have more prisoners---but they also have several Wardens to administer their FCI.

Earlier, I said Fort Dix is one of the toughest prisons, but there are plenty of rougher and more dangerous prisons than Fort Dix. In fact, Fort Dix is a cake walk compared to higher-level security prisons and some other institutions in the United States.

But, Fort Dix is filled with violence and is loaded with drug dealers and criminals, who earned their living off the streets. There were many dirt bags, for sure, but also many good men who made bad choices---primarily because they were trying to provide for their families. This doesn't make their crimes "right," but these individuals are outstanding targets for rehabilitation---if they could learn real, employable job skills.

As I continued my march through Fort Dix, Bob Schaeffer followed, far behind me. I tried to see if he was alright and I looked back. Immediately, the guard barked: "EYES STRAIGHT FORWARD! MARCH IN A STRAIGHT LINE! KEEP MOVING! HURRY UP!"

Ignoring this verbal assault by the guard, I stole a glance at Bob. He was struggling. He held the items he had been issued at R&D (e.g., tooth paste, soap, etc.), in one hand, and gripped his crutches in the other. He limped badly and was in pain. Ultimately, the guard got frustrated with him and took the items. "GIVE ME THOSE," the guard growled, and he leaned in three inches from Bob's ear and yelled, "HURRY UP!"

I kept absorbing these strange surroundings. I heard the cat calls from the men behind the razor wire giving us a hard time. In reality, I wasn't fearful, and I wasn't upset. I was expectant.

I continued to march, straight ahead, eyes forward, through the prison grounds. I kept my thoughts on my family and loved ones, but couldn't help but wonder:

"What in the world does the Lord have in store for me in this God-forsaken place...and what are His plans for me, now?"

CHAPTER 5

THE CAMP

We could see Fort Dix was a big place, and we had no idea where we were headed. We didn't know if we were going to be split up, or wind up together, but Bob Schaeffer and I kept moving---eyes dead ahead---except for a few furtive glances I took to see if he was keeping up. Suddenly, it became obvious. We were headed for the same building.

The Camp at Fort Dix is laid out military-style, in a barrack's-like building, and its walls are sheet metal, with over 420 men living in this forbidding structure, when I got there. To a man, not one person ever called it "home," even men who had been at Fort Dix for years. "Home" was precious to everyone, because it was where your loved ones were. As a result, inmates assign a certain and special reverence to this word.

As Bob and I entered the Camp building, it was still before the 4:00 p.m. "count." The guards at R&D had let us sit in cold, concrete jail cells for several hours, before they got around to processing us. This was to make us sweat and wonder if we would spend the night in the hole---or not.

Prisoners get "counted" five times a day, two of which require the inmate to stand by their bunks. Counts are taken at 4:00 p.m., 9:30 p.m., 12 midnight, 3:00 a.m., and 5:00 a.m. The 4:00 p.m. and 9:30 p.m. counts are "standing" counts. The BOP counts even more frequently on weekends and holidays, because these times are when men become loneliest and most often have tried to escape, according to the guards and BOP.

The Bureau of Prisons used to count people in their beds, but a guard (at a different prison) counted an inmate while he was in his bunk for a number of days, and apparently, the body began to smell. It was only then they realized the inmate had died! There has been a standing "count" required ever since---twice during the week and three times on the weekends and holidays.

These counts are taken in the sleeping quarters of the men. Once inside the building's sleeping quarters, we could see inmates stuffed into rows and rows of small bunk beds, with about three feet of space between them. I had noticed some men had squeezed a few more inches of space between their bunks, apparently by pushing the beds in their section apart a few inches more. I filed that to memory.

From the very first day, I *hated* being counted, and throughout my entire prison term, my spacemate, Mike MacCaull, would laugh at me, because he could see the distaste for it on my face--- every time the guards would walk by and take count. I was counted usually as number "31," and Mike was usually counted as number "32." The number would vary, depending on how many empty bunks there might be in our row of the "B Wing," which is where we hung our clothes at night.

The guards would usually count out loud, and more often than not, one of the two guards, would get the count wrong. When this happened, they would have to start all over again. For me, it was one of the most demeaning things which could happen to a man---having to stand there and be ordered like a slave, to shut up and be counted. Mike and I would always be grateful when what we called, the "A Team," did the count. These guys always got the count correct. No one liked delays in the count, and we appreciated the A Team's accuracy.

On this first day in the late afternoon, around 3:30 p.m., the scene inside the Camp was one of bedlam. Men were darting down the hallways, and many inmates were trying to make last-minute phone calls, before count time. The bank of prison-monitored phones was located along the wall, as you entered the main hallway of the Camp. I could also see men rushing to take care of their personal business, before the guards came marching out and started counting. One thing I had already learned from men passing by---you don't want to be late for count. It spelled big trouble for inmates in prison.

I was ordered to line up and wait for the C.O. (Camp Officer). He would assign me my bunk and issue me sheets, a blanket and a pillow.

He must have been busy, because I waited outside his door for about twenty minutes, and it was approaching the hard count time of 4 O'clock. Suddenly, he directed one of the prison orderlies (which is one of the easier inmate jobs in the Camp), "Issue that man bedding and towels." I would learn the officer's name was Mr. Steele, who was a counselor at the Camp.

It was now about 3:50 p.m. As the orderly led me to my bunk, I could hear at least a dozen guys "offer" to help me:

"HEY, NEW GUY...DO YOU NEED ANYTHING?"

"CAN I HELP YOU GET SOMETHING?"

"DID YOU GET MONEY INTO YOUR COMMISSARY ACCOUNT, YET?"

"IS THIS YOUR FIRST BID, OR YOUR SECOND?"

"I AM YOUR GUY IF YOU NEED ANYTHING..."

It was an unending barrage of salesmanship. Typically, nobody does "nothin'" in prison, without expecting "something" in return. I had read about this and I knew there was only one way to survive this kind of arm twisting. I would refuse any and all offers of assistance, except for a few items from the Evangelical church (i.e., toiletries), which were offered to me my first night, along with a few other minor items during my stay at Fort Dix. Of course, I also accepted the help of the magnificent inmates who saved my life on October 7, 2015.

Otherwise, despite my repeated declines of all offers to "help" me, several guys continued to press and ask if I needed anything---for days afterward. I finally rose my voice, way too harshly for my tastes, and half-snarled, "I don't want friggin' ANYTHING! But, *thank you*, I do appreciate the offer!"

The inmate I had directed my response to just looked at me, and then asked, incredulously: *"Did you just say, 'friggin'?"* Every other word in prison is the "F" word...and I don't mean "friggin'." This man was just shocked I didn't say, "FUC_***!"

A few guys kept coming at me sideways, but I continued to refuse anything and everything offered. This got some of the guys pissed off, but they finally all got the point. I didn't want to fall into the trap of owing the wrong guy anything, and I had no interest in violating prison regulations, which bars inmates from giving another inmate, anything at all.

You have no idea, as you walk inside a prison, who anyone is---plenty of "rats" abound the prison population. The best bet is to mind your business and stay out of the way, until you know what's up---and even then, you always mind your own business.

After my harsh refusals, I was pretty much left alone. I would like to think it was because I spoke up, but I'm also certain I would be wrong about this. Throughout my stay in prison, God sent various guardian angels to watch over me...seriously. Maybe angels pushed men to take certain actions, or respond in certain ways---I can't be certain.

What I am extremely sure of is the men around me WERE affected by a powerful God-loving spirit, whether they wanted to admit it, or not. Some pretty crazy stuff happened at Fort Dix, which can only be explained as the hand of God working in, and around, me.

One of the most important guardian angels sent my way, came in the form of my "spacemate," Mike MacCaull. For some reason, Mike always looked out for me. From everything I observed over nearly two years, Mike had a heart of gold. He helped a lot of guys in prison, and he never asked anybody for anything in return, as best I could tell---and we lived three feet apart from each other (plus a few more inches we would squeeze out between our beds, after my arrival!) for 21 months.

I hope Mike gets a chance to get out early, find a great woman, settle down, and have a family. I think he would make a great Dad. He has that instinct, as he's always looking out for others.

I was assigned to an upper bunk (Mike was in the lower bunk next to mine, on the left, as you sat in my bed). My bunk number was 120U. It had a good perch, and I could see all around the "B Wing" of the prison---the side I was on. While there are only a few windows in the building and I was in an "inner" row of bunk beds, there was a slight draft which flowed across the top of my bed. I didn't realize this would save me from the mercurial temperatures inside the Camp during summertime. With no air conditioning in the hot, muggy, east-coast weather from May to September, summers are brutal on the men at Fort Dix. The building is made of metal and acts like a hot box, or tuna can. When it got hot, we smoldered.

It was nearly 4:00 p.m. and I scurried about and made my bed, just in time for count.

I stood, waiting to be counted for the first time, of the over *3,000 times* I would be counted the next 21 months. I looked around and discovered Bob Schaeffer, the guy I came in with, was assigned to a lower bunk directly across from mine.

I can say during Bob's time in prison, he milked his broken leg for everything it was worth! I don't think Bob had to get a job, until there was about a month left on his prison term. Fort Dix is a work Camp---everybody is supposed to work and you get paid----$0.12/hour was my starting wage. When Bob was finally forced to get a job, he sat in the chow hall (you don't call it a "cafeteria" in prison) and rolled napkins around the plastic sporks men used at chow time. He did this a couple of hours a day but, I really just remember him playing cards in his lower bunk all the time, with some of the Puerto Rican guys.

Sometimes when they played cards, the scene was fairly comical, because from my view in the upper perch of my bunk, Bob would frequently get into arguments with them over the

46

game. The Puerto Ricans would accuse him of cheating but, the problem was, Bob didn't speak a word of Spanish, and the two Puerto Rican guys didn't speak a word of English. You can imagine these guys going at it, with none of them having *any* idea what was being said, but everyone knowing, *exactly,* what was being discussed (i.e., "YOU'RE CHEATING!").

This became hilarious, because they weren't ever going to fight--it was just the macho manner in which the guys played the card game. I speak Spanish, and I was called upon, every now and then, to arbitrate their disagreements.

Puerto Ricans, as do most men in prison, take their game-playing very seriously. I tried to stay out of all their disagreements, but, at times and in such close quarters, it was impossible to not say *something* when asked. As a result, I became a peace-maker sometimes, as far as their card games were concerned. For the record, I don't think Bob ever cheated, but whatever game they were playing, they had each learned a set of slightly different rules, which created and caused commotion every time the cards were shuffled and dealt out!

As a result of my translating for Bob and the Puerto Rican guys in the card game, word got out the new "Gringo" spoke Spanish. This would serve me well in prison, and over time, many of the Spanish-speaking men became friends of mine.

Getting through prison is a tough experience. It really helps to have guardian angels. As I look back, I see how they were constantly present, and I can also see other ways in which God prepared me to meet the challenges I would face, head-on, and which were coming right at me.

Fortunately, in my lifetime, I had also played the game of football. I started playing organized, Catholic-league ball in the fourth grade, and I didn't stop playing until my junior year in College, when I transferred schools. In between, I had played on many an integrated team, including high school in California, where my football brothers hailed from in, and around Watts, one of the toughest neighborhoods of L.A.

None of this mattered to guys on a team. On all my football teams, men *learned* to be teammates. We learned to *get along, joke with each other*, and we learned to *rely on each other*. Attending 14 different high schools also helped me learn to adapt to changing situations.

A long time ago, I learned to accept every man who came across my path in exactly the same way he met me---while judging no one. As a quarterback and outside linebacker, I was also used to leading men. As a CEO, I was used to leading men and women.

But, as an inmate---I wasn't used to ANYTHING!!

I let my instincts kick in, and I stuck to my guns. This, at times, was a delicate operating task. As a CEO in prison, everyone wanted to try and do you a favor. I continued to keep my distance, which long term was the best course of action I could have taken. I'm sure it kept me out of trouble.

Not to beat a dead horse, but if you take something from prisoner "A," you "owe" them. I didn't want to owe anyone, anything, and I have a big "thank you" to give my "little" brother Scott, and his wife Al. They helped me at the very beginning of my incarceration avoid this trap.

But, to my significant other, Heidi, who made sure I always had enough money in commissary to make ends meet for the next 21 months, even when she couldn't afford it, thank you from the bottom of my heart. I had been wiped out financially, but somehow, Heidi always found a way to provide for me when I was at the weakest moments of my life.

Sometimes, the mere knowledge you had pillars of strength behind you, provided the confidence to keep moving forward in prison. In my case, in addition to Heidi, Scott and Al, I also knew my son Ryan, my older brother John, my brother David, my brother Michael, Tara, Craig, Nita, Sonya, Strike and Vic, supported me unconditionally with their love and support.

Tara and her husband flew 2,500 miles to visit me at Fort Dix, and Vic flew up from North Carolina. Every person who came to visit me has a special place in my heart.

Many men in prison don't get any visitors, at all---I was lucky.

Collectively, these people were cornerstones of my existence. I knew because of them, I would be able to serve others and follow God's will for my life, under challenging circumstances. I also knew, regardless of whether I had money, or not, my time at Fort Dix would *not* be a time when I would be changing my stripes with respect to my Christian faith.

Prison is sort of a special animal and is way different than what most Christians experience at home. Prison is, quite naturally, an unholy place. There are divisions among men and not everyone is nice---to say the least.

Probably out of self-preservation, prison is broken down into what I call, "tribal camps." Roughly speaking, prison is broken down first by race, then by country of origin, then by religion and last by area of interest (i.e., weight lifters hang together, smart guys hang together, sports guys hang together, etc.).

Guys would intermingle, of course---we were all living together in close quarters. But, I knew one of my big jobs would be to break barriers down, by placing the Lord first in everything I did. I was color-blind anyway, in more ways than one.

What I knew I couldn't do, however, was cow-tow to any other faith. I was *determined* to make a strong stand for Jesus Christ, especially because I was surrounded by Muslims, Jews, non-believers and yes, pure evil. As everyone knows from abundant TV coverage, real evil lurks around and inside every prison in America.

I could sense the tension in Camp from the very first day. I wasn't sure what would happen in such a rage-, hate- and testosterone-fueled place. I knew a great deal of this was satanically driven, but I took a deep breath and forged ahead. This would become a test of faith, and the Lord would hold me accountable for my attitude, actions and example among the men, while I was incarcerated. I was as sure of this, as I was of the sun rising in the morning.

I knew it would take a long time to earn the trust and confidence of the hardened souls I would interact with in prison, and the process wouldn't be easy. However, I thought if I could work with men and build a good relationship with them, then they *might* come to trust what I had to say. Then possibly, just maybe, they might look forward to a different and better way of living in the future---but only time would tell.

CHAPTER 6

CLASSES START & CHAOS REIGNS

I didn't know what to expect the first night, but I didn't sleep a wink. I discovered my mattress had a huge hole cut out of the center of it (i.e., the new guy always gets the worst mattress in the prison, and with three back operations from an old football injury in college, I would get little, to no sleep during my stay at Fort Dix). As I thought about this huge hole in the middle of my bed, it dawned on me some other inmate had probably hallowed out this mattress and had stored contraband there before I got to Camp. I wondered if any contraband was still inside. That would be just great---getting busted on the first night in federal prison and blamed for someone else's hidden cache of illegal goods!

I would wind up using this mattress for the first six-months, and it truly sucked.

Despite this issue, I tried to adjust quickly to these strange surroundings and within a few days, I had figured my way around. I wasn't assigned a work-duty yet, and each day I headed directly to the "library."

The library wasn't much, and was about the size of a small New York City living room. I shook my head and remember thinking the first time I walked in, *"How are 420⁺ men supposed to learn and/or perform legal research in here?"*

Within this tiny library, as well as in the classroom and in my bed over the next two years, I would spend thousands of hours researching books, writing briefs for other inmates, writing home, creating classes, solving math problems, tutoring, teaching and reading.

In those early days at what would become my "spot" in the library, I poured over many books, including some I had read earlier in my life about God's word. I wanted to prepare my mind and soul to be extra sharp in this knowledge, and have it ready to go for what I believed God wanted me to do.

Heidi, as loving as ever, sent me some books I requested because the library had very few resources when it came to religious, academic, research, or other serious reading materials. It was loaded with fiction novels, for sure---but, not the kinds of books I needed at the moment. The word of God is sharper than any two-edged sword, and I needed to make sure I was prepared to use this mighty weapon, when and if, needed.

Some of the books she sent were: Evidence that Demands a Verdict, Volumes I & II, by Josh McDowell, Who Moved the Stone?, by Frank Morison, The Bible, and other books relating to the financial markets and software programming.

I had met my share of hard men in life, and I knew to reach any of them, I needed to be prepared. When the Spirit provided the opportunity, I wanted to move with the conviction of King Kong and be unabashedly, unafraid.

This initial work in the library went on for a few weeks, non-stop. During this period, I met a number of other inmates. You figured out pretty quickly who you could easily speak with, and with whom you could not.

One of the first guys I met was Alberto Vilar. Alberto became a friend of mine and is easily one of the smartest guys at Fort Dix. He had some problems with his money management firm, and he was sentenced to a long term in prison. I subsequently learned, after meeting him, he had always been an extremely generous and pious man. He had given millions, upon millions of dollars to charitable organizations, especially to the Arts.

A couple of other guys I met during my first couple of weeks, Randy Rahall and Tom Thorndike, asked me if I wanted to see about a job they said would be super easy. It involved being assigned to the "tool shed" and sitting at a desk all day, where I could read and play cards with the guys, as Randy described it.

Not knowing anything, I told Randy I would be happy to speak with the Officer in charge of the position. In order to be hired for a special job at the Camp---like at the tool shed, the Officer in charge typically wants to "check out" and interview any inmates who might request placement in the position.

I really did appreciate Randy trying to help me. He was, and is, a gracious man---as is Tom.

Deep down, however, I really felt God tugging at me---hard. For some reason, I believed he was pushing me to try and teach. I didn't know how to go about being a teacher, but believed God would have his hand in it, if it were meant to be.

As things progressed with the tool shed, I hit it off with Randy and Tom's boss, the Officer in charge of their operation. I also believed a job offer would be forthcoming, and I didn't want to be in a situation I didn't feel right about, especially as nice as Randy and Tom were to try and line up the job for me. After contemplating this dilemma, I decided to visit my Case Officer, Mr. Cole. I thought maybe I could ask him about the prospect of teaching and get some advice.

Case Officers are very important people to an inmate. They keep all the records and have a great deal of pull inside, as do the Counselors in a prison. They can create opportunities for inmates who are doing a good job, and they can create pain, if an inmate is misbehaving. Either way, most guys try to get along with their Case Officer and Counselor.

Mr. Cole was a real professional at Fort Dix. He was a very busy guy and even though a lot of inmates didn't seem to like him, he always dealt straight with me. In my initial encounter with him, he suggested I speak with Education and he gave me the names of some programs I might become involved with, while I was imprisoned.

One of them, "Save Our Youth" ("SOY"), turned out to be a great program. It did reach out to youths, but in reality, this class was designed to help teach inmates how to be better people, how to be better men, and how to be better Dads. There are many guys in prison who never had a Dad or Father-figure, especially if they came from the street. This program was really designed to try and help them, and despite its name---the program made a positive impact on many a grown man at Fort Dix.

I graduated from this class with about twenty others, in the spring of 2015. Officer Simms, who founded SOY, does an amazing job, and is another great professional in the BOP at Fort Dix. He is a real man of God, as well, and a Christian.

After we had graduated, he selected a few of us to speak to kids in high school. I spoke in front of about 100 youths from New Jersey, who had enrolled in various high schools' ROTC programs around the state. This event occurred on the military base at Fort Dix, where the students were bussed in.

Marine Corps Junior ROTC
Character and Leadership Academy 2015

Certificate of Appreciation
Presented to

Mr. R. Kelly

THANK YOU FOR YOUR EXTRAORDINARY PRESENTATION WHILE SUPPORTING THE MARINE CORPS JUNIOR ROTC CHARACTER AND LEADERSHIP ACADEMY. BY SHARING YOUR PERSONAL EXPERIENCE WITH THE CADETS YOU HAD A SIGNIFICANT IMPACT ON THE LIVES OF 100 MARINE CORPS JUNIOR ROTC CADETS. THE PRESENTATION RESONATED WITH OUR CADETS IN A WAY THAT WILL LEAVE A POSITIVE INDELIBILE MARK ON THE LIVES OF THESE IMPRESSIONABLE YOUNG MEN AND WOMEN WHILE AT FORT DIX. THE PERSONAL MESSAGE YOU PROVIDED WAS A WONDERFUL WAY TO SEND OUR CADETS ON THERE WAY WITH SOME VALUABLE LIFE LESSONS. PLEASE ACCEPT OUR SINCERE THANKS AND APPRECIATION FOR A JOB WELL DONE.

Signature Blocked

James S. Stayer
Lieutenant Colonel USMC Ret.
Cadet Leadership Academy Commander

KELLY
56772-056

Cadet Mentor

Counselor J. Simms

"56772-056" was my Bureau of Prisons register number. This was printed and then affixed via iron-on, sticky-white labels, onto all of my clothing to identify myself. A copy of the label is above.

To the left is my "Cadet Mentor" badge from "Save Our Youth."

After my conversation with Mr. Cole, I left his office, turned right and marched down the long, Camp hallway, past the Visiting Room. About twenty-five yards down the corridor, just to the left, was the front of a door marked "Education."

I thought, *"'Education' sure has a tiny office,"* and I could see through the glass there were actually two Officers housed within---and they were packed in like sardines. One was a lady, the other was a man. The names, "K. Lindley" and "J. Lecorchick" were etched into sky-blue, plastic nameplates.

The lady was closest to the door. I knocked. She waived me in from her chair, while she continued staring at her computer.

She looked up.

"Hello, my name is Robert Kelly, and I'm new here. Is this the Education Department?"

The lady said, "I'm Ms. Lindley, and yes, this is the Education Department." As she spoke, she swept her hand away from her body to highlight the glory of her incredibly small office.

I kept from laughing, even though I could see she had, somewhere, a sense of humor. I had learned already, you didn't want to mess with, or get too close to, any Officer at the Camp. If you did, the men automatically believed you had become a "rat" (for those who don't know what a prison rat is, it is a "tattle-tale"). To be known as a "rat" is a very bad thing in prison, especially from an inmate's perspective. Inmates hate rats and make their lives miserable. In some cases, if you are considered a rat, you risk your life.

I continued, "Ms. Lindley, I have an MBA from the University of Michigan and graduated Magna Cum Laude from college. I've never taught before, but was the CEO of a company, on the outside. Do you need any help in the teaching department? I also speak Spanish, but it's a bit rusty, if that makes any difference."

Ms. Lindley nearly fell out of her chair, I think. In time, I learned she is a nice woman who has a good heart for people, especially for those who are trying to better themselves through education.

But, time would also witness me getting shouted at by her, more times than I care to remember! This was usually over stupid things the prison system foisted upon us for the men's education. Some of the BOP's rules, and reactions to my suggestions, were truly remarkable, making the old saying, "I'm from the government and I want to help!" a real knee-slapper.

At the risk of pissing off my fellow inmates, I would like to say, however, Ms. Lindley helped *a lot* of men. Unfortunately, not many inmates really appreciated her, as much as they should have. I certainly had more than my fair share of disagreements with her during my time in prison, but I was always respectful to her, and knew she was probably doing the best she could, given the constraints of the system going on around her.

You see, education in prison isn't an option for the prisoners. Congress has mandated that if you are a prisoner, and you cannot verify your high school degree, you MUST attend classes to receive your GED.

People on the outside, including me before I entered prison, have no idea what this really means.

Translated into prison-speak, this means you have classrooms full of grown, street-tough men, who do NOT want to be in class. They have NO interest in learning *anything*, and believe the education department is *a joke*.

It was only after accepting Ms. Lindley's job offer at $.12/hour (and, by the way, this figure is not a typo---I got paid twelve cents an hour to start), and telling the guys in the tool shed I was going into education, I discovered how difficult it might be to try and teach.

What we are talking about is teaching inner-city and street-smart, grown men (many of whom ran million-dollar drug distribution networks), high school Math, English, Social

Studies and Science. The stories you see on TV about the white guy, or girl, showing up in an inner-city classroom, and trying to teach a highly heterogeneous group of people, have it EASY compared to what you faced in prison. It is nearly impossible to get a man's attention and try to make him think---especially when it is part of the BOP's education program.

Most prisoners just aren't interested, as I came to find out.

As I started my job teaching, I learned a few other things. Most of the other inmate instructors didn't do much. They would drone on and maybe read something, but there wasn't much imagination put into their work. In fairness, some of the guys had been inside prison for a long time and were just tired of it.

One person who taught with me, however, was an absolute jewel of a man, who I also believe is 100% innocent of his purported crime. Joe Kerns is now 76 years old and has been in prison for over a decade---for something I believe he did not do. I tried to investigate, as of this writing, if he had been released, yet. I always pull for Joe, but I read he was transferred out of Fort Dix and to the FCI in Petersburg, VA.

I have no idea why, but this kind of thing occurs in the BOP, frequently. You never know what is going to happen, because the government has complete and strict control over your life. Guys, regularly, would be there one day, and gone the next.

I was fortunate to get to know Joe well, during my two years at Fort Dix. He is also a Christian, and we became teaching partners. I know I irritated him sometimes, because I was relentless at trying to help the men learn something new---every day, but, we soldiered on together, and ultimately made a great team.

Initially, many of the inmates resisted me, and were antagonistic toward my efforts to instruct them. This led to some interesting days ahead, as I tried to earn my stripes and the respect from men I was trying to help. I would discover acceptance would only come with time and great challenge.

Joe and I came to teach nearly all the classes, together. He is a fine man and fine human being, who had been totally screwed in life. He deserves to go home, and he must have a million stars in heaven for all the lives he has touched, while doing his time in prison. He's a very good, honest man, and I hope the bastards who set him up are dealt with in God's mercy, because they are going to need it, as I understand the situation.

Never have I heard of such political skullduggery, greed and apparent vengeance exercised against a defendant, as I believe occurred in the case against Joe Kerns. To this day, I am sorry for him, even though I know he is not sorry for himself. He is one of Christ's true soldiers and true men of God. It was an honor to work with him.

As the initial days went by, Joe and I quickly figured out we were of a similar mind-set, and of similar academic and professional backgrounds and calibers. We also came to realize within a week of my arrival, what we would do, together.

We would teach the men our way, and would pay *no attention* to the absolute crap which was contained in the government education books. The government was transitioning to "common core" and this was a disaster for people trying to learn. The best way to describe "common core" is to describe a process of training people how to take a test---with the same questions repeated in different ways, until the student learns how to pass the test, but winds up learning NOTHING.

I started to really dig in. In the morning, the first class at 7:30 a.m. was ESL ("English as a Second Language"). What I noticed in my first few days at Fort Dix, was this class was being taught 100%, in English.

Joe, and another teacher, Robert Torres, who was close to eighty years old and set to be released from prison quite soon, were the current teachers for the Spanish guys during this class.

Similar to the GED program, ESL is a federally mandated program. If men don't know how to speak English in prison--- they MUST attend class until they pass the ESL exam. These exams (both written and verbal) are not easy, especially if you don't know English and you are between the ages of 21-60!

I have fond memories of Robert Torres, as he was a brilliant entrepreneur and had some really great ideas. We had some interesting conversations during the brief period our terms intersected. Even at his age, his mind was active and engaged--- especially as it related to his interests. However, Robert wasn't too engaged, or worried, about teaching the men. He always had other things on his mind---especially since he was leaving soon.

Teaching this class in English sounds really good on the surface, because the men are there to speak and learn English. The only problem was, with the poor educational background of many men in ESL and Spanish GED (which Joe was also teaching in

English), the Spanish-speaking inmates couldn't (or, wouldn't) understand a word of what Joe, or anyone else, was trying to teach them.

I could see teaching in a language which very few men can understand well, was a monumental waste of time---or at a minimum, an atrocious way to have to teach. I must emphasize, Joe did a great job...he tried hard and really cared about doing the very best he could for the men. He just needed a little help.

As a result of this particular observation, I saw an opening for me to make a contribution, and I became relentless in my use of the white board (which had mostly stood unused at the front of the room, as far as I could tell), and in my speaking Spanish to the men in both ESL and Spanish GED. ESL began at 7:30 a.m. each day, followed by Spanish GED at 9 a.m., Monday-Friday. Additionally, in the afternoon, two English GED classes were taught. One began at 12:30 p.m. and the other started at 2:00 p.m.

Joe and I taught all these classes.

As far as the ESL and Spanish GED classes, by the time I finished my prison term, I had written out thousands of Spanish-to-English translations and math problems, which I had taught the men. I still have the originals of these papers, which were painstakingly penned by me, each day, for class. We were not allowed access to computers for word processing at Fort Dix, and these classroom preparations were done on the cheap, prison-lined-writing paper available at our commissary.

I include a couple of these pages for you to see, as follows.

Very fortunately, I was successful in completely changing how this class and the next period's class (Spanish GED) were being taught. I taught the men in Spanish, which was a game-changer for them. I also believe the men came to see me as someone who really cared enough about them to try very hard (even in my rusty Spanish) to help them improve their lives.

This was perhaps, one of the best things I decided to do for the men in my Spanish classes---speak Spanish! For the next 21 months, the ESL and GED classes were held during the mornings each day, between 7:30 - 10:30 a.m. Of course, in prison, there is no summer recess!

There also is no pay for overtime.

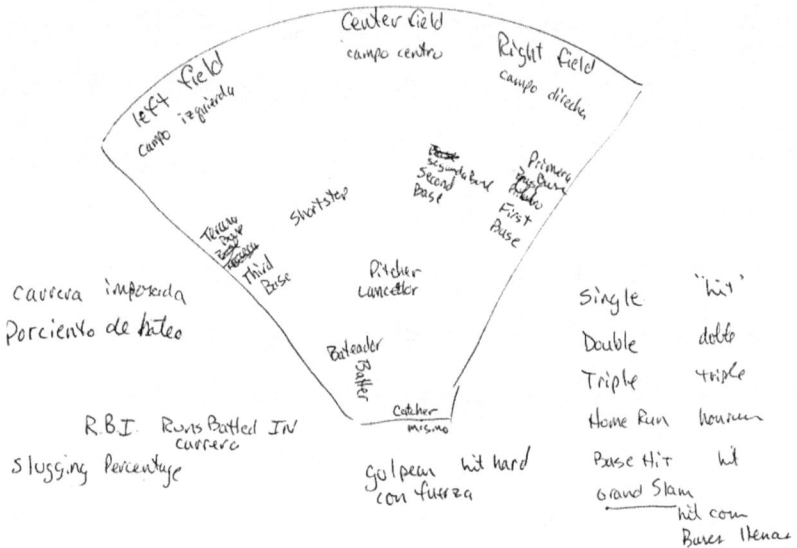

I tried to find subjects the men were interested in, and then wove my teaching around them. Above are all the positions on a baseball field, translated with both English and Spanish---the guys loved their "beisbol!"

For the rest of my life, I'll remember those first days in all the classes, as being quite remarkable.

However, I must say, the first-hour ESL class was simply something out of a television show, where the "children" in high school are completely out-of-control, with pandemonium reigning everywhere. If someone in authority had walked in at times, I swear they would think the inmates were running an asylum!

I kid you not. The situation, when I arrived, was simply crazy!

In the morning, when Joe and I had to teach the guys ESL, which I've told you is a congressionally-mandated classroom requirement for non-English speakers, we were not appreciated--at all. Like it, or not, the men had to sit there while Joe and I tried to teach them something. Talk about an uninspired and unwilling group of students! These guys had NO interest in being in class, and only wanted to fool around and give us a hard time.

I struggled with this problem, tremendously, for the first month I was at Fort Dix. I ultimately came up with a combination of solutions, which helped get many of the men engaged in the classroom.

As I mentioned, before I arrived, Joe had been teaching the class in English, because Joe didn't speak much Spanish. Joe also has a distinctive West Virginia accent and Southern drawl, which caused any Spanish words he did say, to sound really funny.

The guys in class would howl with laughter anytime Joe would try to pronounce a Spanish word, or sentence. As much as I loved working with Joe, he just butchered their language! Joe was great, though, and always seemed to keep his sense of humor about him.

When the guys made fun of him, Joe would just quip (again, at the age of 76, Joe was on his game): "Hey...I don't make fun of your ENGLISH, SO DON'T MAKE FUN OF MY SPANISH!"

The guys would just howl some more, and beg to have Joe read the Spanish words, or paragraphs I had written down on the white board for them. It became a game, of sorts. The funny thing was, nearly each and every day we got someone in the classroom to *read* the English words on the whiteboard. This interaction proved very important in engaging the men, along with me speaking to them in Spanish. Needless to say, this was to the chagrin of many trouble makers in class, who had no interest in being there, at all, regardless if Spanish was spoken, or not!

By means of comparison, if a group of inner-city men from Philadelphia, New York, Baltimore and D.C. could care less about attending a federally mandated GED class, then you can imagine a *thirty-plus* group of men from Puerto Rico and other Hispanic countries had NO INTEREST in learning English---because they *didn't need* to speak English at home in Puerto Rico, the Dominican Republic, Mexico, or any other Spanish-speaking country---they speak *Spanish* there! It made for a challenge in teaching, for sure, and put new meaning for me to the words, "No Hablo Inglés!"

It was under these kinds of hostile environments Joe and I had to teach four, 1½-hour classes each day. Two classes were for Spanish-speaking guys, and two classes were for English-speaking guys. These were the main courses offered at the Camp. A small group of tutors would sit in the library and teach one-on-one, but Joe and I taught the main classes at Fort Dix. Alberto Vilar also had an ESL class. He is a fluent Spanish speaker and he taught a small group of people at 7:30 a.m. (at a parallel time to ours), but he made use of the chapel for his classes. Being brilliant, Alberto is also a very, very good teacher. Charles Daum is another tutor who was exceptionally smart, and dedicated to his small groups. He used his law degree to help inmates learn English, while unselfishly giving of his time and advice in legal matters, to many inmates.

What was it like, you might ask, to be a teacher in prison?

During my first week of teaching, I can honestly tell you, chaos reigned. The Spanish guys, particularly, were unruly. They would talk over Joe and wouldn't listen to anything. Everyone would laugh behind Joe's back.

I took it all in, and primarily observed during the first several days.

I decided to sit in the middle of the classroom, instead of up front, during the ESL class time. This was a real departure from where Joe sat, when he taught class. Joe is very traditional and loved to sit in the big, cushioned red chair at the head of the room, even though I know Ms. Lindley had told him to do just that.

For me, the token "Gringo" who spoke Spanish in the class, I thought it might be better to try and embed myself directly with the men to build their trust. In all my years, this is how I always worked, whether in sports, or as a CEO. I always worked side-by-side with everyone. I thought I would be able to help men more easily this way---by making myself easily accessible to them.

I only had to find out which men wanted to learn. Whether they liked it, or not, I was determined these guys would live with a Gringo in their midst!

By making this decision, I also had to sit on those cheap, red plastic chairs you see in kindergarten rooms. I've had three back operations, and I can tell you, those chairs are beyond uncomfortable, but were the kinds of chairs the men were provided to "learn" in. I know every man came to hate those horrid chairs, obviously the product of some low-cost supplier to the government.

The rowdiness of class transcended pretty much anything I had seen on TV which showed raucous behavior at inner city schools. At least in a school, you can send a kid down to the principal's office and call their parents---and even expel them, in a serious case of unruly behavior.

At Fort Dix, however, we were on our own. We had to manage and motivate the men, while having no authority of any kind. We couldn't rat someone out, either, because someone always found out about rats---and made them pay the price.

I observed whenever Joe wanted to try and teach something, the men's shouting would begin and there would be constant interruptions. One of the inmates' favorite things to do would be to have someone cut a fart when Joe tried to get serious and started speaking. The whole room would explode with laughter, destroying Joe's tepid control of the group.

Initially, nothing would get done, especially when these thirty grown men acted like thirteen-year-olds in a confined classroom space. To them, they only wanted to "play," and the classroom would get wild and crazy, as a result. Since many of the men were very comfortable fighting on the streets, with or without weapons, it was also a potentially very dangerous situation.

You didn't want to get in a confrontation with anyone---whether they were a little guy, or a big guy!

Shivs, shanks and knives, along with other weapons, are ever present in prison, and these objects don't care how big someone is. They all can pierce a man's skin.

One of the best and most classic stories I can discuss occurred about a week after I started. It occurred during the ESL class, when one of the Hispanic guys, named "Omi," got into a heated argument with another Latino in the class, whom I'll call Jose ("Jose" is not his real name).

Omi was a leader among the Hispanic inmate population at Fort Dix, and he was very strong and athletic, albeit quite short. Once, I witnessed (many months later) Omi vault over the tall softball field fence (which is about seven feet tall), with just his bare hands. Omi stood only about 5'5" tall.

These kinds of guys on a football field were always dangerous, from an athletic perspective. They usually made great halfbacks, or were at some other physically punishing position, which also required great skill. They were always considered a threat if they played for the opposing team, and I can assure you, Joe and I were playing for the opposition, as far as Omi was concerned.

Omi didn't give me the time of day when I showed up to class at Fort Dix, despite the fact my seat, now in the middle of the classroom, sat one row behind him—just to his right. As a leader among the Hispanics, the last thing Omi was going to do was get comfortable with a new Gringo!

To this day, I don't know what set these two men off, but Omi and Jose really started getting into it. Men in prison can be very "macho" and this was certainly true with Omi.

A crescendo of screaming, in Spanish, began and things started to melt down. Tempers started to flare, and Omi and Jose's voices rose, dramatically.

Joe had told me previously, Jose had suffered from a head injury and wasn't "all there," but I never did learn all the details. All I really knew was Jose seemed like he was always a very nice man, as far as I could tell. I still have no idea why Omi was mad at him.

From my seat, in the midst of the class, I sat right between Omi and Jose---and I was caught in the cross-fire of their shouting. With Omi always sitting to the far left of the classroom (as he faced the teacher), and the other guy, Jose, sitting behind me and to my right, you could draw a diagonal line between us, with only about seven, or eight feet separating Omi and Jose.

The argument boiled and went out-of-control and they both stood up. I could feel the tension and sensed incredible tension spiking all around me. I instinctively I stood up. I was going to do what I would have always done on the outside---I was going to try and break up, or prevent a fight! The only problem in prison is you NEVER get into someone else's business. It is even against regulations to try and stop a fight between inmates. What you are supposed to do is call an officer.

I really didn't think about any of this and wasn't exactly familiar with all the rules, but I knew by standing up, I could at least try and keep them from tearing each other to pieces.

As I stood between them, I looked at Omi. I could see his wheels spinning a million miles an hour, with smoke pouring out his ears. He was calculating if he should tear right through me to his target, or not! I was naïve, of course, being brand new to prison life and I had NO IDEA what I was doing.

By the Grace of God and an unknown guardian angel, Omi held himself back and both men returned to their chairs and sat down---nobody touched anyone! I secretly breathed a sigh of relief and was relieved it was all over, without a fight occurring. I thought, *"Wow, that was close!"*

Joe and I tried to ignore the situation for a few moments and focused back on what we were doing before the commotion began.

I was looking down at the lesson again, preparing to reengage the class. Suddenly, out of the corner of my eye, I saw Omi jump out of his chair, and in the very next instant, one of the classroom's unoccupied large, office chairs (reserved for tutors) sailed right by my head! It passed, with full force and effect, about 2 inches in front of my nose, on its way to bombard Jose---the poor man with brain damage!

The chair Omi got hold of was stationed in the front of the classroom next to Joe, and was officially reserved for instructors. Omi had effortlessly and swiftly grabbed it and thrown it, as if it were a javelin! After this incident, I tried to lift this chair and it was heavy. It probably weighed at least thirty, or forty pounds---and it is also very bulky. Most people are familiar with the ergonometric office chair in America but, most people don't hurl them ten feet through the air. Omi was one strong dude!

Both Joe and I stared at each other for an instant, which seemed like hours, and the entire classroom was instantly silenced--- stunned, was more like it. Even in prison, heavy chairs don't normally get tossed sailing right across the room!

For one fleeting moment, I got ready to tackle Omi, as I scrambled back to my feet. I could see he was going to make a lunge for Jose to finish him off. I felt my entire body coil, ready to spring, as I expected a complete brawl to break out.

But, magically, as suddenly as the disagreement began, it ended. There was no brawl and the commotion stopped. Omi took his seat, Jose cowered in his, and everyone could see how proud Omi was of himself, even though he entirely missed Jose with the chair---but, almost hit me. It's not impossible to think I was the true target of intimidation in the entire matter---perhaps potential "payback" for standing up the first time. I don't know.

You could also see Omi feeling very good he "got away" with this little stunt. There would be no trip to the hole for Omi either, because we weren't going to rat him out. With only Joe and I in the classroom teaching (we had been left with this responsibility by the Education Department), no one in class was in a position of authority over the inmates. After all, Joe's and my forest-green, Fort Dix uniforms were the same color as the other men's in the classroom. This was an internal inmate matter, which was handily taken care of through the implementation of a flying chair!

I only share this story with such specificity because both Omi and Jose have already been released from prison. Otherwise, they could still get into trouble for what transpired and you wouldn't be hearing about this intense and crazy story from me.

According to BOP policy, we were called "tutors." This title was used by the BOP in our job descriptions, even though Joe and I were all-out teachers, with no supervision during class, of any kind. I think Ms. Lindley, rightfully, came to trust us and let us do our jobs. We appreciated this very much, and never abused the privilege. We tried to honor it, actually, each day.

For our part, after Omi and Jose sat down, Joe and I were mostly stunned. We laughed pretty hard about it later, and never, ever forgot the incident. It was like witnessing a bar fight in the old, Wild West while being caught right in the middle of it!

I knew for sure, at this point, my work would be cut out for me, and I wondered how I could have been stupid enough to turn down the plush job in the tool shed---at least I believed this at the time.

Little did I know, even though I failed miserably in my first attempt to reach the men, God had big plans ahead for me at Fort Dix.

1) Plot the points, Draw the line, Provide solutions for x and y
   Traza los puntos, Dibuja la raya, provee las soluciones para "x" y "Y"   Polanco

2) Find the slope
   Halla la pendiente

3) If not provided, write The equation, $y=mx+b$
   Si no está escrito, escribe la ecuación.

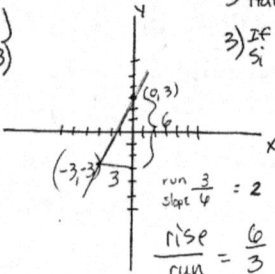

A) $(0,3)$
   $(-3,-3)$

$(0,3)$

$(-3,-3)$ $\dfrac{\text{run } 3}{\text{slope } 4} = 2$

$\dfrac{\text{rise}}{\text{run}} = \dfrac{6}{3} = m$

$y = mx+b$

$y = 2x+3$

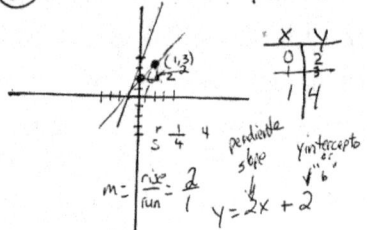

B) $y = 2x+2$

X	Y
0	2
1	4

$\dfrac{r}{s} \dfrac{1}{4}$ 4   pendiente

$m = \dfrac{\text{rise}}{\text{run}} = \dfrac{2}{1}$ $y = 2x+2$ y-intercepto

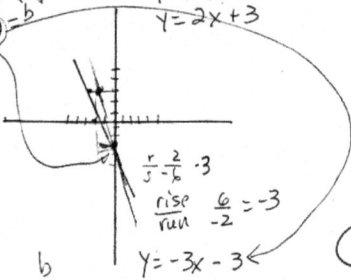

C) $(-2,3)$ b
   $(0,-3)$ b

$\dfrac{r}{s} \dfrac{2}{-6} = -3$

$\dfrac{\text{rise}}{\text{run}} \dfrac{6}{-2} = -3$

$y = -3x-3$

E) m b
   $y = -2x(-2)$

D)

$2y-2x = 4$

$m = 1$
$b = 2$

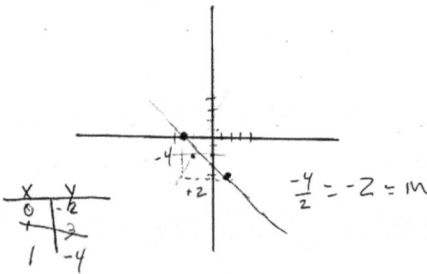

X	Y
0	-2
1	-4

$\dfrac{-4}{2} = -2 = m$

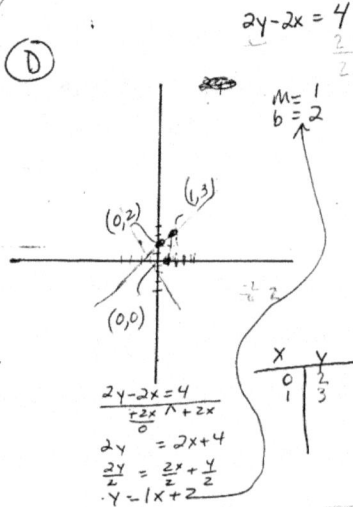

$(1,3)$

$(0,2)$

$(0,0)$

$2y-2x = 4$
$\underline{+2x \quad +2x}$
$2y = 2x+4$
$\dfrac{2y}{2} = \dfrac{2x}{2} + \dfrac{4}{2}$
$y = 1x+2$

X	Y
0	2
1	3

I was also the designated math teacher at Fort Dix. I didn't sugar coat anything and fed the men algebra, geometry and some advanced components of trigonometry, along with a little calculus (concepts only). Often, there weren't any workbooks the men could use, and I had to create problems for them. The Spanish guys, in particular, didn't have much to work with, especially in my early days at Fort Dix. I translated things into Spanish and used these resources for them all the time.

CHAPTER 7

BELUGA CAVIAR

Did I worry about getting beat up, or even worse in prison? I'd be lying if I said, "No."

You wouldn't be human if you didn't worry.

In fact, twice a day, there is a loud-speaker, broadcast warning about "PREA"---the "Prison Rape Elimination Act." Violence is a big problem and the BOP knows it. Evil lurks around every corner in prison---and you have to be on your toes at all times.

Despite my best efforts to avoid confrontation, I encountered some very angry men at Fort Dix, who seemed to look for a reason to explode in rage. Fortunately, I never had a physical altercation with anyone, but this was only because I kept my cool when some men tried to provoke me to violence. I was a pretty easy target at first, too. I was the "new" teacher, no students wanted anything to do with me, and I really seemed to be pissing everyone off, because I was teaching aggressively.

During the winter of 2015, a new inmate showed up to the classroom. He had been in prison two times previously---and this was his third "bid." Despite being a self-admitted methamphetamine dealer, and a big one at that, he had worked his way down from the higher-level security prisons to the

Camp. This was due to his good behavior. He was doing his time, and he was on the back end of an approximate eight-year sentence, in this third bid of his. He was in his 40s and he was the kind of guy you didn't want to mess around with. He was very strong, was a serious weight lifter and runner, and had a distinct accent from West Virginia.

I'll just call him, "Ace," for purposes of this book. Ace values his privacy, tremendously, and I want to protect his identity, because he's still doing his time.

When Ace, or any inmate was processed into the Camp, one of the first things the BOP checks is his educational background. This inquiry immediately lit up Ms. Lindley's computer screen, because it did not show Ace having earned a high school diploma. This meant Ace was heading, immediately, to our classroom. When he walked in, Joe and I tried to be pleasant and greeted him.

Ace looked disgustedly in our direction, half-sneered, and said threateningly, "If you guys try and teach me any of that teaching *sh***, I'll bash you over the head with a brick. Just leave me alone." Ace didn't shout, though. He let those words drop on the classroom in a firm, committed voice, the tone and manor of which was undeniable. He meant what he said and he was obviously a street-tough guy.

Joe and I looked at each other. We rolled our eyeballs and nearly together and without prompting, replied:

"NO PROBLEM!!"

In prison guys swear, they threaten frequently, and the pecking order is all about who is biggest and who is strongest. Pissing contests between the men are always front-and-center, especially for a hardened man when he steps foot in a new classroom. He lets everyone know he is not a wimp and is not afraid of violence. It is just what happens, particularly among tougher men in federal correctional institutions.

Joe and I looked at each other and we shook our heads. We smiled right at Ace---and then paid him no mind. To us, it was pretty funny. Of course, neither of us wanted to be head-bashed with a brick, but to live and survive in an environment like this---well, you have to have keep a sense of humor. We were working in the street, for sure.

Ace would become an interesting story during my time at Fort Dix, but his story would take over a year to unfold. In the meantime, Joe and I went back to the class, where I had some math problems on the white board, and the other inmates turned their focus back on us.

It was an interesting moment, because the other men were ignoring the show Ace had just put on for everyone. Many times, I could feel his eyes checking out the White Board and listening to me, while I was teaching. On his first day in the classroom, I remember thinking, *"I hope this man notices something different in our classroom, which he hasn't seen before."* When I finished my explanation of the problem on the white board, I was sure Ace would be all eyes on me---especially his first day.

Once again, I would prove to be wrong. Ace was in the back of the classroom, and had assumed what would become a customary position. He was sitting in one of the little red chairs, with his arms folded and his eyes closed. He would go on like this for months. I can tell you neither Joe, nor I ever forced Ace to do *anything* and I never got him, or any of our students into trouble---despite having some real issues with several of them.

Some of the men just wore hatred on their shirt sleeves, and these guys found me an easy target because of what I stood for. No matter what I tried to do, I made little or no impact on these kinds of men. But, the winter went on, and I kept trying.

Life inside the Camp building was boring and monotonous, especially if you didn't propel yourself forward, and keep your mind and body active. As you went along, you found there were some important standing rules: 1) Never touch another guy's stuff; 2) Lock your locker, and 3) Don't use contraband.

At least, those are the rules.

The reality at Fort Dix was quite a bit different. Guys would regularly use contraband, whether it was food, cell phones, or other items--- you can use your imagination---as it was all pretty much available at Fort Dix. Also, many men never locked their lockers, but unless you were in a group of trusted compadres, no one *ever* touched another inmate's possessions, unless he was a thief. Unfortunately, there were plenty of those around. Playing football through college, I always was in the habit of locking my locker and I did the same in prison, too.

There were many stories about guys getting "set up" with contraband being planted in, or near, their locker. For me, it wasn't worth the risk. In prison, you must check your shoes (shoes are stored under the bottom bunk, on top of two sets of parallel wires, which are strung down the length of the bed), as well as your bed and area around it for contraband---always. If you got an inmate mad at you, especially if he happened to have a long sentence, contraband could magically "show up" in your area. Many prisoners have their prison terms lengthened, or can be banished to higher-level security facilities, when they are set up like this.

Because the Fort Dix prison system is located on an active military base, and many of the men worked in, and around the military installation on a daily basis, inmates have an easy time bringing contraband into the prison. Alcohol, drugs, cell phones and many other banned items, not limited by the imagination, are found at Fort Dix, all the time.

The BOP constantly plays "whack the mole," to find contraband, too. It was a game, and the inmates were brilliant at playing it. It was funny when a group of guards was going to lock down one side of the Camp building to check for contraband. Inmates would immediately text the other side of the building (e.g. *"Raid---B Wing!"*)----and everyone's cell phone would light up with a group message. No matter how fast those guards moved, they could never quite beat Albert Einstein and the speed of light. Upon receipt of the texts, you immediately heard loud whistling and warning calls of inmates alerting each other--- code for: "Hide your stuff!"

Some inmates were truly ingenious in playing this game. It was common knowledge some made a lot of money dealing in cell phones and other contraband. Cell phone usage was, and still is, an epidemic. I never used them, but many men did. I can hardly blame them either.

The prices for food, drinks, pay phones and emails are a real rip-off in prison. The BOP uses third-party vendors to provide many services, and the quality and costs delivered by them is horrible. As you will see, essential items, on a bare-bones commissary list, are really expensive, are of inferior quality, and are extremely limited in selection.

In fact, wherever the BOP could cut corners, it has. This includes critical inmate food and services including food at the chow hall, inmate facilities, clothing, medical services, and communication capability with loved ones. No one expects a country club in prison, but if you are locking any citizen up for any length of time in the United States, inmates should not be taken advantage of, especially NOT for the benefit of the BOP's employees and their retirement, compensation, bonus and at-work entertainment plans. Collectively, these policies and lack of care breed nothing but rancor among the men.

There is an incredible conflict of interest, which the employees of the BOP have vis-à-vis their treatment of inmates and allocution of spending, which needs to be addressed by Congress. It wastes billions of dollars each year and funnels money intended for rehabilitation and the well-being of prisoners, into the pockets and lifestyles of the BOP employees.

Many BOP staff members have a habit of squandering money to make their jobs and lives more pleasant, to the detriment of the people incarcerated. This is part of the "rob Peter to pay Paul" mentality which goes on at the BOP. Resources are regularly steered away from those incarcerated and directed into the pockets, benefits, parties, vehicles and other perks of BOP personnel. A truly independent third party, who is not subservient to, and not "on a string" to the BOP, is needed to audit, forensically, how monies are being spent.

Additionally, a revision of regulations over union control of federal workers is critical. Government needs to be able to easily fire poorly performing federal workers, without the threat of breaking the law. This is a problem throughout all government.

Law enforcement and Congress should send people *inside* as inmates, "undercover," to multiple prisons *simultaneously*. Let these "undercover inmates" observe the abuse of power and corruption in the system, as well as how money is siphoned off and wasted by federal employees on nearly everything (except for what the money was intended for---the rehabilitation and well-being of inmates).

"Rehabilitation" is key to reducing the recidivism rate. Taking advantage of inmates' health and well-being, to the advantage of BOP employees, merely rubs inmates raw and completely alienates prisoners from the system, long term. It is hard to imagine why inmates are charged for anything, when their starting pay is only $.12 per hour!

The prices for items in commissary follow. You can see the prices for yourself, first hand:

FCI FORT DIX COMMISSARY LIST

PURCHASE LIMITS IN BRACKETS [ ]

Approved Current Date _____
J. Hollingsworth, Warden

Inmate Name: _____   Reg. #: _____   Unit: _____

___Single .21 Stamp

[3]Copy Card $7.50 (50 copies)
[1]Book First Class Stamps
[20]Single First Class Stamp
Single .01 ___ [8] 1.10 Stamp
[6]Photo Ticket $1.00

*LIMIT 48 SODAS*SOLD BY 12 PACK*

BEVERAGES
___[12]Pepsi (K) ___[12]Diet Cherry Pepsi (K)	$	6.00
___[12]Ginger Ale (K) ___[12] Grape Crush	$	6.00
___		
___[15]Water (OU)	$	0.90

SOUPS & RICE
___[24]Chicken Soup ___Spicy Soup	$	0.30
___[24]Low Sodium Chicken Soup	$	0.30
___(12)Veg. Cup Soup$.50 ___[24]Thai Soup	$	0.55
___CRC Chicken $ 0.90 ___CRC Veg Soup	$	1.80
___[12]Brown Rice (K)(H)	$	1.35
___[12]White Rice (K)(H)	$	0.90

[5 TOTAL OF ANY] CHIPS
___Doritos	$	1.85
___Ripples Plain Chips (OU) (H)	$	1.25
___Buffalo Wing Chips (OU) (H)	$	1.25
___		
___Corn Tortilla Chips	$	2.35
___Pretzels (OU)	$	3.20
___White Cheddar Pop Corn	$	1.05
___Plantain Chips	$	1.65

SNACKS & CONDIMENTS
___Mustard (OU)	$	1.25
___Asian Sweet/Hot Sauce	$	1.95
___Squeeze Mayo (OU)	$	2.60
___Cream Cheese (H)	$	0.40
___Garlic $.55 ___Salt & Pepper (K)	$	1.50
___[3] Honey$3.90 ___Sriracha Hot Sauce	$	1.70
___Sugar Substitute (OU)	$	1.55
___Olives $1.10 ___Chili Garlic Sauce	$	2.25
___Chopped Onion (OU)	$	1.10
___Salsa Sauce $1.95 ___BBQ Sauce	$	1.90
___Soy Sauce (K)	$	2.60
___Pizza Sauce$2.55 ___Italian Seasoning	$	1.10
___Jalapeno Pepper Slices	$	1.75
___Peanut Butter (OU)(H)	$	3.00
___Parmesan Cheese	$	3.55
___Adobo $1.70 ___Mrs. Dash (OU)	$	3.15
___[3]Cheddar Squeeze Cheese	$	3.35
___[3]Jalapeno Squeeze Cheese	$	3.35
___Mozzarella Cheese	$	1.05
___Goya Sazon	$	1.55
___Vegetable Flakes	$	1.25

MEATS & FISH
___Bacon	$	1.85
___[12]Hot & Spicy Beef Sausage	$	2.25
___[12]Turkey Sausage	$	2.15
___Chorizo Sausage	$	1.40
___		
___[12]Chicken	$	2.65
___Spam	$	1.45
___Pepperoni	$	1.90
___[12]White Tuna	$	2.95
___		
___[24]Mackerel (OU)(H)	$	1.00
___[12]Light Tuna (OU)(H)	$	1.55
___[12]Yellow Fin Tuna	$	2.10

COOKIES & CRACKERS
___[3]Oatmeal Cakes & Cremes (OU)	$	1.75
___[3]S/F Cookies (Vanilla Wafers) (OU)	$	2.70
___[3]Chocolate Cream Cookie	$	2.20
___[3]Chocolate Chip (OU) (H)	$	2.35
___[3]Vanilla Wafers (OU) (H)	$	2.35
___[3]Peanut Butter Cookies(OU)(H)	$	1.70
___[3]Duplex Creme Cookies(OU)(H)	$	1.70

COOKIES & CRACKERS CONT.
___Chocolate Cream Cookie	$	2.20
___		
___[3]Goya Tropical Crackers (OU)	$	2.70
___[3]Ritz Crackers(K)	$	4.10
___[3]Unsalted Crackers (OU)	$	2.15
___[3]Matzo Crackers(K)	$	3.50

PASTRIES & WRAPS
___(10) Sweet & Salty Snack Bar	$	0.70
___[25]Cream Cheese Cake (OU)(CRC)	$	0.60
___[12] Honey Buns (K)	$	0.95
___Cupcakes (K)	$	2.75
___Buddy Bars (K)	$	1.75
___[3]Whole Wheat Tortillas(K)	$	2.00
___[3]Flour Tortillas (K)	$	1.95
___[3]Corn Tortillas (K)	$	1.15

MEALS & DRY FOODS
___Refried Beans (K)	$	1.60
___Pizza Kits (H)	$	3.65
___Mac & Cheese (H) (K)	$	1.00
___CRC Cholent with Beef (OU)	$	5.45
___CRC Beef Rib Steak (OU)	$	8.70
___CRC Stuffed Chicken	$	5.05

HEALTH FOODS & NUTS
___[3]Granola Bars	$	3.05
___Granola Mix $3.15 ___(10) Fruit Snack	$	0.60
___[4]Unsalted Peanuts (K)	$	2.80
___[4]Mixed Nuts (K)	$	2.80
___[4]Almonds	$	4.05
___Cashews (K)	$	3.40
___Trail Mix $3.35 ___Dill Pickle Pouch	$	0.65
___[8]Ultra Fit Bar	$	1.80
___Unsalted Peanuts	$	2.15
___Honey Roasted Peanuts	$	3.10

HOT & COLD CEREALS
___(3)Variety Oatmeal (OU)	$	3.60
___[3]Wheat Germ	$	3.80
___[3]Oatmeal (OU)	$	1.80
___[3]Raisin Bran (K)	$	3.60
___[3] Cocoa Roos	$	3.10
___[3]Oat Blenders (K)	$	2.55

CANDY
___[6]M&M Peanuts $0.80 ___[6]Snickers (OU)	$	0.80
___[6]Reese's P.B. Cup (OU)	$	0.85
___[6]Chocolate Peanuts	$	1.55
___[6]Chocolate Bar	$	1.30
___[6]Twizzlers (OU)	$	1.30
___[4]Jolly Rancher	$	1.50
___[4]Asst. Candy	$	1.00

SUGARFREE CANDY (K)
___Just Chocolate	$	2.20
___Butter Scotch	$	2.20
___Tropical Fruit	$	2.20

DRINK MIX, COFFEE & TEA
___Cocoa Mix (K)	$	1.70
___S/F Cocoa Mix	$	1.80
___[6]Coffee Creamer (K) (H)	$	1.10
___[4]Colombian Coffee (K) (H)	$	3.25
___[3]Folgers	$	7.45
___Decaf Coffee (K) (H)	$	3.45
___[4]Powdered Milk (K) (H)	$	4.05
___S/F Hawaiian Punch	$	1.30
___S/F Iced Tea (OU)	$	1.65
___Tang $2.25 ___Espresso	$	3.90
___S/F Raspberry Drink (OU)	$	1.65
___ Tea Bags (K)	$	5.25
___Gatorade	$	1.45
___Herbal Tea (OU)	$	2.95
___Egg Powder	$	3.00
___Soy Milk $6.20 ___Breakfast Drink Mix	$	7.15

VITAMINS
___Daily Vitamin	$	4.30
___Vitamin C	$	2.60
___Vitamin D & Calcium	$	4.50
___Vitamin B Complex	$	4.25
___CRC Multivitamin (OU)	$	6.60

HAIR PRODUCTS
___Comb	$	0.85
___Afro Pick	$	0.50
___Vent Brush	$	1.00
___Boar Bristle Brush	$	2.25
___Pink Luster	$	5.80
___Murrays	$	3.15
___Hair Food	$	2.35
___African Pride	$	6.65
___Sulfur 8 Shampoo	$	4.10
___Sulfur 8 Hair Grease	$	3.85
___Head & Shoulders Shampoo	$	7.05
___Suave Shampoo 2 in 1	$	3.25
___		
___Therapeutic Shampoo	$	2.95
___Styling Gel	$	1.95
___Braided Ponytailers	$	0.85

DENTAL CARE PRODUCTS
___Soft Toothbrush	$	0.95
___Oral B Toothbrush	$	3.30
___Toothbrush Holder	$	0.50
___Colgate Total	$	3.25
___Cool Wave Toothpaste	$	1.50
___CRC Toothpaste	$	3.45
___Sensodyne Toothpaste	$	6.75
___Fixodent	$	4.45
___Denture Cream	$	4.40
___Dental Floss	$	1.95
___Mouthwash	$	2.20

BODY CARE, SHAVE & SOAPS
___Magic Shave Cream	$	4.25
___Shave Gel	$	1.55
___M5Razor $6.45 ___M5 Blades	$	6.45
___Gillette Razor $9.85 ___Blades	$	13.35
___Bic Disposable Razor	$	2.25
___Shave Bag	$	6.00
___St. Ives Facial Scrub	$	4.80
___After Shave Lotion	$	2.85
___Cool Zone	$	2.55
___Degree	$	3.90
___Mennen Active Fresh	$	2.45
___Clear Roll On	$	1.55
___Dry Idea	$	4.25
___Noxema 2.20 ___Chapstick	$	1.60
___Blistex	$	1.95
___Cocoa Butter Stick	$	2.05
___Baby Powder	$	1.60
___Sunblock Lotion	$	3.90
___[3]Ambi Medicated Soap	$	2.30
___[3]Neutrogena Facial Bar	$	3.65
___Q-Tips $1.10 ___Palmer's Cocoa Butter Cream	$	6.00
___Soap Box	$	0.70
___Kleenex Tissue	$	3.30
___[3]Dove Soap	$	1.80
___[3]Dial Soap	$	1.40
___[3]Lever 2000 Soap	$	1.25
___[3]Tone Soap	$	1.10
___[3]Shea Butter Soap	$	4.90
___Tone Coco Butter Lotion	$	3.60
___Aloe Lotion	$	1.65
___Shea Butter Lotion	$	2.25
___Jergens Lotion	$	4.85
___Lubrisoft Lotion	$	3.70
___Body Wash	$	4.50
___Clearasil Face Wash		$7.90

82

MEDICAL ITEMS

___Tums $3.15	___Visine Seasonal	$ 6.20
___Halls Reg $2.40	___Halls S/F Cherry	$ 2.40
___Natural Fiber/$6.30	___Breathe-Right Strips	$ 6.60
___Omeprazole (Generic Prilosec)		$ 20.25
___Simethicone (Anti-flatulant)		$ 2.30
___Triple Antibiotic Ointment		$ 2.35
___Loratadine (Generic Claritin)		$ 1.70
___Antacid (Generic Mylanta)		$ 3.25
___Cough Syrup		$ 2.45
___Chest Rub		$ 2.10
___Milk of Magnesia		$ 2.55
___Allergy Tabs		$ 1.60
___Hemorrhoidal Ointment		$ 3.70
___Hydrocortisone Cream		$ 1.40
___Cromolyn Nasal Spray		$ 8.85
___Nasal/Saline		$ 1.85
___Muscle Rub		$ 2.50
___Ibuprofen 2.65	___Pink Bismuth	$ 2.10
___Aspirin 1.45	___Non-Aspirin	$ 2.35
___Terbinafine (Anti-Fungal Cream)		$ 9.95
___Bump Stopper Liquid		$ 3.65
___Anti-Fungal Foot Powder		$ 2.60
___Anti-Fungal Cream		$ 1.70
___A&D Ointment		$ 2.50
___Artificial Tears		$ 2.40
___Ranitidine 150 MG (Generic Zantac)		$ 4.30
___Ear Drops		$ 1.90
___Lactase (Lactose Supplement)		$ 5.00
Corn Pads		$ 3.30

CLEANING PRODUCTS

SIMLINE	$1.60
___Ajax Dish Detergent	$ 1.35
___Tide Laundry Pods	$ 7.10
___Bounce Dryer Sheets	$ 2.55

BATTERIES

___[2]AA 4-PK	$ 1.10
___Watch Battery #2016	$ 2.50
___Watch Battery # 2025	$ 2.50
___[2]D 2-PK	$ 2.55

All used batteries must be returned to Commissary Staff

SPORT ITEMS & CLOTHING

___Elbow Support (*)	$ 7.15
___Wrist Support (*)	$ 7.15
___Knee Support (*)	$ 11.05
___Ankle Support (*)	$ 8.45
___Lifting Strap (*)	$ 4.55
___Waist Trimmer (*)	$ 11.05
___Wrist Band ___Head Band	$ 1.30
___Rain Poncho Clear (*)	$ 3.60
___T-Shirt 3PK M - L XL	$ 10.65
___T-Shirt 3PK 2X-3X	$ 13.65
___T-Shirt 2PK 4X - 5X - 6X	$ 17.05
___Tank Top 3PK M - L - XL ( )	$ 8.60
___Tank Top 3PK 2X - 3X ( )	$ 13.65
___Briefs 3PK S - M - L - XL	$ 7.55
___Briefs 3PK 2XL - 3XL	$ 12.35
___Briefs 3PK 4XL - 5XL	$ 13.55
___Boxer Briefs S - M - L - X L - 2X	$ 7.25

GROOMING & SHOE ACCES.

___Nail Clipper		$ 0.90
___Toenail Clippers	___Tweezers	$ 1.15
___Mustache/Beard Scissors		$ 5.15
___		
___Shoe Shine Brush		$ 5.00
___Shoe Polish Black		$ 2.15
___Shoe Lace Black	___White	$ 1.15
___Odor Eaters		$ 3.90
___Boot Lace Black		$ 1.95

OPEN HOUSE ITEMS

During daytime sales, on scheduled day

Russell Shirts MED.to 3X SIZE___	$ 5.70
Russell Shirts 4XL to 5XL SIZE___	$ 11.05
Work Boot ( )	$ 64.90
MP3 PLAYER	$ 88.40
Classic Nylon Reebok (*)	$ 42.85
Running Shoe ( )	Varies
Cross Trainer Shoe ( )	Varies
Basketball Shoe (*)	Varies
SoftWalking Shoe (velcro)	$ 49.40
Multi-purpose Cleat (*)	$ 36.40
MP3 Cover	$3.25
Sony Radio( )	$ 42.15
Mesh Shorts 5XL TO 6XL SIZE___	$ 9.65
Mesh Shorts Med. To 4XL SIZE___	$ 8.95

As you can see, you had to work long hours to purchase anything at the commissary. For example, it took 35.8 hours to purchase a bottle of cheap vitamins (i.e., generic garbage, by the way) and 17.9 hours to buy a little turkey sausage! It took ten hours of teaching to purchase a small bottle of mustard, and if you needed Tums, it would take thirty hours of work. If a person needed Visine, it would take about fifty hours of work--- requiring nearly an entire work week to obtain. From these examples, you get the idea. The pay schedule implemented for working inmates is simply inhuman. No wonder there is contraband all over the place in prisons across the land!

Most inmates refer to the prison wage rate and work, as systematized slave labor. I can't say I disagree with them. Inmate pay scales haven't been adjusted in decades, and are commensurate with the minimum wage paid *before* 1938, when the Fair Labor Standards Act was enacted by Congress:

History of Federal Minimum Wage Rates Under the Fair Labor Standards Act, 1938 - 2009

The table of federal minimum wage rates under the Fair Labor Standards Act, 1938 - 2009 is also available in a PDF Version. In order to view and/or print PDF documents you must have a PDF viewer (e.g., Adobe Acrobat Reader v5 or later) available on your workstation.

Minimum hourly wage of workers in jobs first covered by

Effective Date	1938 Act [1]	1961 Amendments [2]	1966 and Subsequent Amendments [3]	
			Nonfarm	Farm
Oct 24, 1938	$0.25			
Oct 24, 1939	$0.30			
Oct 24, 1945	$0.40			
Jan 25, 1950	$0.75			
Mar 1, 1956	$1.00			
Sep 3, 1961	$1.15	$1.00		
Sep 3, 1963	$1.25			
Sep 3, 1964		$1.15		
Sep 3, 1965		$1.25		
Feb 1, 1967	$1.40	$1.40	$1.00	$1.00
Feb 1, 1968	$1.60	$1.60	$1.15	$1.15
Feb 1, 1969			$1.30	$1.30
Feb 1, 1970			$1.45	

Source: U.S. Department of Labor.

This is precisely one of the reasons there are many violations of the contraband rules. When you pay men slave-labor wages and don't feed them properly, and then charge them through the nose to buy food and medicine, while denying them proper medical care, as well as the ability to economically reach their loved ones---something is going to give.

At Fort Dix, what "gave" was obedience to the rules. A total breakdown with respect to the ingress of contraband was in full force and effect, while I was a prisoner at Fort Dix.

In at least one instance, word got out the guards found *bags* of pre-paid cell phones, located just outside the open fence of the Camp's back exercise yard. Men walk out of the Camp at Fort Dix, freely during working hours, to go to jobs on the base, or other jobs around the prison. Somebody would pick up the phones and sell them for a couple of thousand dollars *each, to inmates.* This was a big money business for someone.

One of the more clever inmates, whose name was "Alex" (who was a nice, Jewish guy, originally from Russia) had a job to keep the prison grounds at Fort Dix clean of debris. One day, Alex was on his bicycle making his check of the grounds.

On this particular day, there was a really big party and reception taking place at the Warden's administration building. The Warden's building is near the entrance to the prison, and the room where they were holding the reception had a big picture window, which looked directly out onto the street. This street ran from the Warden's building down to the Camp and other prison facilities at Fort Dix. The road also had a drainage ditch, which ran along beside it, and debris often collected there.

As the time for the party approached, a couple of BOP Officers were walking over to the Warden's building. As they approached it, they noticed a garbage bag in the ditch.

They didn't think much about it, at first, but curiosity took over and they decided to check it out. They opened up the bag. With eyes bulging like saucers and incredulous, the men couldn't believe what they were seeing. Crammed into this large, dark-plastic bag were some of the world's finest food delicacies!

There was caviar, desserts, smoked salmon, and other unimaginable, scrumptious morsels---a veritable treasure trove of goodies, fit for a king.

Initially, the Officers thought some of the guys from the food warehouse had stolen the food from delivery vehicles and then stowed the food into the bag---throwing the bag into the ditch for "pick up" after work.

As the Officers went through the stash, they were going to confiscate the goody bag and haul it away. But, after thinking about it, they decided to leave the bag in the ditch and wait *inside* the reception room of the party to see who might pick it up. The window in the room provided a perfect view of the ditch---and bag.

They wondered, *"Who would come along and retrieve this gold-mine of goodies?"* The Officers also told the attendees of the party what was going on, and the result was quite predicable. Dozens of sets of eyeballs were now fixated on the dark-plastic trash bag in the ditch, in front of the party room!

Within about a half-hour after the party started, the room became eerily quiet. All eyes were now definitely locked onto the bag in the ditch, as the attendees could see someone approaching it! Like they were watching a movie, dozens of people started laughing, out loud and hidden from view, as they observed the scene in front of them. It was better than a drive-in theater! They watched, as who other than Alex the Russian, casually rode up on his bicycle---faithfully doing his Camp job of collecting trash around the perimeter!

They watched Alex's every move. They saw him stop, directly in front of the "garbage" bag, then dismount, and then very carefully look around.

Of course, unbeknownst to Alex, fifty people had crowded around the reception room window, all having been apprised of the "goody bag" in the ditch, and savoring the moment of catching Alex in the "act."

Alex once again, looked carefully around. He then bent over, and looked quickly inside the bag. He then hoisted it into the hopper on the back of his bicycle, remounted his bicycle and casually pedaled slowly away. Nothing to see here, folks...The room then exploded and erupted in great laughter!

Now loaded with a full bag of "garbage," Alex was simply going to finish his day, go back to his bunk and relax. There he would stash his treasure trove and enjoy his caviar and smoked salmon on Russian crackers! I can only imagine the raucous laughter coming out of that room. I heard everyone was in stitches!

Despite the great laugh they had, this really got the guards, the Warden, and every other person in the BOP, pretty worked up. Many of them had never even tasted Russian Beluga Caviar before!

Poor, Alex. They couldn't wait to get their hands on this guy. They caught Alex, all right, and promptly sent him to a more "secure" prison. We never saw him, again.

This is how things went at Fort Dix. Some guys would get busted for a cell phone, for gambling, for alcohol, for food, or for some other infraction and then they would just disappear.

Others, however, somehow managed to magically return to Camp. These men were quickly identified as rats, or worse, because inevitably, somebody else would get in trouble, shortly after their return.

Alex was special, though. He held a special place in the minds of the inmates at Fort Dix because apparently, he had been playing this game for a long time and had never been caught, until this day. I felt badly for him---but, I have to admit how funny the story was, when I first heard it. Alex and his caviar IN PRISON! I mean, he had a brass pair of balls---that was for sure.

Alex had also been one of the guys who was required to attend an education class in the library, by law. Alex was super smart, but he couldn't show proof of his high school diploma. He didn't study much of anything in his education classes but, one thing he did do every day, was diligently work on his Russian crossword puzzles. He loved those things, and it drove Ms. Lindley crazy.

Alex always refused to engage in a classroom environment and kept to himself, but, whenever his instructor got sick, he was ordered by Ms. Lindley to come into my class to "work." Somebody had to babysit him, apparently. But, Alex was always quite nice and very polite to me, and I just let him do his thing. He never bothered anyone.

Being Russian, and growing up when his country was firmly in the hands of the Communists, I was certain he must have a unique perspective on politics and political systems. But, I had no idea what his political beliefs were.

I wondered, even though we had never really spoken, if I could ever call upon him to make a contribution to the class one day. I thought he might be able to share about his native country and perhaps make the class more interesting and "real" for the other students. Thinking of ways to get the classes' attention was a challenge, and I thought Alex might help at some point.

Often in the afternoon, Joe and I would teach our GED class (which was loaded with "liberal" students), "Social Studies." This inevitably would move into the realm of politics. Those debates got really crazy, sometimes. I personally tried to stay as neutral as possible, but provided economic reasons as to why an economy, or political system, had worked, or hadn't worked, historically. I learned a long ago it is difficult to change anyone's mind when it comes to politics. People have to come to their own conclusions.

When it got to a discussion about Hillary, Bernie Sanders and liberal politics, most of the guys were absolutely for them. They believed socialism was the best thing since sliced bread.

As one of these debates progressed, I sensed an opportunity. I knew it was risky, from a teaching perspective, but thought it was worth a shot. Alex was sitting off to the side, quietly working on his Russian crossword puzzle, like he always did, when he had to be "babysat." He was ignoring everyone and was minding his own business, just like usual. From my perspective, Alex didn't need to be in school---this seemed sure.

As he sat there, not bothering anyone, I half-shouted, to get his attention, "Hey, Alex. You grew up in the Soviet Union, right?"

Alex answered with his heavy accent, "Yaaa, I deed."

All the men in that 12:30 p.m. class turned to Alex and then moved their eyes back to me. I continued, "Alex, can you do me a favor? I don't know what you think of Communism, or socialism. You and I have never discussed these subjects, or anything else, for that matter. But, if you could, would you mind telling the class what you think of these political systems? The guys are convinced socialism is the way of the future."

Alex looked at me, and in his hardened street persona, growled in his thick, heavy Russian accent, "Communism and socialism are 'sheet' 'seestems!'" He raged on, "There is nothing to eat, prices are sky high." Then pointing to the students, he said, "You guys are 'eedeeots' to want 'thees' 'sheet' 'seestem!'"

Joe and I just about lost it. We laughed and laughed. I turned to the class and said, "Guys, I try hard NOT to give you only one side of things, but listen to someone who has actually lived with and through, these flawed economic systems. Socialism is a disaster for nations. Economies collapse because of it."

I continued, "Just look at Venezuela, Argentina, Brazil, and the entire Eastern Block. They were destroyed by these policies. Europe is going down the tubes for the very same reasons!"

Yes, Alex was taken out of the Camp at Fort Dix, shortly after this amazing contribution to the class, but I will never forget what he did for the men that day. Alex was a true entrepreneur, and avowed capitalist---even in prison!

CHAPTER 8

SOME GUYS JUST GROW UP TOUGH

As a Christian in prison, it is easy to be underestimated. Many inmates assume because you try and be nice and even try and help other prisoners, you are just a wuss and will likely wilt when confronted---even in trivial matters. Once an inmate goes down the wussy-road trail, it is downhill from there.

You can never, ever be afraid in prison and you can't be a wimp---whether you are a Christian, or have some other religious philosophy. The law of the street rules prison. You have to stand your ground when pushed and you must push back---hard, when and if, necessary, while maintaining your integrity and values.

Additionally, no matter how nice you might be, no matter what you try and do for others, some men are just "dicks" and are always looking for trouble. "It is what it is," as they say. I know it's not "Christ-like" to think this way, but it is the truth of prison life.

The fact is, many inmates have lived and survived off the streets, for much of their lives. They may not have been caught with a weapon when they were arrested, but many men were used to them being around. This was obvious from their trash-talk and the way they carried themselves. Many of these men had lived lives filled with danger, and were true mismatches for satellite camps, which were created originally for a true, "low-risk" prison population.

Directly because of the BOPs budget-saving decisions, and self-serving need to stay "in budget" and pay for their benefits, bonuses, pensions and salaries, the BOP at Fort Dix, like other prisons, created an inter-mingled mess of men. Danger is the *key* word in any prison, and it lurks around every corner.

For this reason alone, when anyone decided to ever push back, or confront anything with another inmate, warning flags immediately were raised...and when this happened, you can also actually feel your pulse quicken.

I had a number of run-ins, with a number of guys, while doing my time. It was inevitable when you were teaching assertively to a population of inmates who generally didn't even want to be in the same room with you.

You quickly became a target out of anger, resentment, envy or just "because." "Because," could have been due to a bad day, or because of my skin color (or lack, thereof), or educational background, or because I got in line before someone else did, or changed a TV channel. It didn't really matter. "Because" didn't need an explanation.

As I said, during my first week in class, I was very naïve. When I arrived at Fort Dix, I thought I would go out and serve my fellow man, survive and maybe even help some guys while I was there. Hah-hah! That joke was really on me.

I started out with this "desire to serve" attitude in the area quite close to my bunk. Each week, the men would clean up and mop the floors (Mike and I mopped twice a week), and in my first week, I thought I would just mop the space between all the bunks in our little "neighborhood." I didn't think anyone would possibly have a problem with just helping other guys out.

Turns out, I was wrong...big time.

It was early on a weekend morning, and I began sweeping the floors and aisles, around the bunks. To sweep, as everyone knows, you sweep dirt up carefully (when you are indoors) and put it into a dust pan---then you mop. It's pretty straight forward.

Or, so I thought.

On this morning, one of the big guys at the far end of the aisle was observing my activities. After all, I was the new guy on the block. Out of nowhere, he started screaming at me, "What in the HE** are you doing? You don't know ANYTHING!! KEEP THAT SHI* OUT OF OUR SPACE!! WE ALREADY CLEANED IT UP EARLIER THIS MORNING!! GET OUT A' HERE!!"

I was pretty shocked, to be quite honest. Not only was he big, but I could sense I was being measured. I also knew him to be one of the leaders of a bunch of the men at Fort Dix.

I don't know what got into me, but I knew I hadn't really done anything wrong. Anyone knows when you sweep you clean up the mess, and then mop. This guy, though, was looking for trouble.

While he was screaming, trying to break me down and belittle me, I just calmly and piercingly, stared back at him---right in his eyes, and I could feel my adrenaline start pumping---my blood rushed up through my face and neck. When he was done with his tirade, I belted one right back at him. I shouted, feeling my eyes nearly pop out of my skull, with about thirty *other* sets of eyeballs now locked onto me, by the men in our 'hood:

"AND JUST <u>HOW</u> WOULD I POSSIBLY KNOW THAT???!!! ALL I AM DOING HERE IS TRYING TO MOP THE FLOORS!"

He didn't expect an aggressive volley back from me, and I'm sure he was at least somewhat shocked I responded in this forceful manner, because he was a lot bigger than me.

You could have heard a pin drop, too, along both sides of the aisles in row after row of bunk beds. Everyone grew silent. This looked like it was going to turn into a big fight and a major situation.

Fortunately for me, this guy was getting ready to go home soon, and he decided to let the situation drop. I think he hated my guts afterward, because he never gave me the time of day, right up until he left the Camp, about a month later.

I had nothing against him then, or even now, but these kinds of small things have a way of causing potentially big trouble in prison. Men are very frustrated, and most have good reasons for their frustration, exactly because they *are* in prison.

After we both calmed down, one of the guys across from the big guy's bunk, silently lip-sync'd a "Thank you" to me. This man could see I was only trying to help guys out and mop the floor. I appreciated his gesture of thanks, because I truly thought I was in a crazy house at the time, where no one appreciated much of anything.

After thinking about it and talking with my spacemate Mike, he convinced me to just clean up our area and not do anyone else's, anymore. It wasn't worth the trouble.

I didn't either, until the big guy left. I really don't remember his name, but after his release, I picked up the broom and mop and continued to clean up around other guys' bunks. Many, many guys appreciated it, and I didn't mind.

In fairness, initially, I didn't mop floors very well. Mike always made fun of me for this, because my first mop-jobs used way too much water (which left small pools of water in the cement aisles), which took far too long to dry...irritating the men!

With this lesson learned, I tried really hard to focus on my own business and do the best I could with what I had to work with. I had to give up on serving all the men around me, at least temporarily, until things cooled off. I was determined, however; I would help anyone I could, regardless of race, creed, or color.

Over time, these men would cast judgment upon me, and after my first few bad experiences, I thought it would be interesting to see what their verdict would be in the future.

One of the craziest things about prison is more often, than not, issues are resolved by violence. It is in the culture. Also, the guards (generally speaking) look the other way.

I saw numerous fights, with serious injuries inflicted on men, while I was at Fort Dix. In big altercations, men would use hand-made weapons. The most serious characters always packed some kind of weapon within easy reach of themselves, at all times. Months later, another incident occurred in the TV room, with another very serious guy, named "Richie."

When you get several hundred men, all brimming with frustration, and all living under incredibly confined quarters, tempers frequently boiled over. A major source of those problems would center around the TV---or rather, what was being watched on the TV.

The basic rule is whoever is in the room first, gets to watch the channel he selects---with several caveats. The first caveat is no one can touch the Spanish TVs. They had to remain tuned to Univision and Telemundo. After a while, with many of the Spanish guys becoming supportive of what I was doing for many of them in the Camp, they allowed me to change these stations to the news---but only on the weekends in the early morning, when no one was awake yet. I was grateful to them, and would turn the station back when I was done.

For all the other TVs, they were open. At night, when a regularly televised series was going to be broadcast, or "Love & Hip Hop" was on (or, some other widely watched show), the TVs had to stay on those channels, regardless of who was there first. Of course, you were taking your life in your hands if you changed the TVs dedicated to sports...

A new inmate had to feel his way through this system, but the easiest way to avoid trouble was to watch TV as little as possible. This is what I decided to do. I read a lot, worked on my class preparation and wound up being one of the guys men turned to, when they needed help.

Anyway, this afternoon, an inmate named Richie was watching TV without ear phones. TVs required radios *and* earplugs to listen to television broadcasts (together, these cost about $50 at commissary, and at $.12/hour, represent about 416 hours of work!), because TV speakers are supposed to be turned off at all times. Multiple TVs in each room meant you couldn't hear a thing if all their volumes were on at once---hence the need for ear plugs and a radio to watch TV.

I needed to do an email and I entered this particular TV room, where Richie was watching TV. The email terminals were located in the back of the room and I went and took a seat. I ignored everything around me as I was doing my email, and when I finished, no one else was in the room. Richie had left.

I looked at my watch, saw I had some time to kill between classes, and thought it would be nice to sit down and watch TV for a few minutes. Amazingly, I had some "private" time, as no one else was in the room.

I changed the station.

This turned out to be another big mistake. Richie, apparently, had only left to go to the bathroom. When he returned, he completely lost his temper.

When he yelled, "Who changed that channel?!" I turned around, looked at him, and said, "I did. I thought you had left."

Richie must have had a bad day because he started really raging at me, in front of another inmate who had come in and sat down, after I changed the channel. Richie came right up to where I was sitting in my chair, watching the History channel. He towered over me, and projected a tone of near-violent intimidation, as he began to shout me down. He raged for at least five minutes at how I was "disrespectin'" him.

While he was shouting, he lowered his face to within four inches of mine, clearly egging me on to take a swipe at him.

I stared at him, right in the eyes, never batting an eyelash, and remained calm. I honestly didn't know he was returning and he hadn't said anything when he left. Guys enter and leave TV rooms all the time, but once again, this had turned into another sidewinder incident, which looked like was about to spin out of control.

Once again, God was at work, because Richie in his old life would have just punched me first, and asked questions later---or maybe worse, I don't know. But, he calmed down after I talked him through it, and all friction between us, stopped. Later, I learned he had some tough times happening on the home front.

In due course, after this confrontation, I would often speak with him out in the yard during the spring and summer. Richie had become a Christian and I encouraged him in his faith. I told him to keep his eye on the prize---on being released and focusing on the new skills he was picking up in prison.

During his prison term, Richie had become one of the best physical therapists and weight training coaches at Fort Dix. He and my buddy, "Dr. Shah," were absolutely amazing. They worked hard to help many men who needed physical therapy and were helping them build a better and healthier lifestyle.

I was honored, about six-months after the TV-room incident, when Richie asked me to help him write a petition for his early release from prison. Like other men I would help, he briefed me on his situation, I read his paperwork, and then I drafted a plea and petition. Richie reviewed it, we made some minor edits, and then he sent it up the chain-of-command. To do a good job for a person, you have to think of doing the task, as if you were doing it for yourself. Maintaining this attitude helped me do the best job I could, by remaining super-focused on their issues and adopting them, as my own. Men had begun to trust me to help them regain their lives, and I didn't want to knowingly mess something up.

After Richie sent his petition in, about two months later, we were elated to hear Richie would receive a 10-month reduction in his prison sentence. This is an eternity to a man who just wanted to get back to his family and see his Mom, who was in poor health.

Word spread and a lot more men started asking for help---which I always tried to give.

Another interesting situation happened to me, with an inmate named Bonilla. Bonilla didn't speak English very well, and couldn't write it, either. After he explained, in Spanish, what was happening in his situation, I created a petition and request for Bonilla's early release, like I did for Richie. Bonilla's case was totally different, of course, but when we were done drafting the petition, Bonilla sent it directly to the courts and his judge. I didn't know Bonilla well, but he felt comfortable with me because he was told I could be trusted by the other Hispanic men.

The Latinos are like a family, and they really do have great family instincts in prison. I was honored at being accepted as part of their trusted circle.

In any event, petitions and "letters" you send to a judge always require you to get familiar with the legal documents of a man's case. You then made sure you could recite, succinctly, a defense and/or request for a reduction, or elimination of a sentence, before delivering it to the inmate for his review.

I wrote the letter and petition for Bonilla, and then recited it back to Bonilla in Spanish, and he was very grateful and gracious. I gave the letter to him, and he sent it off in the mail.

But something strange happened. We were shocked to hear, about one-month later, Bonilla was unexpectedly *removed* from prison.

I got word through the grapevine, guards came and grabbed Bonilla, and ordered him to pack up. He was ordered to *leave* the premises within two hours because he was *immediately* being sent directly HOME!

The BOP has insurance, liability and strict regulatory concerns and procedures regarding releases. Apparently, the judge ordered for Bonilla's *immediate* release and the guards ordered him off Fort Dix premises within a strict two-hour timeframe.

None of us ever found out all the details as to why he was abruptly released. Without the dramatic sentencing change and order by the judge, Bonilla had quite a bit of time left to serve. He was so excited to be released early, and in such an unexpected fashion, he hardly had time to say goodbye to anyone and I never had the chance to say goodbye. It didn't matter though, I was thrilled for him, as most other guys were!

It was all part of God's plan, this I knew.

This situation was interesting because when you don't think anyone is watching what you are doing, it is usually when you get surprised. As I walked to my bunk, with the entire Camp lit up and abuzz with Bonilla's early release, my spacemate Mike was talking about this shockingly great news with another inmate. Mike didn't know I was passing by, and his back was turned to me, but I heard Mike say: "All I know is, Bonilla was here for years. Bob Kelly wrote a letter, and now he's gone!"

Word got around with this event, too. I could see God working on a number of souls, and it was a great quench of my spiritual thirst to see something really good get done while I was being incarcerated. I thank God for this still, today.

Another amazing story regards a nice man who approached me one day, named Orlando Ayala. Orlando was in his twenties, and had already served over six years of a long sentence for drugs. He came to me and said he had some circumstances in his case, which he was wondering if I could review. He thought they might help him request a reduction in the length of his sentence. Orlando also had a young family at home, and he was active in the Evangelical Church. I never cared if a man was in a church, or not, either. I helped those who asked---no strings attached.

After reviewing his materials, I decided to put my shoulder to the wheel, and see if we could make an impact on his case. I haven't included his entire legal brief, but what follows is a copy of the letter I wrote to his judge, and part of his legal petition. They both request a sentence reduction, on his behalf. Orlando had an attorney, years before, but many times things get stuck in court, as was the situation in his case. I found it helped frequently to send a petition, along with information which demonstrated real change in the inmate's life, while he had been incarcerated.

About two months after we sent these documents to his judge, Orlando was informed he had received a *three-and-a-half-year* sentence reduction! Orlando was beyond happy, as was his young family. With a huge smile on my face I said to him, "Daddy will be coming home, very soon!" He grinned hugely and gave me a manly hug. He understood the English, too!

Orlando will not come back to prison, either. He loves his family too much to even think about it.

Prison typewriters are notoriously horrendous, and please forgive the typos in Orlando's letter.

I guess the judge didn't seem to mind, though, thank God.

Holding the Fort

Granted 3½ years off sentence!

February 28, 2016

The Honorable Senior Judge Juan M. Perez Gimenez
United States District
Room 150 Federal Building
San Juan, Puerto Rico 00918-1767

Dear Judge Gimenez:

I am writing to make an inquiry into the status of my motion requesting a modification of sentence pursuant to 18 U.S.C. §3582(c)(2). I am deeply grateful for the courts consideration of my petition, as I have been working very hard in prison to turn my life around.

As documented in my Pro Se petition for my consolidated cases: 09-297(PG) and 09-173(PG), I was sentenced, originally to 168 months, based on a Total Offense Level of 35, with a criminal history category I (range of 168-210). If the two (2) point reduction were granted, based upon my eligibility and the manner in which I have been conducting my life, since entering prison (please see below), my total offense level would be a "33" with an applicable sentencing range of as low as 135 months.

I have already served 6 years and 4 months of my sentence, and have made great progress toward becoming an excellent and honest contributor to society, upon release.

I know a key consideration in your decision to grant me the 2-point reduction is my post-sentencing conduct which has occurred after the imposition of my sentence. I thought it might be helpful to provide the Court with this list of successfully completed programs I have completed while incarcerated. Being able to learn and grow, away from the streets, have made me a better man, and a man ready to "hit the ground running" and obtain honest employment, upon release. I know this is the only way I will be able to help my family, and myself, while allowing myself the ability to earn an honest living.

Date	Program
1/4/2011	Walking For Fitness
4/15/2011	Relay For Life-Cancer Warriors Team
2012	Fort Dix Softball Champions
2012	Coach-Fort Dix Softball Champions
12/21/2012	Parenting
8/21/2014	English As A Second Language (ESL)
12/2/2014	Demonstrated Reentry Skills & High Praise For Work over a long period of time (2 1/2 years as of this date of achievement)

Education information and FCI Fort Dix transcript also attached.

As you can see, I have kept very busy while in prison, every day preparing myself for reentry. I continue to work in my current job and continue to perform at a high performance level.

Importantly, I have had no disciplinary actions, while incarcerated.

Finally, Judge Gimenez, I have learned a trade where I can not only make a good living, when I am released, but I can also help other people and the environment.

As you can imagine, with Fort Dix on one of the biggest military bases in the United States, we get experienced with a very wide variety of materials and recyclables, which have to be dealt with. Obviously, some are quite hazardous, and have to be disposed of thoughtfully.

I just wanted you to know that with this skill, in particular, which is in very high demand, because of the contribution it makes to society, I believe I will be gainfully employed soon after release.

Thank you again, for your consideration of my motion, and I hope this letter helps to shed further light on my case, allowing you to confidently grant me the 2-point reduction.

Thank you for the chance to change my life. Prison has accomplished that!

Sincerely,

Signature Blocked

Orlando Ayala
Criminal Nos. 09-297(PG)
            09-173(PG)

There were many other stories and some really exciting ones, too. Some really toughened, hard men came to appreciate my frankness and directness when it came to the Lord and my work with them. I know many of them used their time in prison to try and improve themselves, by planning to be the best they could be, when they would return to society.

At the end of the day, I really just tried to encourage the men around me, as best I could, and helped out where and when called.

It is hard to describe, but these activities at this time in my life, saved *me*. The guys thought I was helping *them*, but in reality, it was the other way around!

```
           IN THE UNITED STATES DISTRICT COURT
            FOR THE DISTRICT OF PUERTO RICO


UNITED STATES OF AMERICA,              :
                                       :
                                       :
              v.                       :      Criminal Nos. 09-297(PG)
                                       :                    09-173)PG)
                                       :
                                       :
ORLANDO AYALA, aka "NEGRITO"           :
                                       :
_____:
```

MOTION REQUESTING A MODIFICATION OF
SENTENCE PURSUANT TO 18 U.S.C. §3582(c)(2)

Petitioner Orlando Ayala, Pro Se, respectfully request this Honorable Court to modify his sentence pursuant to Amendment 782 of the United States Guidelines and 18 U.S.C. §3582(c)(2).

CASE SUMMARY

On September 9, 2009, Petitioner Orlando Ayala was charge in two separate indictments. In Criminal Case No. 09-297, United States v. Orlando Ayala Medina. Petitioner Ayala, along with two (2) other co-defendants, were the subject of a three-count Indictment issued by a Grand Jury in the District of Puerto Rico charging the defendants with drug offenses.

On September 29, 2009, in Criminal Case No. 09-173-016(PG), Petitioner Ayala, along with sixty-four (64) other co-defendants, were the subject of a seven count First Superseding Indictment issued by a Grand Jury in the District of Puerto Rico charging the defendant with drug offenses.

To me, most inmates at Fort Dix were very good men, who had made poor choices in life. I came away feeling lucky to have been able to meet them, because I know I got the best end of the deal. They really helped me stay strong in the Lord, and kept me focused during my prison term.

Having said this, none of us wanted to be in prison---I mean, even Saint Peter was broken out of jail by an angel.

God knows, it's not a nice place to be!

Every man in prison aches for his family and loved ones. All of us missed home, terrifically. We were all alone---except that we had each other, and among us, God moved some mountains, while we were there.

Despite the obvious hardships, and separation from family, interestingly, each prisoner discovered some things about Fort Dix, while he was doing his time.

Some took longer than others, and many could care less, but all of us, regardless of background, found we had several things in common. They included:

1) Everyone was trapped at Fort Dix, together;
2) Many men were sentenced harshly, and in many cases, innocent men were prosecuted and thrown in prison for long periods of time; and
3) We all wore the same color. Our prison uniforms were forest green and were issued with standard military-style, steel-toed boots---the standard uniform of the convict at the Fort Dix Camp.

No matter what walk of life a man would come from, no matter if a man hated another man, or resented him, we would come to know we were all part of a brotherhood which society had left behind.

This knowledge was little solace for most men, but, nevertheless, it was a tie that bound us, together.

I hope anyone reading this doesn't ever, ever go to prison. It is dangerous and you could easily lose your life, as I almost lost mine (I cover this near tragedy in a later chapter).

But, if you ever find you have to go, carry with you the sword of the spirit, the helmet of salvation and the whole armor of God. I truly tried to think in this way, each and every day...and lived life like this, while in prison. Please notice The Bible says nowhere in this passage, things will be *easy!*

The Armor of God

[10]Finally, be strong in the Lord and in his mighty power. [11]Put on the full armor of God, so that you can take your stand against the devil's schemes. [12]For our struggle is not against flesh and blood, but against the rulers, against the authorities, against the powers of this dark world and against the spiritual forces of evil in the heavenly realms. [13]Therefore put on the full armor of God, so that when the day of evil comes, you may be able to stand your ground, and after you have done everything, to stand. [14]Stand firm then, with the belt of truth buckled around your waist, with the breastplate of righteousness in place, [15]and with your feet fitted with the readiness that comes from the gospel of peace. [16]In addition to all this, take up the shield of faith, with which you can extinguish all the flaming arrows of the evil one. [17]Take the helmet of salvation and the sword of the Spirit, which is the word of God. (Source: The Bible, Ephesians 6:10-17, NIV).

Holding the Fort

CHAPTER 9

TEACHING MEN TO FISH

As November rolled into December, during the winter of 2014, I was getting an eye-full of the challenges faced by men in prison---especially for the ones who might want to change their lives.

As I settled into teaching, many of the Hispanic guys came around first. I have always had a heart for Spanish-speaking people, as nearly all the ones I have known during my lifetime, have great hearts. At the end of the day, most of them live their lives around their families and are devoted to them.

I'm not sure if their coming around was because of my commitment to excellence in the classroom (as far as my preparation for class), or if it was merely my genuine affection for people---I really don't know.

We had a huge Spanish GED class---easily over 30 students, and after a while, Joe and I thought it would be a good idea to split the class up---he would take some and I would take some. The only catch was, Joe told me, I would have to teach in the small "Rec" room.

All I really knew about the "Rec" room was it had a white board and some tables, which I would have to set up each day, in order to teach.

After we discussed it, all I could think was, *"This is a great opportunity. Divide and conquer!"*

The Spanish GED class had been nearly as crazy as the ESL class (ESL, the class of the "sailing" office chair!), and there were plenty of jerks running around causing problems each and every day. Classroom interruptions were standard fare and something the men engaged in, at will. The biggest trouble makers would do virtually anything to make it impossible for anyone to learn *anything* during class time. This was how the class had always run itself before I showed up, and was the solid history of the Education Department at Fort Dix, until I started teaching.

The big difference now, was when I was in front of the group teaching, I spoke *Spanish*. This made a huge difference to the men, and a group of the Dominican, Puerto Rican and Mexican guys had sort of bonded with me. These were really a group of great men, and although they did not want to be in class, I think they realized all the work I was putting into preparation to try and make math, science and all the other courses more interesting for them. Fort Dix had nearly no Spanish materials, of any kind, and I wound up translating everything into Spanish, at night. Unfortunately, though, I didn't get paid my $.12/hour for homework!

I mean, it would have added up. Think about it, one hour of translation time and I could have put a whole twelve cents in my pocket! I'm sure I could have retired, especially if I had been paid overtime. If they paid me to work 24-hours a day, 7 days a week for the 21-months I was in prison, I would have walked away with a cool $1,844.40. Yea! Party on, Garth...

As I worked with the men, I realized math was particularly difficult for them, and with Ms. Lindley designating me, the "Math Guy," I tried to create new materials the men might find useful.

I was shocked one day, when we were in the Rec room and I was teaching a math word problem to the class, when one of my favorite students, Ricky, asked me a question. Normally, everyone in Camp called me, "Kelly." But, this time, Ricky, who is about forty years old, began his question like this:

"MAESTRO, tengo una pregunta, por favor!"

For most Americans, this is no big deal, but for a person in the Hispanic culture to properly call a "Gringo" in the front of the room, "Maestro," within the federal correctional institution known as Fort Dix, it was a subtle, but *huge* compliment. He was giving me huge "respect," in front of the other men.

"Maestro" simply means "teacher," in Spanish and Ricky was merely saying he had a question---but, it was the *way* he said it, which floored me. Up until this day, no one had ever called me "Maestro," or "teacher."

The world changed for me, every day, thereafter. From then on, many of the guys in my class called me, "Maestro" and sometimes would use the English form "Teacher," when they wanted to get my attention. They would affectionately use the term to speak with me in the yard, by the bunks, in the library, or someplace else. I never felt comfortable with the title---in my mind, that title was reserved for the likes of Aristotle, Socrates and Plato---certainly not for a hack teacher, like me.

I was simply overwhelmed and humbled by Ricky and the men, as they continued to use this nickname for me. I never let on how it made me feel, and I always let it slide right off my back.

Generally, I tried to keep things upbeat and super casual---albeit, super-focused. I thought it was really important to honor the age-old tradition of what a "good" teacher should be. Good teachers always committed themselves to their students and always tried to make things interesting for their classes. At least, this had been my experience.

I'll always cherish the moment, when Ricky first used the term, because I know these guys don't give respect out, easily. All of the guys were tough men, but they knew I could see through their outer toughness and realized they all had great hearts.

You could see the Hispanic guys' family attitudes and natural warmness if you bothered to look closely, especially in prison. They really stuck together and took care of each other.

They cooked together, pooled their resources, and generally treated each other like family. I sort of got adopted, but was always careful to make sure I kept my position as their "teacher," a serious one. It was my God-directed course to set a good example for the men, while also providing them an education they never had the opportunity to receive before.

Many, many inmates have grown up poor, financially speaking. This is one of the roots of the problem, with respect to recidivism and incarceration, in the United States. Poverty, and a general lack of employable job skills by children's *parents*, pushes kids out the door at an early age and onto the streets, where they are forced to work and help support the family.

Yes, many people wind up in prison from good homes and from all classes of "wealth," however, one of the biggest problems lies right here with this word---"wealth." With a lack of education and lack of employable job skills, and no "wealth" backing them up to improve their lives, the unfortunates find themselves forced to take risks to feed their families, in their pursuit to build better lives.

Until we fix this problem, all the politicians in the world---with all of their pontificating---will not make a dent in the issue of recidivism. They will continue to waste billions of dollars in taxpayer money, and allow a corrupt system continue to hire questionable, outside parties to perform the business of imprisonment of the destitute. What they should be focused on is serious rehabilitation and education, which arms inmates with employable job skills. These could provide men and women with great jobs---perhaps even as good as someone's job on Wall Street.

This is a very tough problem, but when I was thinking it through, during my first two months in captivity, I knew this would be my goal.

Never one to think small, I decided I would try and make a *big change* in somebody's life, if I could. Then, I thought:

"If I could get a group of committed students, who really studied and worked hard, prepared to get a great job by obtaining a unique skillset, I would feel like I was doing something worthwhile---even during the period of my life where my world had been turned upside down."

Again, it came down to the Biblical principal of what Jesus taught, where he didn't just give men fish, but he taught them *how* to fish, and how to be fishers of men.

Unfortunately, there was no playbook to achieve this at Fort Dix, especially with respect to arming men with real job skills. I thought night and day: *"How could I really reach these men?"*

I had earned the respect of many of the Hispanic inmates, and this was great. As a result, many of them would go on to receive their GED diplomas and ESL certifications. In fact, during the 21 months I was at Fort Dix, 25 men graduated with GEDs and their high school diplomas, a record at Fort Dix, along with a huge number of ESL certifications. I honestly can't remember how many ESL certifications were awarded, but it was well in excess of 25. I was moved when the men attended their graduation ceremonies, or received word on their passing the GED exams, many of these "tough guys," cried. Many a time, tears welled up in my eyes, too. It was always fantastic when one of the men would pass!

Ms. Lindley did an incredible job of honoring the graduates, too. They were able to invite their families to graduation, and this was an important event at Fort Dix. The graduates received real high school diplomas from a Washington D.C. high school, and wore their caps & gowns during graduation ceremonies.

I have included a pamphlet from one of the graduations, which follows.

English as a Second Language

Campusano, Rigoberto

Claudio, Alexis

Cruz, Luis

Guzman, Leriel

Lisboa, Edwin

Martinez, Sergio

Rodriguez, Jose

Serate, Esteban

Torres, Jay

GED Graduates

Cruz, Pablo

Emanuele, Giuseppe

Henderson, Michael

Johnakin, Wayne

Jones, Reginald

Robinson, Percy

Sims, Eric

Summers, James

Suriel, Levis

Zenelaj, Agron

I provided the men with the "best-of-the-best" (or, at least, as best I could), and didn't take crap from anyone, not even the really tough guys. This caused some of even the most hardened men, to sit up and take notice.

Joe and I took it on our backs to push the men forward, and we prodded them, cajoled them, prayed for them and worked hard to try and help them.

A couple of men in one of the afternoon classes, were two of my favorites. They were Larry (McCeevy) and Taylor (Sidney Taylor). Each had been in prison for too long, and while Joe and I wished they could just go home, we *loved* those guys being in our class. They were real, honest and didn't give anyone a problem. They were also really funny---and really smart.

They didn't usually pay much attention in class, because they were both around 60 years old, and were just waiting to go home. I can honestly say I didn't blame them...they had had enough of prison life.

I was always impressed with Larry, who every morning at 7:30 a.m., when I would be entering the ESL classroom to start the day, would show up at the bank of phones to make a call to his wife---just to tell her he loved her. I called him, "The faithful man," when he would walk by. He made sure she knew---each and every day. I don't care what anyone says, that's a good man there.

The other favorite, Taylor, was a true friend, and beyond funny. He was brilliant when it came to English Literature and he had a real gift for it, which is quite amazing since he grew up in the inner city of Philadelphia.

We would read some of the great authors, including Edgar Allen Poe, Charles Dickens, Shakespeare, Samuel Clemens, Tolstoy, Michenor, many political speeches (e.g., Lincoln, Kennedy, Churchill, etc.), as well as important historical documents. Taylor would often shock other guys when he answered a complex question posed from the materials.

What I personally really appreciated was for months, these two men watched me spend time with the young guys who really wanted to change...and apparently, Larry and Taylor noticed something.

They noticed my persistence, against all odds---and against all the trash talking and stone-throwing which would go on against me by the "disinterested" inmates, initially. Larry and Taylor saw my efforts to provide an outstanding education for the men, day in, and day out, and each day, I would flat out TEACH. This is something none of the men were used to.

Other prisons don't even require an inmate to study, or do any work during class, at all. The teachers kick back and read, or do something other than teach. I frequently heard complaints from the men, "Why can't we watch movies in the classroom? That's what they would do in other prisons!" I doubt seriously, if this was Congress' intent (i.e. to allow movies during federally mandated class time), but this is what transpires, without question.

Joe and I never forced anyone to do anything, either. In fact, we would often help guys fill out their work for Ms. Lindley.

This prevented the guys from getting into trouble and it was a good feeling (for the men, Joe and I) to know everyone could relax in the classroom, even if they *didn't* do their work. We got to teach them something, even if we filled out their work with them. They were at least listening!

On the flip side, this allowed me to focus on the men who really *wanted* to learn. This is exactly what Larry and Taylor had noticed. Larry and Taylor were and are, very careful men, and they don't state things lightly. Hardened by life and wise as foxes, they could spot B.S. from the real deal, in about two nano- seconds.

Every day, they would give me the respect of letting me do my lesson plan, as would most of the other disinterested students. This was an important breakthrough, because when I got to Fort Dix, the classrooms were complete and utter disasters, from a noise and organizational perspective. The guys would think nothing of talking over an instructor, and the general order of business was to resist and disrupt the classroom, at all costs. Classes were sort of like an anti-Trump rally!

Nothing was perfect and disruptions would still occur from time to time, but I would never stop talking. This irritated a lot of men, particularly at first, but when hardened criminals began to see several men pass their GED exams, and noticed they knew answers to some pretty tough math problems, even some of the truly "tough guys" started to pay attention.

For the record, the GEDs the men earned were no cake walk. We made the men learn algebra, geometry, and even a bit of trigonometry and calculus for certain math problems. We dove into the great work of brilliant literature minds, the importance of written communications and how to create them, and went full force into science and social studies.

This was exciting stuff, inside a place where they had previously only been graduating a few people a year.

In any event, as I've said, while the Spanish-speaking guys called me "Maestro," the inner city guys just called me "Kelly," except my friend, Taylor. He had created a special nickname for me, which, of course, was self-styled in his own precocious manner and sense of humor. This name stuck with me, too, at least as far as Taylor was concerned, the entire time I was at Fort Dix.

In Taylor's really great Philadelphia, inner-city accent, he just called me:

"Kihllah."

...As in "Killer." Taylor had a way of slurring this word and he always had a toothpick in his mouth, so the pronunciation of "Kihllah," could have been easily defended by him, as being "Kelly." This is how Taylor played...very clever!

As I said, he and Larry were also really very funny guys. I told them they should get on a radio show, someday, and just start talking. They had real gifts in the communication area. Joe and I would laugh with them, very, very hard, sometimes.

They are truly missed, as are Spence, Chet, Dillon, Mr. Love, Rickie, Rosado, Pablo, Sr. Roman, Chet, Mr. Gray, Mr. Jeffrey Eugene, Mr. Brown, Dee Williams, Mr. Battle, Perez and all the other guys in our classes.

I was now beginning to see clear evidence I could make a difference with the GED program and help guys with their ESL certifications, but I really wanted to try and do something powerful---something potentially even more significant. I wanted to try and change drug dealers' and other criminals' lives, forever, or at least give them the tools to do so.

I knew this was one of my missions.

This was one of the reasons God sent me to Fort Dix.

CHAPTER 10

DECEMBER 2014 –EUREKA!

My bunk at 120U was surrounded by an ocean of other bunks. If you looked out, all around, you could see most of the other two-hundred bunk beds in the "B Wing" from my perch. There were bunks on both sides of me, double-stacked, as well as below, behind, and in front of my bed. The bunk at the head of my bed, directly behind me, was where another man would sleep in his upper bunk---with his head separated from my head, by about eighteen inches. This separation was made by way of the grey, metal poles across the heads of both beds, along with a bit of open air space between them.

I was lucky when I first arrived, because the bed behind mine was empty. No one was there. I knew at Fort Dix this wouldn't last long---and it didn't. Around the beginning of December, this really tall black guy, with long dread locks and a face full of tattoos, showed up.

While our beds were close, they were not as close as our lockers. My seven-foot tall, narrow-grey-metal locker (like the kind you see in a football locker room), bumped up right against the new guy's locker. There was even a slit of space between my locker and Mike's (they sat side-by-side in our space), which allowed this new guy and I to see each other if we were both standing in front of our lockers. You could definitely say, we were close "neighbors!"

When I first saw this man, I was standing in front of my locker eating some peanuts I had bought from the commissary. I introduced myself, in the best spirit of the "Welcome Wagon." "Hey, what's up?", with a nod of my head, "I'm Kelly---What's your name?"

This tall man looked at me kind of funny, as in, *"Why is this white cracker introducing himself to me?"* He stared, sizing me up, for about five seconds before responding, and then he smiled this huge smile and said, "I'm Contee. Wasuhp?"

The man's full name, I would learn later, was "Sean Contee."

From this day forward, we would become good friends. I would also learn he was a pretty funny guy---and really, quite smart, as it turns out.

As luck would have it, Sean Contee never received a high school diploma. Life went by as a child, and he was forced to make a living on the streets. He was never allowed the opportunity to finish school and this only meant one thing at Fort Dix---he had to attend the afternoon GED class, which I taught.

Sean was amazing---he actually paid attention in class, even if it didn't look like it. I noticed this, straight away. He had a keen mind, but had learned to fake it in a classroom---probably a long time ago. Because of this tactic, other guys didn't realize Sean *knew* pretty much *everything* going on in class. He had been incarcerated for a while and he was no stranger to higher-level security prisons, and Sean knew how to play the game.

By the way, "friends" in prison is way different from "friends" on the street. We are not allowed to communicate with each other once we are released and leave the prison grounds---those are the regulations. If you violate them, you are in violation of your probation and subject to resentencing, and other penalties. The bottom line is you have to remember those "Kodak moments" of friendship with inmates for years afterward, without ever being able to see those guys again. This tugs at you, for sure.

It was during this time period, in December of 2014, I would decide to ask Ms. Lindley if I could teach an "Adult Continuing Education" ("ACE") class, during the evening.

I had been really beating my head against the wall to try and figure out something I could do to teach the men, which might change their lives---beyond high school subjects. I knew, whatever I was going to do, I needed to teach them a skill which the men would clearly see might be used to earn *more money* than what they might earn by selling drugs, or committing some other illegal act on the street.

During my first month at Fort Dix of non-stop teaching and helping the guys, I assessed their raw skills, capabilities, and made a few general observations to myself. First, I noticed an uncanny knack, by nearly all the men, to sniff out "B.S." ---very quickly. I also noticed the men were direct, honest and open, generally speaking, about nearly everything.

The other thing I noticed was a function of our environment. Out of necessity, there was a great deal of bartering going on inside the prison.

I guess if you think about it, these are obvious traits and activities you might expect from men of the street. Most men in prison have nothing left to hide---they had already been "caught," and as a result, seemed less guarded than people who might work in a "normal" workplace environment. The inmate population talked openly and assertively. In prison, men don't have anyone else to talk with directly, and tend to open up with their buddies...and classmates---but, only the ones they felt close to, and could trust.

Bartering in prison is a time-honored tradition, worldwide, but it is also totally against BOP policy and regulations. Nevertheless, a blind man could see the massive amount of bartering going on at Fort Dix. It was a way of life there, as it is in all prisons across the land.

When I layered these observations on top of the fact nearly every man inside Fort Dix originally made his living off the street (i.e., A really miraculous and amazing accomplishment, even though for most, it was also illegal...), I thought these men had some interesting capabilities---capabilities very hard to learn in suburbia, grad school, or at Harvard Law.

I wondered, *"How can I tap into them?"* I pondered this question, over and over, in my mind. Then, I put some of the pieces together:

"Huh...at the end of the day, these guys made their living off the street. By definition, this means they are street smart, quick on their feet, direct in their communications, unafraid, fast and quick-thinking. They weren't polished in the "white shoe" sense of the word, but they were certainly polished warriors of the street---and they had skills. Maybe they didn't have great

traditional educations, but they were innately talented. They had to be---they survived on the streets for years---on their own!"

This was particularly true among drug dealers at Fort Dix. Suddenly, it dawned on me---these men might make amazing traders...as in *Wall Street traders*!

A light bulb went off in my head, and I literally said out loud: "Eureka!"

A couple of guys were standing nearby, and looked at me funny. They thought of me as the "crazy professor" and just sort of continued to stare. I didn't care---I knew at this instant, I would create a class which taught inmates how to MAKE MONEY---and make more money than they could ever dream of making by selling drugs! I started thinking hard and fast about how to get a class organized for the 1st quarter of 2015, as ACE classes would start at the end of January. It was now the moment to speak with Ms. Lindley.

I needed BOP approval for the class, and try to figure out, and create from scratch, a teachable, real trading system and class plan. I thought, *"How am I ever going to do this in prison?"*

I had excellent experience trading and investing, and had been immersed in the financial markets my entire adult life. I knew my book, D'Apocalypse Now!---The Doomsday Cycle, was receiving recognition, with its amazing forecasts coming true. But, I continued to rack my brains.

"What to do?"

A trading system must be "bullet proof" to mistakes. Ideally, it should be based on a system which had documented and profound success. The system also needed to be created without access to a computer, and without access to the Internet. These are not legally available to inmates at Fort Dix.

I thought even harder. Previously, I had architected an S&P futures trading model for Morgan Stanley, but I needed something which would be easy to learn, without computers.

Finally, it came to me, *"Could I figure out how to teach the men to trade like the world-famous Turtles?"* The world of trading knows "The Turtles." Curtis Faith became famous for making $34 million in about four years, after starting out with only $2 million...and he was only 19 years old when he started using the system.

I continued in thought, *"Could I teach the guys this system? How could I learn the Turtle system, if I had never used it before?"* With no access to the Internet, or a computer in prison, anything I did for class would have to be done by hand. This would mean hours, upon hours, of documenting daily data and updating databases from about twenty markets, in all probability. I would also have to manually tabulate and track profitability, trading, stop losses and do countless other calculations.

Furthermore, the system had to be created on paper and provided in a format which the guys could learn and understand---all without any software, computer, or printer.

This meant *everything* had to be written on the old electric typewriters in the prison library...and then copied on the copier.

The mission began.

CHAPTER 11

THE BLACK CRACKER

The first step was getting approval for the class. I didn't think this would be a problem, until I hit the "red tape" of the BOP. I knocked on Ms. Lindley's door, and explained my plan to try and teach the men a potentially important, new skill, to trade on Wall Street. I said, "If the men apply themselves, they could learn to earn more money honestly, than they ever could by selling drugs, or committing other crimes, when return home."

Ms. Lindley was supportive, and immediately turned to her computer. She said, "Geez, I'm really sorry, but there aren't classes in the computer approved for trading on Wall Street."

I looked at her, I'm sure, as if she was an alien, or something. Here, I thought I had a great idea for a new kind of class, which really might help change men's lives, and I was getting stymied by the "approved" BOP class list she was reading off of her computer monitor.

I was about to leave, defeated, but then spun around and asked, "Ms. Lindley, what classes *are* approved by the BOP?"

She clicked on her mouse and started scrolling down her screen, "Let's see, we have African Studies, beginning Spanish, Algebra, Alcoholics Anonymous, Seven Habits of Highly Effective People..."

I interrupted her, because we were going nowhere in a hurry with those classes. "Ms. Lindley, are there any business classes listed on the computer?"

"Uhhhh...Let's see...Yes...We have Real Estate, Marketing, How to Write a Business Plan..."

I interrupted, again. Ms. Lindley didn't like to be interrupted, but I was really trying to sort this out, quickly. I don't like to waste my time, either.

"Ms. Lindley, what if I were to teach a course about 'How to Write a Business Plan' for a Wall Street trading company." She looked at me, skeptically. I continued, "Seriously---it wouldn't be very realistic to learn to write a business plan without a business running, would it?"

A smile came across her face. She said, "I think *that* will work!"

Ms. Lindley always tried hard, within the constraints laid upon her by the BOP, to provide the guys the best education possible. She had a tough job, because she usually didn't have many teachers who cared, and typically she had a hundred[+] students with no interest in being in a classroom, at any time.

I responded, probably a bit too loudly, "That would be GREAT!" I think she thought I had lost my marbles, because nobody thinks anything is *great* in prison. As you will learn, I would promise the men who took the class, I would only teach it in prison, one single quarter---during the 1st Quarter of 2015.

These are examples of other "ACE" classes taught at Fort Dix. These were the classes being taught during the spring quarter of 2016, right before I was released:

ACE CLASSES SECOND QUARTER 2016

Monday April 11, 2016 to June 27, 2016
5:00 pm to 7:00 pm Business Law with Boyce
7:00 pm to 9:00 pm Household finance with Mahato

Tuesday, April 12, 2016 to June 28, 2016
5:00 pm to 7:00 pm Product Import/Export with Finazzo
7:00 to 9:00 pm Screen Writing with Shipley

Wednesday, April 13, 2016
5:00 pm to 7:00 pm 7 Habits of Highly Effective People with DeSimon
7:00 pm to 9:00 pm African Culture/Social Science with Sharif

Thursday, April 7, 2016 to June 30, 2016
5:00 pm to 7:00 pm Typing with Goetz & Pereiro
7:00 pm to 9:00 pm Business Planning with Kaitz

*****For class completion credit *****
must earn a minimum of 70% on final exam AND miss no more than 2 classes

Ultimately, I came to respect Ms. Lindley, greatly. Don't get me wrong, I had some real issues with her, too, but I guess this is what happens when you're focused on excellence and you fight for the men---and you're only a convict to boot.

Sometimes you just rub people the wrong way!

I had now obtained the Education Department's approval for the class, but I had to figure out the Turtle system, create an entire curriculum to teach it, and make sure what I was teaching was *exactly* what Curtis Faith had learned and used---or darned close to it!

I first had to obtain books, and other research and data materials. My loving Heidi was the key to this success. She was my eyes and ears on the Internet, as I schooled her in what I was seeking.

If you don't violate BOP regulations by using contraband cell phones, inmates only have a very limited number of minutes each month to use the pay phones to call home. You get 200 minutes a month, and 300 during November and December, over the holidays.

Because of these strict talk-time limitations, every call I made to Heidi over the next 570⁺ days, would be timed on my prison-purchased stop watch. This was to make sure we didn't run out of time to speak to each other before the end of each month.

This became an art form, because emergencies at home would occur, and of course, being separated from loved ones, extreme sadness and anxiety can often prevail. Lots and lots of tears were shed over those 4,200 minutes during the nearly two years I was away from home. My heart just died when I would hear her cry.

Heidi was a trooper, though, and incredibly strong and supportive. She never abandoned me and has always been loving to me. She had witnessed all that had happened during my drama with the federal government, and had seen it up close and personal.

She knew how I had worked four years straight for WWEBNET, without a single pay check, after 2008. This went on right up until the day of my arrest. I did this in my belief in the software's capabilities and my personal commitment to shareholders. She also knew I never foreclosed on WWEBNET either, which was my right when it couldn't pay the bills to my 100% owned software company, Rymatics, which I had started in 1999. At one point WWEBNET owed Rymatics over $1 Million for past services rendered..

She also witnessed the attempted destruction of my entire life and the attempted assassination of my character. This saddened her greatly, but it also made us stronger.

I explained to her, over the phone, what I was going to do, and I laid out in a detailed email, what it was I needed. In the email, I asked if she could get me a list, and a short, descriptive summary of some of the many books written about the Turtles and their trading exploits. I had never read any of them, and I was taking a real gamble the right resources could be found to build the class materials I would need, *quickly*.

I also told her it would be critical to obtain a subscription to the Investor's Business Daily ("IBD"). IBD is a daily financial publication, which contains the best data of any daily newspaper in the U.S. I also knew money was really, really tight for us, because I hadn't had a salary in so long and the lawyers had wiped me out during the period of time when I was trying to defend myself.

After I finished explaining, Heidi didn't blink an eye and was faithful to the core. She found a great list of publications and then started investigating IBD costs. She found a decent introductory rate, and subscribed. IBD was my lifeline for the class during prison. The publication's data would become mission critical for all the trading we would be doing in the Turtle class I would ultimately teach.

From the list of books she read to me, I selected a book on technical analysis (which I had read and studied before), and a few books about the Turtles. The most important one was the missive written by Curtis Faith, himself, <u>Way of the Turtle</u>.

When the books arrived and I started receiving IBD, I began to get really excited. I was bound and determined to decipher the various obscure descriptions of the Turtle System, contained in the pages of the books I received. The system's secrets were buried in words written by several different authors. Together, they would form the basis of my class and would create a concrete battle plan for "How to Trade Like a Turtle," the informal name of my class.

I read these books multiple times, took notes, ear-marked pages, and developed a system on paper, in hand-written form, which could then be typed and then copied for the course. I would do this work at night, and in the late afternoon when I was finished with GED classes.

The two main problems were deciphering everything correctly without the aid of the Internet, or a computer---and, the COLD.

The winter of 2014-2015 at Fort Dix experienced outside temperatures dropping to nearly *20 below zero* in January (with wind chill). Fort Dix was a place frozen like an ice cube.

Unfortunately for us, the heaters also *failed* during the second week of December in 2014 on the "B" Wing side of the Camp, which is where I slept.

They were not repaired for a *month*.

Unfortunately, this also meant there would be no heat in the library, where I was doing most of my work. You can see the weather calendar for January 2015, as follows:

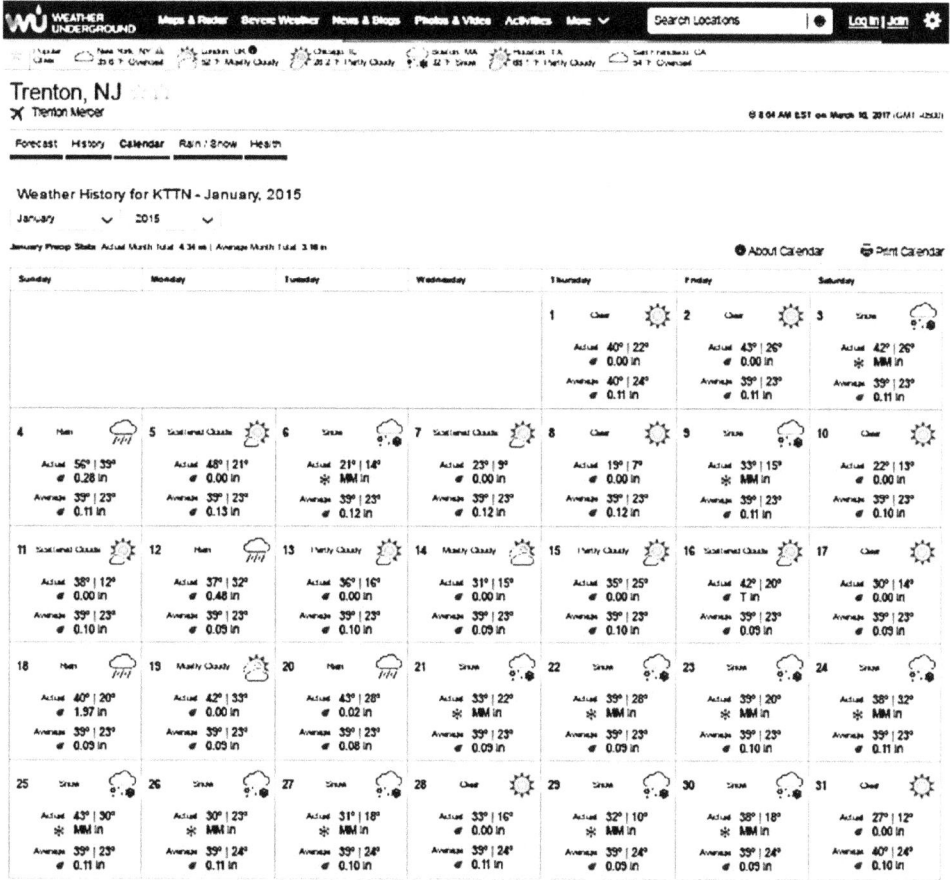

Source: Weather underground web site

https://www.wunderground.com/history/airport/KTTN/2015/1/10/MonthlyCalendar.html?req_city=Trenton&req_state=NJ&req_statename=&reqdb.zip=&reqdb.magic=&reqdb.wmo=

The failed heater, which heated the library and our living quarters, was a European model and probably from some low-cost supplier to the government. It sat on the roof, atop our "B" Wing living quarters, which became extremely cold. During the second full week of January it was worse than an unheated igloo---and the men would have to sleep with their clothes, winter coats, hats and gloves on. You could clearly see your breath when you exhaled in bed.

Things got pretty ugly, and the men's tempers ran short, as the hand of a bitter, and icy cold winter gripped down upon us. We lived in these conditions for over a month, before the BOP acquired a replacement heater. This was a big source of contention for the men, as most readers can probably understand. The guys got super mad, which only contributed to behavior problems and a refusal among the men to obey the rules. The BOP doesn't broadcast these kinds of issues, but it is an understatement to say the Camp was close to rebellion.

I was also having trouble writing and taking notes, because my fingers would be *freezing* while in the library, or in my bed.

The building which housed our living quarters, the chow hall, administration, classroom, chapel and library is built out of the least expensive materials you can imagine. The building itself looks nearly identical to an army barracks, which is no big surprise, since the prison sits right on a military base.

There was little, to no insulation and without a heater, the frigid arctic air pierced the thin metal walls and ceiling, as if there was nothing there. This made for freezer and ice-box-like conditions. Two hundred men suffered with this cold, for weeks.

My breath would expel itself from my body, and a cloud of white vapor would appear before my eyes. This would be true in the library and in my bed, or anywhere in the "B" wing.

It was especially true in my bed, at night.

I have never been as cold during the nighttime and early morning, as I was at Fort Dix---and I've lived in some cold places, too, including New York, Minnesota and Colorado. Unfortunately, the winter of 2014-2015, outside of Philadelphia, Pennsylvania, was bitterly cold that year. It made things just a little bit tougher.

I felt like a guy from the old West, studying hard to go to school at nighttime on the cold prairie, except I didn't have a fire to warm my hands, yet needed to continue my work through all hours of the day and night.

Any spare second between classes, after classes and in the evening, was devoted to preparing my class materials. I knew, especially inside the enclosed walls of Fort Dix, there were no secrets---and if the class was a failure, word would get out, fast. As the old saying goes, "Failure wasn't an option!"

I needed to develop a cogent, teachable system which novice traders could easily learn, with a bit of hard work and practice, even if some of them had suspect math skills. I asked myself, *"Could I develop a trading and risk management system which could be taught to the dregs of society?"*---at least I knew this was how society thought of us, anyway.

We were the true deplorables which everyone had cast aside.

I set out to do the impossible. Against Goldman, Morgan, BofA, and the hot shots from the hedge funds...I had to develop a system where my guys, whoever signed up for class and stuck it out---could WIN. This was the only way to really help these men, tangibly, and maybe provide them with some tools to make a better living, once they were released from prison.

Seeing 25 GED degrees and high school diplomas be awarded, along with an untold number of ESL certifications was great, but if men couldn't *leave* prison without some *real, employable skills*, which could *really* earn them a good living legally on the street, the odds were stacked against them. They would probably become another returnee to incarceration---and another added statistic to the recidivism table.

Fort Dix is woefully inadequate, as is the BOP in general, in preparing men with real skills for when they are released from prison. In fact, at the Camp, these programs were pretty much non-existent.

The exceptions were a few guys (meaning 3-6 out of 400⁺) who got selected to attend a culinary school each quarter, but those selections were limited to only Pennsylvania residents.

Everyone else was screwed. The BOP kept talking and talking for years about getting a commercial driver's license program initiated, but this program never materialized either, while I was there.

Lots of money goes into the BOP, but where it goes, is a really good question, because it doesn't come to the men for rehabilitation, and it sure doesn't come for food, shelter, or clothing! A recent court case has revealed *millions* of dollars have been paid to BOP administrators and wardens as bonus money.

WASHINGTON — The U.S. Bureau of Prisons paid more than $2 million in bonuses to top administrators and wardens during the past three years while the agency was confronting persistent overcrowding, sub-par inmate medical care, chronic staffing shortages and a lurid sexual harassment lawsuit that engulfed its largest institution, according to government records and court documents. (Source: "Execs at troubled federal prisons received bonuses totaling in the millions" USA Today, by Kevin Johnson, April 9, 2017).

The word is the BOP is more interested in maintaining its pensions and bonuses than it is in helping incarcerated people get training. The training available to the men is atrocious and is essentially, non-existent.

A major review of all compensation and pension plans is a must for the entire BOP system, because the system does nothing to rehabilitate the men, but seems to be designed to make *certain* every BOP employee is well paid---with everyone looking forward to sweet-heart pensions, in the future.

As I started my work to prepare for the class, I knew the best way to keep a man out of prison was to teach him *how* to fish. This was how Jesus did it and I thought, *"Well, if it was good enough for Him, then..."* But, in the cramped quarters of prison, nobody does *anything* without others knowing about it--- especially at Fort Dix. With 420⁺ guys stuffed into a barracks-style building, originally built for 200 men, eyeballs were everywhere. There was no privacy.

This was particularly true for a new guy writing night and day, and not saying much about what he was up to! This breeds curiosity, and...suspicion. Mike, my spacemate, who is highly intelligent and a man who always treated me right, got curious about what I was doing. He must have thought I took the Socratic oath, because I was always compulsively teaching, reading and writing. One evening he looked up at my bunk.

Mike has one of those great Long Island accents and he barked at me (i.e., Mike had an affectionate way of raising his voice, accusingly at people, when he wanted to find out something...a skill he picked up inside prison at some point in time, I'm sure):

"BOB!!---WHAT AH YA' DOIN'??!!!"

I was sitting in bed poring over about a half-dozen books, taking notes, looking at the IBD, and not saying a word to anyone. It was also frigidly cold. I looked down at Mike, and I responded nonchalantly, "I'm trying to create a class, where virtually any inmate who can calculate an average, can learn how to successfully trade FUTURES contracts on Wall Street."

Before this, Mike thought I was a pretty smart guy. But right then, he thought I was an idiot, I'm certain, because he started laughing his butt off! I can still hear him chortling, "Good luck with that!! Bob...you're NEVER gonna' teach these guys ANYTHING in here! TRUST ME!! "

Mike is a classic, tough, New York Irish, Scotch and German guy---funnily enough, the EXACT same DNA makeup as my own. Even though our personalities were quite a bit different, we got along well.

On more than one occasion, Mike steered me clear of big trouble. I owe him a huge debt of gratitude. No matter what he did in the past, today, I believe Mike has learned his lesson. He would be better off on the outside, paying back restitution. Men are jailed for far too long in the United States.

As Mike's laughter died down, I calmly continued to stare at him. I was determined, "Well, I'm sure going to give it my best shot...I'm going to teach them to trade like a Turtle. Do you know who 'The Turtles' were, Mike?"

I felt compelled, or at least thought it was the appropriate time, to confide in him, a bit. I let Mike know my plan, forcefully and with conviction, because I knew this is what God wanted me to do, at least for this stage of my experience at Fort Dix.

When a New Yorker hears someone speak with conviction---no matter how loudly they themselves normally shout or intimidate, they usually listen---and listen attentively.

Mike was no different, but because he was really quite brilliant, he could also be quite skeptical. This time, however, it was as if God, or an archangel, whispered in Mike's ear, *"Listen."*

Uncharacteristically, Mike stood there and patiently waited for me to stop speaking. He knew I had written five books and in one of them, had made some amazing prognostications about the currency, equity and gold markets but, Mike had zero patience to hang out and chit-chat. And I do mean, ZERO. Mike holding still for three minutes in a conversation was a minor miracle!

I recounted the Turtle story of Curtis Faith, his peers, and their amazing, consistent success in trading. Many of the original "Turtles" are leading hedge fund managers in the world, today.

Mike had also actually run a fund on the "outside," and was one of the few men inside the prison I could talk to about serious Wall Street matters, particularly involving things a bit more complicated, which included futures, currencies, hedging, risk management, economics, the market, gold and other topics.

Money almost always catches a prisoner's attention, and I noticed the story about the Turtles was having an impact on Mike. Not at first, but I could see his wheels turning.

Mike hadn't known me too long, yet, but he had been silently observing me. First-hand, he had seen the amount of effort I put in to try and help the men learn. I knew he appreciated my work, even if it didn't directly affect Mike, himself. I think this was because he had already seen some of his friends, who were in GED, become impacted positively by my teaching influence. Many of the guys looked up to Mike because Mike always helped other guys out.

When I finished speaking, he continued to stare at me for about three seconds. Then he flatly stated:

"I'll make sure all of my guys are there..."

To this day I don't think Mike really fully bought into the possibility of teaching neophytes how to trade at a level which could compete with Goldman Sachs---but he trusted me---and that counts for everything in prison.

I was now honor-bound to dig in, even more aggressively, and make sure these men learned how to trade and win on Wall Street. I didn't want to let Mike, or any other man down!

Everyone gets measured by what he does and what he stands for, and I was a bit of a conundrum to many around me at Fort Dix. My mission was to aggressively be there for men who had never before had a decent teacher, or effective advocate, in their lives, period. I didn't want, or expect, anything in return.

All I wanted was to honor God, and all those people who had taught me and been there for me, during *my* lifetime. Many had given of themselves and helped me become a better man. I believed it was important to carry on this spirit and tradition of selflessness, particularly in prison, despite the fact it flowed against the tide of normal behavior among most inmates.

As December turned into January, even Sean Contee started asking me what I was doing for all those hours in my top bunk. I had been hunched over, in the freezing cold, writing out a system of tables, charts, and data which could be used for the class. I was also creating a "text book," containing the secrets I had uncovered to help the men become great traders. When completed, it would be nearly 200 pages.

Inevitably, the word got out---"Kelly was going to give a class to teach guys how to trade on Wall Street!"

I would be lying if I didn't tell you I used every ounce of publicity this generated inside the prison to gain the attention of every man I could during my GED and math classes, particularly! I used the tools for making money on Wall Street to convince hardened criminals it was IMPORTANT to LEARN. I told them, "If you want to learn how to make big money on Wall Street, you HAD TO KNOW MATH, and I will teach you a system to do this during Winter ACE classes."

I began also working hard on one Sean Contee. Sean, my head-to-head bunkmate, was a great guy, with an easy-going smile. The guys nick-named him "Snoop," but I always just called him by his real first name. He was very smart and would stay up for all hours of the night (e.g., 4 a.m.), playing Sudoku.

Over the next year, Sean and I became friends. He would ask me questions which only real, deep-thinking men would think to consider. Once we got to talking about a restaurant Sean wanted to open---he's a pretty good cook from what he told me. We also often joked around quite a bit, and I brainstormed, one day, "Hey, Sean, if you and I opened a restaurant together, and the judge approved it, we could call it, 'The Black Cracker.'"

He thought this was hilarious. I was sort of nick-named, afterward, "The Black Cracker," at least between me and Sean.

Sean wound up enrolling in the ACE Class, too, which was now called unofficially, "How to Trade Like a Turtle." Sean attended every one of them for twelve weeks straight. This was no small feat in prison. Guys pretty much do what they want regarding night classes---and there were no requirements with respect to anyone attending the ACE courses.

Sean was a mere boy when he had to help his family pay bills and had become a high school dropout, but I can tell you, the man who played Sudoku until 4 a.m., nearly every single night in his bunk, became a true star of the Turtle class---but, more about this story is yet to come.

And there were a couple of other cool things about Sean.

He received his GED and high school diploma while at Fort Dix, and even got married to his long-time girlfriend, under a BOP-sponsored wedding ceremony. He told me in confidence, inmate-to-inmate, he never, ever wanted to go out on the streets again, and NEVER wanted to go back to prison.

I truly pray for God's greatest blessing to be on this man, and his family. He is a great guy who changed his life.

CHAPTER 12

HOW TO TRADE LIKE A TURTLE

As a teacher, like it, or not, since the time of Socrates and Plato, the example you leave your students makes a lasting impression.

I'm sure everyone reading this book remembers vivid associations with teachers and instructors from grammar school, junior high school, high school, college, university and beyond. These associations go way beyond academia and also include instructors in sports, theater, dance, etc., as well. I knew even in prison, by becoming a teacher, the time-honored spirit and tradition of responsibility and caring should be brought to the position. I felt honor-bound to do my very best.

We all know great teachers make some of the greatest and longest-lasting impressions on our lives. But, I'm also fairly sure, as we all look back, probably not a single one of them taught for the money!

With my initial starting salary of $0.12/hour, I was confident I was off to a good start---there certainly was no incentive from a monetary perspective to teach.

There also would be NO reduction in my sentence if I taught well, nor would there be any other magical "perks." The only thing to look forward to would be more work!

The BOP is bound by regulation. No matter how creative I got, no matter how good the class was, or how many students graduated with GED and ESL certifications, there was no advantage or incentive for hard work, even if it went above and beyond the call of duty. This was certain.

Like the millions of teachers who have dedicated their lives to others in the course of human history, I didn't think about the money, or lack thereof. In my case, I did it for the men, because it felt like the right thing to do.

In the business for which God brought me to Fort Dix, I still was hoping and praying, *"How could I help change lives?"* I knew I probably wasn't going to get very far by brow-beating guys with The Bible, especially in prison. These men were hardened by tough lives, and found themselves only trusting certain people they grew a bond with, or were convinced wouldn't try to screw them over, in some way.

I had become a Christian and believed in Jesus Christ, while growing up Catholic. However, my strong motivation to drill down into what was the truth of The Bible during college, led me to the even stronger conviction that Jesus Christ and The Bible were not only true, but the facts of Jesus' resurrection and the facts of The Bible, were beyond doubt. Armed with this knowledge of truth in my life, I have always tried to apply the principals of those truths in everything I have done, no matter where I have been.

Given my background, experience and abilities, I felt an overwhelming force of conviction to share this knowledge and truth of Christ in prison, through my work. One of my first major salvos at Fort Dix, outside of normal teaching, would be disguised under the auspices of "Business Management" and "How to Write a Business Plan."

In the classroom materials, I quoted directly from The Bible in the "text book" I created for the course:

> "I am come that they might have life, and that they might have it more abundantly." (Source: John 10:10, The Bible, KJV).

...and I didn't really care if there was supposed to be separation of "Church" and "State," even if I was teaching in a government-controlled facility.

With the cold pressing in all around me and the other men in January of 2015, the prison library exit door to outside, was *frozen* from the cold. The frigid draft flowing through the crack at the bottom and sides of the door, was merciless, but I soldiered on. I began typing the documents for the class from my hand-written notes, and created the tables and work-flow documents the students would need to trade like a Turtle.

Key to the whole course would be the data sheets. These probably don't sound important to someone outside prison. On the street, a person can easily query a data retrieval service, or even Yahoo Finance, and suck down years of digital pricing information to an Excel spread sheet in about two minutes.

But, in prison there is no Excel spread sheet, Internet, word processor, or computers to compile anything on. There certainly isn't Yahoo Finance, or investing.com, either.

All I had was my cheap, white, hand-held calculator, which cost $9.99 from the prison commissary (representing 83 hours of work at $.12/hour!), which sported only the basic functions of adding, subtracting, multiplying and dividing. I also had cheap, prison-lined paper and access to the 1980's era, Brother electric typewriters. These required a ribbon and correcting tape, both of which had to be purchased in the commissary and yes, you guessed it, probably represented another 100 hours of prison work---price and time wise. Finally, I also had pens and pencils I had purchased, also from commissary.

I did save money on copier paper for typewriting purposes. I got these from Education for "free," since it was for the class. While the paper was "free" for me, it probably cost the taxpayers $1/sheet (that's a joke, but you never know who is supplying what in the BOP...). Everything else had to come out of my meager commissary account at Fort Dix.

A commissary account at a federal prison is like a small bank account. You get charged for everything through this account. Phone calls cost $.20-$.30 PER MINUTE, which is a complete rip off, emails on the terminals cost $.05 PER MINUTE--- another complete rip off, and food, clothing and healthcare items at commissary, are also another total rip off!

The prices at commissary were sky-high. If you have been to New York and gone into a CVS, Walgreen's (i.e., Duane Reade), or other drug store, prices on the commissary list were comparable to these high-cost stores. Commissary also had a very limited number of items at Fort Dix, and the quality of food was simply atrocious.

The guys would say, rightfully, "Dogs eat better than the men in prison." This is a little bit grotesque, but, if you can imagine never having one solid bowel movement during a nearly two-year stint in a BOP FCI, you know something is wrong with the food they are feeding the men. I know this for a fact, because I lived with this condition for 21 months.

The food they serve and sell at commissary and the chow hall is complete garbage. It is also one of the reasons why there is a huge amount of theft from the base, from the BOP itself, and why many, many men find it critical to have food contraband smuggled into Fort Dix.

If the BOP upgraded the food, the massive costs associated with theft from within the BOP system would largely disappear. As the Mission Impossible movie says (as stated by both Alec Baldwin and Jeremy Renner), "Desperate times, require desperate measures..." Many men in prison are, indeed, desperate.

While nearly everyone complained about the cold, the food and everything else, it wasn't helping me to focus on the shortcomings of prison life. I had to press on.

I kept writing and typing. I had now experienced Christmas and New Year's alone. You looked around, and you could see the worry and loneliness on men's faces, all too easily. The holidays are really hard for men in prison.

I typed some more and stayed incredibly focused.

One page had become ten. Ten pages became twenty. My fingers were numb, my butt was sore on the hard-plastic seats of the Fort Dix library, and I could see my breath! I kept typing.

My stack of typed paper got bigger and bigger. Twenty pages finally turned into two hundred, and the books I had ordered were dog-eared in a hundred different places.

I suddenly realized I was just following the same process I always did before, in my life. I found myself thinking *"This is exactly the same feeling I always had when I thought of a product I believed was a real breakthrough."*

So far, in my career, the ability to innovate had allowed me to take three companies public from scratch. Along with whatever else I received from my family tree, I got a strong dose of my Great-grandpa's inventor genes. He invented vulcanized rubber and he ran the Hewitt Tire and Rubber Company out of Buffalo, New York, back in the '20s.

As the ideas flowed from my own personal experience and knowledge of investing and trading on Wall Street, along with my experience as a CEO, the Turtle system took root. I realized I had completely cracked the code on the Turtle's trading system---and armed with this capability, I could help some less fortunate men try and learn something extraordinary!

I was hoping I could give them a real path to make more money, legally, rather than have them return to the streets, untrained in anything, and contribute to the sky-high recidivism rates we experience today.

I believed what I was doing may be a key to reducing recidivism, which most of the BOP and our glorious politicians do not "get." Men need to learn how to provide for themselves, with the ability to earn a good income for their families. If they don't, inmates return to incarceration in the majority of cases.

Whether an inmate learned to trade, or learned some other practical, income-earning skill, it didn't matter; giving a man a legal way forward in life to earn a good living—is one of the keys to turning the corner on recidivism.

Men in prison need to learn a new way to make a good living, other than by breaking the law.

Naturally, many guards and other BOP personnel could care less if men return to prison. In fact, their pensions *depend* on plenty of inmates doing just this! By keeping the prisons full, Congress will continue to fund operations of the system. This includes the BOP's generous salaries, bonuses, benefits, expense accounts and of course, sweet retirement plans.

I challenge anyone to actually look at the ongoing pension obligations for these and other government (City, State and Federal) employees. This burden, along with salaries and benefits, creates a serious conflict-of-interest in the care of prisoners. It pretty much *guarantees* men and women in prison receive the <u>lowest</u> quality, at the <u>lowest</u> cost—of <u>anything</u>, while they are incarcerated. It also contributes hugely to the problem of inmates returning to prison after they are released, because no one is rehabilitated and no one is retrained.

Because of this, most inmates have an axe to grind—even when they leave prison. They saw what was going on around them, and realized resources intended for their rehabilitation, and successful return to society, were being squandered and taken by BOP employees.

Unfortunately, because of the BOP's employee cost structure (which needs to include all the prisons managed by private contractors, as well), the BOP has no great incentive to *train* inmates with *real* skills, which would guarantee good-paying jobs upon release. Overall, if the prisons are full, people with cushy, government jobs are set for life, and the private prisons, managed by non-governmental personnel, grow fat with profits.

This represents a serious conflict of interest and it must be addressed. Private companies should never run a prison. This conflict of interest should be obvious to everyone. BOP employee pay, benefits, expense accounts and all other discretionary expenditures, should be overseen and directed by outside, arms-length parties. These parties should be incented to ensure the monies Congress has designated for rehabilitation and training, as well as the care of those incarcerated, comes FIRST. No one in the BOP will like this, but if the country is serious about curbing the recidivism rate and its tremendous cost on society, big changes are REQUIRED at the BOP.

In any event, seeing these conflicts going on around me, I felt quite alone in my personal battle against recidivism. I couldn't change the world, but I was sure hoping a couple of guys might be helped. I continued working and I completed my course syllabus, and the "text book" I would be handing out to the class. I started getting excited to see what would happen when ACE classes started for the quarter.

I posted a one-page summary of the class right on the glass door of the library. The library had two entry doors from inside the building. The one I posted the notice on was a locked entrance. The guys would always lean up against it, when they waited for "chow" at the chow hall.

The notice was only up for about a day, because somebody ripped it down. I'm not sure if it was a guard, or a jealous inmate. I don't have a copy of it, but it said this:

"Want to change your life? Want to learn how to make real money when you leave prison? Then, come and learn to 'Trade like a Turtle.'

Robert Kelly will be teaching an ACE class in the first quarter of 2015 for any students who know how to calculate moving averages, and use other fundamental math skills.

Who were the Turtles? The Turtles were a group of Wall Street traders founded by Richard Dennis and William Eckhardt, who had a unique way of trading the financial markets. One individual, Curtis Faith, earned more than $30 million over an approximate 4-year period of time with this system.

If you are willing to commit to every class and work hard...come and change your life. Space is limited."

I had no idea what would happen, but I was confident I had nailed the system down. If God wanted this to work, he would send guys my way and they'd be able to understand what I had "translated" for them, into easy-to-understand course materials.

Another thing I was confident in: this had nothing to do with the "love of money;" however, it had *everything* to do with the bottom tier of Maslow's hierarchy of needs. When guys have nothing, they are purely focused on making sure their families can eat. Most men in prison indeed, have absolutely nothing.

It was now the middle of January and I was sitting in my regular seat in the library, when suddenly, someone screamed:

"They're outside! There's a crane outside!"

Several of us burst open the frozen library door, and ran outside. It was freezing, but we could see a crane was hoisting our new heater into place, on top of the roof. It took most of the day to get it installed, but nearly all the guys went outside in the cold to take a look.

We could see a couple of men on the roof, who were actually doing the installation, and about twenty BOP personnel on the ground, just staring up, contributing nothing at all.

We all got a good chuckle out of this, because you could always see an abundance of government waste, all around the prison. Suffice it to say, the inmates got their laughs, despite the hardships. It was just part of survival.

I continued my final preparations for class and realized, the next day, my fingers weren't numb. This was certainly a good sign. I also knew, despite the fact I had done everything in my power to guarantee I had created the Turtle Trading system perfectly, the system was completely UNTESTED.

Especially in prison, if this thing blew up in my face, my entire credibility as a teacher would be destroyed. All the work I had put into everything else, could be laid to waste.

Because of this, quite a bit was riding on the system working.

On January 22, 2015, I was on pins and needles. I ate a quiet bite-to-eat in the chow hall and high-tailed it to the classroom. The quarter-long class would run on Thursdays, from 5:00 p.m. to 7:00 p.m.

As the clock approached five, I wondered if anyone would even show up to the classroom.

Chapter 13

A Sea of Faces

I sat in the classroom watching the clock. It was 4:40 p.m. and no one else was there. I had finished teaching GED classes at 3:30 p.m., and now I awaited the arrival of students for my ACE class. I got a little nervous---it was like I had felt before a big football game in college---my stomach would always get butterflies until the first hit of the game!

If anyone showed up, I would have to speak to the men and introduce the class. I knew inmates were not only merciless in their appraisal of speakers in any venue at the Camp, but most men would also immediately make a decision to stay, or leave my ACE class, based on the first fifteen minutes of me opening my mouth. Inmates have extremely short attention spans!

I knew this because of my experience teaching the GED and ESL students. You can lose respect in a hurry if you don't back up what you say---and you don't maintain your credibility. It became doubly important in an ACE class, because there was no obligation for *any* man to attend.

As a result of this reflection, I made another important decision. I decided to treat any of the men who showed up, exactly as if they were at Goldman Sachs, or some other big Wall Street firm.

I would be tough as nails, and not put up with any crap. If they couldn't cut it, they had to be weeded out of the class.

Since I was only an inmate, and had no authority over anyone, or anything, this would be a bit of a trick. I was certain, in order to make real change, the men had to *want* to make a real change, and this takes *commitment.*

In the materials I created, I made sure I didn't put everything into the first big set of handouts I had prepared. I wanted the men who ultimately would receive all the course materials, to be "*all in.*" I also wanted to ensure they would stick with the twelve-week program, if they were going to be the recipients of all the important information I had put together for them.

Twelve weeks worked fairly well, because it would take this long to compile the daily data we would need from the Investor's Business Daily, learn the system (over a several week period), and then come to grips with how the system worked, and actually use it to trade over a significant period of time.

I still had no idea what would happen, or what the results would be. We would be testing the Turtle Trading system, "live," with it developed under Arctic conditions in prison, using only a cheap calculator, a few books, a note pad, cheap paper and an electric typewriter---in front of an unknown number of eyewitnesses---if anyone attended the class.

I was thinking about all this and I wasn't paying attention to the classroom. I again wondered, "*Will anyone even show up?*"

I glanced up from my papers, where I had been lost in thought. It was 5:02 p.m. and I could see in front of me, every single seat in the class was taken. Some more guys were standing in the back of the room. All the men had been waiting for me to start the class.

During the day, the men were required to wear their prison uniforms (ours were forest green in color), as I've discussed. But, after 3:30 p.m., the workday was over and the men could dress down and wear their sweats, or something more casual.

This early evening, the 22nd of January, 2015, I stood in front of my classroom. The men were, indeed, casual. They had their sweats on and were comfortable, but for every one of these Turtle Trading classes, I made sure I suited up in my "dress greens," because I wanted to show respect to the men for taking the course.

I started the class:

> "I want you all to look around. Not many of you will likely be here at the end of the quarter. But, I want you to know, for the guys who stick it out, you will learn something amazing---and for those of you who do stick it out, I will make you this promise: I will never teach this class, again, while I'm here at Fort Dix."

This caught the attention of *everyone*. They hadn't expected me to say *that*.

This was a calculation on my part. Most prisoners who showed up at the first (or second) class would do what inmates usually always do in prison: they abscond with the course materials, and then have their buddy sign them in for each class. This way, they could receive "credit" for the class in their "jacket"--- without ever actually having taken the course!

The "jacket" is what their Case Officer uses to summarize an inmate's activities, progress, disciplinary history, etc. in prison. It can be used as a factor in good behavior and good time, in some instances.

Inmates are very clever, and I knew most of the guys who attended the first class were only there for the fake-out credit.

What they didn't know, however, was I am a stickler on truthfulness, and I wouldn't allow people to sign into the class, without actually attending it. I didn't believe this was intellectually honest.

More importantly, I wanted to make sure the guys who *did* stick it out, knew I was going to teach them something very special. If they tried, I would be there for them, and would not abandon them. Some of the concepts were going to be a challenge for many of them, this I knew, and they would need help after "school."

Of course, by promising to only teach this class once, this was also my "carrot" for trying to get most of them to not act in the "same 'ol," "same 'ol" manner. I wanted the men to stick it out. I wanted the men, frankly, to be men.

At this, I failed miserably.

Of the forty, or so, faces which showed up originally in the classroom, when the dust had settled and graduation occurred--- with a real, final exam administered and taken by the men--- there were only twelve people who would learn the system. But, I guess that was a pretty good number, because Jesus started with twelve disciples, so in the end, I was in good company.

The only problem? I was one of the "twelve." Ultimately, only eleven guys would make it through the class when it ended in April, who really learned the system. But, I guess after Judas betrayed Jesus, he was down to eleven guys, also...

I continued with the introduction to the class:

> "The Turtle Trading system will empower you to execute trades, diversify your positions, manage your risk and track your trading portfolios. You will know *for real* if what I am teaching you is either a bunch of B.S., or if it might very well help you change your life.
>
> As most of you know, I am a Christian, and you must be wondering why I am interested in teaching you these secrets. For me, the answer is driven by God above, 'I came so that they could have life, and they could have it abundantly.'" (Source: John 10:10, The Bible, KJV).
>
> But gentlemen, please listen up...Wall Street is a *brutal* employment battleground and the last thing you need is an unrealistic learning experience. It will not help you.
>
> You will first spend the next several weeks learning the system, and we will collect data from about twenty futures markets, in order to create the database we will need to trade from. Once this database is compiled, you will each be given $1 million in your classroom capital accounts."

Laughter immediately rippled around the room. Inmates can never touch real money in prison, it is against regulations. These men would be provided a $1 million account, alright; it just would NOT be in their commissary accounts!

Throughout the twelve-week period, however, we would use our classroom's theoretical bank accounts to meticulously track our performance and equity balances over the course of the quarter.

The trading was as real as it could get, because we used the closing prices and data which were published by the Investor's Business Daily---the same IBD which Heidi had purchased for me during December. I started recording data from the very day I began receiving it. As a result, our classroom database started from the beginning of January, 2015.

We utilized pre-established stops, limit orders, and used the closing prices to measure results, as needed, to minimize any slippage in the numbers. The only thing which wasn't counted in the figures, were commissions; however, in our case, these costs would not be material because we were going to base our trades in, and around, futures contracts. Commissions would be relatively inexpensive for the kind of trading we would be doing and we were not engaging in high-frequency trading.

Additionally, we selected our markets *before* any trading was to begin. Each man had to pick the markets he would track. These became important in tracking a man's individual performance and ensuring the results of the class could hold up to outside scrutiny. If any of the men were to ever try and obtain a trading position with a private equity, or proprietary trading firm, their trading sheets and history would show exactly what they accomplished and learned.

The students included people of all religions and pretty much, all colors. We had Hindus, Muslims, atheists, Catholics, Evangelicals, black men, white men, yellow men, etc.

The majority of these students was from the inner city, and had come to the class because most had met me at some point, over the previous two months. Once again, like most things in prison among the men, things came down to trust...and once again, these men were placing their trust in me, in matters of importance. In this case, it might even lead to a new way to live their lives, with the new skills I would teach them.

The biggest payoff for me after the first session was when my spacemate Mike (who kept his promise and brought himself and a few other guys to the class) came up to me, and said matter-of-factly, "I can see you're used to leading men."

I can't remember my exact words, but my surprised response was: "Thanks, Mike...I just don't want to screw this up...thank YOU for bringing your guys..." Mike is a man of few words, but the words he says, he means.

For me, Mike was and is, a great guy who deserves another chance in life. I know he will get it!

Holding the Fort

CHAPTER 14

THE ELEVEN DISCIPLES

Only time would tell if I could actually teach these men something very valuable, which might improve their job prospects when they left prison.

Because of the unique, fierce, unyielding and merciless environment of a federal prison, especially one as diverse as Fort Dix, I was hoping God *didn't* have it as His plan to provide me with yet another humbling experience in my life.

I'd lived through enough of those, I figured.

I mean, it would be fine, if He did, but I was *sure* hoping good would come out of everything which had happened to me.

During the trials and tribulations of my life since the credit crisis unfolded, one of my greatest sources of inspiration had been the Book of Job. Now, this man had it bad. Most of our problems are nothing in comparison with what Job faced. The most important lesson the Book of Job teaches is to never, ever waiver in our faith toward God, no matter what.

I had been determined to take this lesson to heart, all through the turmoil in my life, especially over the last several years---and now, confronted with this situation inside of prison walls---I was determined to be no different. I would work hard---and put my faith in God, above.

No matter what---even in something as trivial as a class, and its ultimate success, or failure, I would always point to Him and say "Thank you, Lord."

This definitely enhanced my ability to teach---I am certain. Any teacher will tell you, teaching is tiring work. I started teaching each day at 7:30 a.m. and taught six hours of classes each day, Monday-Friday. Teaching yet another two-hour class on Thursday nights could be a bit tiring, for anyone.

However, I can say on every Thursday night at 5:00 p.m., for the next twelve weeks, I felt like I just woke up and got out of bed! I was excited to at least try and make a real difference in these men's lives, and I completely forgot about being tired or needing sleep.

As I've shared, I had a huge hole in my mattress and I was not sleeping at night. I was waking up four or five times, each night, with my back barking at me---because of degenerative disc disease and three previous back operations. Secretly, I was in pain all the time. It takes a toll on you.

What sleep I did get, I kept telling myself something my older brother always told me from his days in the Marine Corps: "Sleep is a weapon!"

I used this saying every day in prison, and have used it also, throughout my adult career. Thanks again, John, for the many wonderful things you taught me---the most important of which was, and how to be, a real man.

In trying to make the class as interesting as possible, I made sure each of the guys took ownership of their trades, and could independently track and verify their results.

As I've stated, of the forty guys who first showed up, only eleven made it, but each of these men was determined to learn one of the most powerful trading systems ever invented. I can say this, because I didn't invent it!

I just figured out what they did, and created a usable system which would prove incredibly profitable during the next several months.

As I've also explained, many of the guys were from the inner city, and struggled with the math and the process of using some important risk management techniques. But, they didn't quit. They asked me to spend extra time with them in the library, in order to make sure they could understand what was going on.

In short, they were becoming the lesson. They truly wanted a way out of their previous lives and could see the tools I was freely giving them could make a huge, positive impact on them, and on the lives around them.

At this point, I have to say thank you to Curtis Faith, Richard Dennis and William Eckhardt. I wonder to myself sometimes, *"Will they ever know their work was used to try and help guys in prison find a better way of making a living?"*

I hope so, because they deserve to know their work exceeded the monetary motivations in which they originally intended it. They had a major hand in providing needy men tools, which if these men continued to work hard at, could certainly make a huge difference in their lives.

Collectively, the math skills of the group were marginal, at best. Officially, they had to know how to calculate an average.

That's right, you heard me---they had to know how to add up a column of digits and divide by the total "number" of digits being counted and get an "average" for the column.

The students worked diligently from January 22, 2015 until graduation day, the day of their final on April 10, 2015. Mike's guys stayed until they learned the system, and then left, with a few classes remaining. However, their portfolio coverage and trades could be tracked, because they had already selected the markets they would be trading throughout the course.

Only a few people even went to college, who stuck it out. To outsiders, looking in, they would think I was truly teaching the "dregs" of society, because all of us now had the "Scarlet Letter" of "F" for "Felon" branded on our chests, and most men were from the street. Against all odds, though, we persevered.

I had to start at the very foundation of the markets, and then build up from there. The first thing I did was explain what futures and commodities were. I had written out, in detail, the definitions of the commodities, currencies, and other futures markets we would be covering.

For my part, I used the markets listed in IBD, and selected the most interesting and liquid markets listed. Liquidity, in the real world is critical, and I drove this point home with the men.

I let them select their own trading markets; however, one person in the class was provided markets chosen at random, and I was assigned markets which were largely left out by the other men. I needed this to occur, because I wanted to test the system across as broad a range of markets, as we could.

After all, if it worked, I had to figure out a way to make a living when I got out, also. I had been devastated by the upheaval, legal fees and legal defense costs I incurred for years, in the build up to my decision to enter into a plea bargain.

As I've discussed, prison is a pretty tough place and if you try and B.S. your way through, you are sussed out in a real hurry--- especially by a bunch of "street smart" men. This is why, only after the men learned the basics of the system, were the men permitted to select their markets. These were then tracked meticulously, and the men could see and verify they were receiving truthful and unalterable data and results.

It was how we began class each week, even before we went about the evening's lesson---we tracked the weekly performance of each person's trading.

The men took it really seriously, also, even though we were using theoretical bank balances. They could see, with their own eyes, the movements in the markets and where the profits and losses were going in their selected, diversified portfolios.

Turtle Trading has very specific rules in which traders make trades. Once their markets were selected (my guys were allowed only ten markets to track, exactly the same number Curtis Faith was allowed to track, according to his book), trades were made in strict adherence to the rules I had provided these men in the course materials.

It was interesting to see the men want to be in class initially, but it became *extremely* interesting to see the men *dying* to be in class to find out how they did during the week! I knew at this point, they were hooked and convinced the lessons they were learning were beyond real, because they were witnessing them, first hand.

This was really great because it made them pay even more attention in class, and allowed me to introduce other skills they might need when they returned to society.

Once the students selected their ten markets, these were "in stone." The SYSTEM dictated, automatically, according to the Turtle rules I had constructed, what market to trade, where stops should be placed, as well as where entry and exit points should be placed on all positions.

One of the interesting aspects of Turtle trading is it does *not* have much utility for very large institutions. This is because of potential drawdowns, which can occur through the course of trading in the futures markets. For individuals and private funds, however, the payoffs can be enormous.

Many institutions would not use this system of trading because it can, and ultimately will, be subject to "price shock." This is due to the leverage used in futures markets. Typically, all futures traders face this risk.

The risk management system I taught the students, however, focused on risk management in two specific and important ways. First, it *limited* and adjusted the *size* of trading a trader may do, and second, it taught the use of *"stops,"* religiously.

The reader knows the system was created by me without the benefit of a computer. What the reader doesn't know is this meant I had 6-7 hours of prep time for each and every class!

I had to manually record pricing data and calculate performance results by hand. As you know, the data was obtained from the IBD and/or the Wall Street Journal (sometimes, an IBD would get "lost" in the mail and I would have to run around and borrow someone else's Wall Street Journal to obtain pricing information).

All trades, out of necessity, were based on "end-of-day" trading information, using price data from the aforementioned reliable news sources.

These are all the markets we tracked. Ultimately, I had decided on 19 total markets we would officially cover, instead of 20+. By market, these are their profits and losses (not annualized) by product contract, for the trading period January 30, 2015 – March 31, 2015:

Futures Market Traded	Theoretical Profit/(Loss)
Nasdaq	$24,872
10-Year U.S. Treasury Bond	-$78,063.20
British Pound	$77,756.25
Euro	$102,025
Sugar-World	$164,214.40
Cocoa	$149,881.80
Wheat	-$70,323
Soybeans	-$65,250
Natural Gas	-$30,350
Light Sweet Crude Oil	-$72,210
Heating Oil	$144,001.20
Gold	$34,408
Swiss Franc	$25,900
Coffee	$69,660
Orange Juice	$115,798.50
S&P Mini	-$20,359
Copper	$24,850
Silver	-$33,404
Corn	Did Not Trade
Total Theoretical Profit:	$564,337.95

As you can see, these would have returned $564,337 over the quarter. You can also see how some markets had losses, and others had gains.

Finally, the Turtle system is designed to take many smaller losses---and to take some big gains. The key is *staying* in the markets long enough whereby you increase the odds of winning on very large market moves.

The risk management system was also designed by the original Turtles to withstand a market catastrophe, or "price shock." The Turtles knew if you were in the markets long enough, you must plan for them, and the rigorous rules on position sizing help minimize the impact of these kinds of "black swan" events.

The summary results of the students in the class are in Chapter 17, "Results of Turtle Trading." I also included various copies of some of my original hand-written, prison notes, typed classroom materials, tables, and even data we used. There are also comments from many of the students, in their own handwriting and own words.

As you will quickly see, nothing has been altered in these documents. The many "scratch marks" and scrawls on the paper are from cross-out errors, or hand-written notes I made during my time in prison, or I needed to quickly write up performance results in class, and...unfortunately,

---I didn't have a "Backspace" key to erase mistakes!

CHAPTER 15

THE WHEAT'S KILLING ME, BOB!

Another reason I made the guys select their markets was because I wanted to inject some competitiveness amongst them. I knew they were instinctively competitive---many men in prison compete in their workouts, at card games, at dominoes, at sports and get really crazy over big games on TV.

Being competitive in prison is a healthy way to blow off steam and keep some kind of semblance of a "normal" life, whatever that is, in prison.

After they had learned the Turtle Trading System, initially, it turns out the decision to allow the men to select their own markets to trade, was a great one.

This was the extra spark which kept the guys engaged, every single week. As markets went up or down, they engaged in the triumph of victory, and the swift blow-to-the-gut of defeat!

Before we selected the markets, however, I taught them some basic, but very important skills in chart watching, and technical analysis. I told them, "What we are looking for, are markets which are about to 'change.'"

The Turtle system simply doesn't care if a market is going up or down, but the trend-following system I decided upon for the men, would be most profitable if trends occurred in the markets they were trading.

To allow them a greater probability of actually benefiting from markets which start to trend, and potentially becoming profitable, I had them each follow ten markets, of their choosing.

This was the same rule given to Curtis Faith and the rest of the Turtles, when they learned to trade. Again, I wasn't trying to reinvent the wheel for this class. I wanted to teach men how they could change their lives. The challenge was trying to distill the concepts down to their most simple form and make it possible for these dedicated individuals to learn the system.

Once this was achieved, and the men learned the rules, the "prison-proof" Turtle system would virtually run itself. Don't' get me wrong, my guys were actually pretty smart, but without any real background in trading, I had to make the system as easy-to-use as possible.

With the trading decisions made for the men by the system, the men could then become more engaged in the rudiments of risk management. This ensured their stops were set, and made certain their exit points were lined up, ready to go.

This also got the men super focused on their performance!

Each and every week, I would roll in with the data sheets, along with the profit and loss statements for each market. Since each man had inscribed in "stone," (i.e., put down in writing to me before we started trading on January 30, 2015), which markets he was committing to---each person could quickly determine his profit and loss, depending on the makeup of his particular futures' portfolio.

As you can probably guess, one of my favorite students was Sean Contee. He was a pretty funny guy, as I've already tried to share.

Sean originally got my attention when he arrived at Fort Dix because he bunked by me. But what really got my attention was during the GED class he attended at 2:00 p.m. each day, the man made an effort to be interested---even though he was dead tired from staying up all night playing Sudoku!

It's usually not too smart to be goofing off at all hours of the night and have your teacher bunk right next to you---especially when the teacher doesn't sleep much!

The problem was Sean was only interested in sleeping during class! His famous position was to sit in his tiny, red chair and tuck his head down in his arm---which he had bent to form a pillow. I never gave him a hard time about this, and Joe and I would always try and warn the guys when we saw the classroom door start to swing open (i.e. this meant Ms. Lindley, or some other Officer, would be entering right behind it). We didn't want these people to catch Sean, or anyone else, napping!

Joe and I went out of our way to try and make sure no one got into any trouble during class---even among the guys who gave us a hard time---or had zero interest in doing anything. We would provide them all with answers and work papers if we knew Ms. Lindley wanted to review their work or, she was going to show up "unexpectedly." The men then put their names on the documents, and turned them in...and PRESTO!

No trouble in our class!

This also allowed the men to show us a great deal of respect. The older guys didn't begrudge the younger guys who really wanted to learn, and many of the older men actually became huge fans of ours, as a result. They had begun to realize Joe and I didn't have to put forth the effort we did, and we were doing it only for the men.

We weren't going to be rewarded for it---this was obvious to all, as everyone had to do their "time." At the end of the day, people in prison try and help each other out. Ultimately, the older guys decided Joe and I were, "OK."

As time went by, I treated my classes exactly like a college professor might. I would use the Socratic Method and hammer home important subjects, concepts, discussions, and of course math equations, at random and on point with what was on the white board.

If you asked any of my GED students what the Pythagorean Theorem was, they might say, "I don't know." BUT, if you asked them what does $a^2 + b^2 = c^2$ represent, or, what is the slope of the line (e.g., $y = mx + b$), or what goes on at the Federal Reserve System---they would tell you, straight away. In fact, they would know the answers to these questions and a whole lot of other ones, too.

We enjoyed wide-ranging discussions on topics of interest to nearly everyone---in nearly all my classes. Joe was really great in this process, as well. He would often tell the class, in his West Virginia drawl, "Well, whatever I don't know, Kelly knows, and vice versa!"

172

Joe never said this to boast, either. You would never meet as humble a man, as Joe Kerns. He was just explaining to the students, that between us, *the students* had a great resource and could achieve a great education---*if* they engaged.

Many men did engage, too. There were 25 men who graduated while I was at Fort Dix, but what I haven't told you, was there were two whole other groups waiting to take their GED tests, when I was released from prison on July 28, 2016.

At Fort Dix, this was really something. But, in over a decade of Joe's work in prison, he had seen many, many more men graduate than most.

Given my propensity to use the Socratic Method, Joe or I would go around the room and ask the class if they knew the answer to certain questions. Frankly, most of the time, we would get answers all over the playing field. Some guys would shout out, "A." Others would shout out, "D." Others would read the answer they thought was correct to a problem in math, or recite a passage for English, Science or Social Studies.

While we would be asking these questions and receiving answers all over the map, Sean Contee would be at his desk and in his little red chair, sleeping away.

At least we thought so, at first.

Sean's head would remain tucked in the crook of his elbow, and his long dread locks would be dangling down to almost touch the floor. He would be dead silent---obviously to me, catching up on his much needed sleep. After all, it's tough staying up all night playing Sudoku.

But then, suddenly, after everyone else had provided answers, Sean would frequently scream out his own, and in his deep, baritone voice, would say:

"C!"

He wouldn't add anything, he never moved his head, and his dread locks didn't quiver. He just belted out his answer. This happened *all the time*.

Joe and I would just look at each other, shake our heads, and smile. Sean would be right---almost always. There was a pretty smart guy hiding out in class all right, this much I came to know.

This was also one of the main reasons I aggressively recruited Sean for the Turtle class.

To me, he was the perfect candidate. A guy who had to drop out of high school, he got into trouble selling drugs---and I guess until he was caught, was pretty good at it. But, he had confided in me he never, ever wanted to go back to prison, and he wanted to get home to his son and girlfriend. Sean ultimately married this woman in a Fort Dix-sponsored wedding ceremony, the following summer.

When trades started being made and we would announce the results each week, with the tabulated profit and loss for every student's positions, Sean pulled out in front of EVERY ONE, initially by quite a distance.

I don't know, maybe his picking my brain about what kinds of markets he should track helped him, but I really think his street smarts did, too. He just had that rhythm to understand a good thing, or a bad thing, when it came to trading.

Sean led the class, by a mile, when he started out. By February 25, 2015, he had racked up $477,302.50 of "PROFIT" in our classroom Turtle Trading accounts. His markets were Gold, Orange Juice, the Euro, Copper, Wheat, the Swiss Franc, Coffee, Silver, the S&P and the Nasdaq.

This was really a cool thing to watch. Sean and the other guys could see the system *working*. This made them pay attention even more, because they knew and could see live, first-hand, what I was teaching them was the real deal.

The men could see the Investor's Business Daily, and could even follow their markets on CNBC, which was usually always broadcast in the small exercise room inside the Camp.

The one who was probably proudest in the room was my spacemate Mike. When a man puts his name and reputation on the line, and *twists* arms of other inmates to attend a class (i.e., no one really wants to attend prison night classes), he certainly doesn't want to be embarrassed...and I was really happy I didn't embarrass Mike.

Also, Mike was great during class because inevitably, you would get questions from someone and Mike would back up what I had to say about it. This helped reinforce the discipline of respect in the class.

One of the unique things about the Turtle system is it was designed to take many more losses, than profits. The risk management system keeps a stop loss in place on each and every trade. It also *limits* the exposure in a particular contract group,

175

as well. This is calculated by adjusting the size of each "unit" for each market traded. A "unit" is simply the number of contracts we were allowed to trade, each time the Turtle system gave us a "Buy," a "Sell," or an "Add-to-Position" signal.

I really stressed the importance of the character of markets, as a result. I wanted the guys to understand most of the time, they will have LOSING trades. But, the system would show them how one huge winner (or more) can make up for dozens of small losses in short order.

I also taught them an important lesson about trends. They don't happen very often, and they are frequently the result of buyers and sellers exhausting themselves. I lectured them, "You want to try and find a market, which has been basing for a long time, if you can. This will help you improve the odds something will change for the particular contract analyzed."

I looked around the room, and knew my advice wasn't really sinking in, very much. I went on, "You MUST be in these markets---know this in advance. Some of them take months, or even YEARS, to break out, either up, or down. Just when you are pissed off at losing too many times in a particular contract market, it will take off. If you are not in it, and give up on it, you will have lost, big time. Because when they break---they make a break in a hurry!"

This was perhaps the greatest challenge I had in the class, after I got through the first few weeks. As a group of street guys, they knew one rule---never *lose* money! It was too precious to them.

Even acknowledging such a thing would be anathema to them.

They had no choice though, at least not in my class. They were locked into their positions (Curtis Faith's original Turtles were locked into ten markets, and were forced to stick with them for a full year, before they could change them). Using this strategy would help improve their odds of catching trends. If they bounced in and out of markets, continually second-guessing themselves, they would miss big moves, at just the wrong time. Markets work against the human psyche and using this system is critical in fighting off the temptation to use your feelings.

As Sean hit nearly ½-million dollars in profits after the first month of trading, he started to slip back, a bit. A couple of his markets had provided him entry signals, and he was dutifully entering those trades.

The only trouble was...one of them was the Wheat market.

At first, Sean was real calm and looked at his performance, and said, "Oh, I lost money in Wheat this week."

I would assure him this was how the system worked and he had to stay in markets which were unprofitable, in the near term, because he would have a higher probability of earning big money when the markets in question, finally broke out.

This went on for a couple of more weeks. Finally, as all the students were reviewing their profit and loss sheets three weeks later, Sean had had enough.

He screams, at the top of his lungs, interrupting the entire class:

"THE WHEAT! THE WHEAT!!

THIS WHEAT'S <u>KILLING</u> ME, BOB!"

Sean was one of the few guys in prison who called me by my childhood name, growing up---i.e., "Bob."

You had to be there to get the picture, but the entire class burst out laughing...*hard.*

Sean understood what was up, and he didn't like it one bit. He had dropped out of first place in the class!

I again, tried to reassure him, saying, "Sean, you will maximize your probability of profit in wheat in the future, by being patient and trusting your trading signals. It's like a being a trained pilot---you have to trust your instruments."

Sean just rolled his eyes at me, disgusted---but grudgingly continued to believe.

This was a major home run, from my perspective, because at this moment in March, a few weeks before class would end on April 10, I knew I had won their minds. They had all seen how they could change their lives and earn more money legally than they ever could by selling drugs, or by making an illegal living otherwise, off the streets.

There were still a couple more weeks to go in the class, and I had some other important lessons and preparations to teach the men, before they took their final exams.

Most of them had never interviewed for a job before, and I knew we had to spend some time on this.

I also knew this would prove to be a real challenge for most of the inmates attending our "Trade Like a Turtle" class!

CHAPTER 16

THE INTERVIEW

What happened to the men when they realized they were making big money, in a real hurry---and it was legal---was really cool.

With major successes using the system now apparent to everyone, I was able to become even bolder with the class. I started planting the seed in their minds they could actually *use* the knowledge gained from the course, both the system of risk management and the business plan, to start building their own plan to get a *job* when they got out of prison.

I told them they wouldn't be able to work on Wall Street directly, because we were all black-balled by the powers-that-be, however, they could potentially work for a private person or entity, who might be more than interested in their prison-learned trading skills.

To this end, I had the students participate in mock interviews. Some guys had never been in any interview experiences before, ever---particularly the guys who grew up poor and were from the inner city. They became super apprehensive sitting in front of me, while I conducted mock interviews before the class.

I was touched at how such serious men had become so suddenly, seriously nervous men!

It was endearing to realize something nearly everyone in the working world takes for granted (i.e., an "interview") was an activity unfamiliar and uncomfortable for many inmates. The thought of having to participate in an interview seemed to rattle the normally macho and self-confident manners the men had learned on the street.

The interviews were enlightening, because I discovered very few of the men had any kind of interpersonal, "corporate" communications skills. This is hard to teach and was the result of not being educated in, or very exposed to, this skill set.

This was true because these men were the real deal---they made their living off the street. It is unfortunate most people sitting in the ivory towers at the financial center in New York City, consider them barbarians.

But, I pushed on, anxious to see if we could make some improvements in this area of "The Interview," in the greatest tradition of "YOU'RE HIRED!"---and, yes, I copied Donald Trump. Remember this was *long* before he would become President of the United States and months *before* he would even announce his candidacy for President on June 16, 2016.

In the first quarter of 2015, the whole "YOU'RE HIRED!" slogan was not politicized. "The Apprentice" was one of the most popular shows on TV, and the guys were starting to get a kick out of the process. We had some fun with it.

I tried to lower the obvious nervousness of the men stepping up to be interviewed. I told the guys, "Don't worry about interviewing---just be honest and tell me what you know. Don't worry about the things you don't know, and don't worry about being perfect in everything you say. Just *focus* on what you *do* know."

I was trying to take the pressure off them, because none of the men were anxious to make a fool of themselves in front of the other guys. If you were made to look a fool in prison, word spread quickly among 420+ other men, and you would never hear the end of it!

The first man who volunteered to come up for an interview was my friend, John Barnes. John is a Christian brother and yet another person who changed his life around, in prison. For this class, he especially studied very hard. He and I would sit in the library, going over the formulas and the methodology of calculating our volatilities and position sizes, frequently. John was a great student.

John also used to be a drug dealer and boxer, and I knew he was tough as nails. He is on the backend of doing a 20+-year prison sentence for dealing drugs. In other words, he's a serious dude, Christian, or not.

Before his interview began, I looked around the class and I reiterated my warning to the men: "Wall Street is brutal and you *must* be prepared to go up against the best-of-the-best and WIN!"

John then sauntered up and sat down in front of me. We engaged in the interview and I was pretty tough on him.

The interview, by any normal measure, didn't seem to be going well. John was unsure of himself and he was incredibly nervous. John's a very strong guy, and as an ex-boxer, he doesn't scare, or intimidate, easily. But, this was new territory for him. I must say, he was facing the situation with courage, for sure, but he was drowning---or, I thought he was, anyway.

He had just been bounced around the boxing ring of a very tough interview, and John appeared on the edge of defeat. He was really downcast because of his poor interview performance.

I could see it written all over his face.

I decided I had lit into him enough, and I didn't want to crush the self-confidence he found in learning how to use the system. I thought I should graciously let him down from the interview and let him return to his seat.

I couldn't bear the thought of saying, "YOU'RE FIRED," to my friend, John. Also, he had his bunk near mine, and I didn't want to get beat up in the middle of the night (*Hah, hah...just kidding, Johnnie*)!

At the end of a laborious interview, in front of all his peers, I would ask John one final question and send him packing.

"John, *why* should I hire *you*?"

At this moment, suddenly, like a black version of Rocky Balboa, John got the "eye-of-the-tiger." He swiftly lifted his head up. He looked me directly in the eyes, and with all the street-smart, ex-boxer-bravado, inner-city-instinct a guy from the 'hood can muster, screamed to the whole class:

"BECAUSE I JUST MADE TWO-HUNDRED-AND- FIFTY-THOUSAND-DOLLARS...

IN ONE <u>WEEK!</u>"

I didn't pause, I didn't fake a thing. I just immediately screamed out and pointed my finger in brash excitement, aggressively at his chest, and yelled right back at him:

"YOU'RE HIRED!"

The entire classroom became pandemonium and everyone was clapping for Johnnie.

I was so proud of him.

For a man who had been in prison a long time, who had given his life to Jesus and who had become a completely reformed individual, those words he heard, "YOU'RE HIRED!", even in our classroom environment, meant the world to him.

John beamed and had the biggest smile on his face. The class, I think, was really proud of Johnnie, too. He took a situation in which he was unfamiliar, relied on what HE KNEW, and used it to land a job!

I thought, *"Not bad, Johnnie, not bad at all. Great friggin' job!"*

John had confidence in the numbers. He had confidence in the process we had learned, and yes, John had confidence in his instructor, a fellow Christian and fellow inmate at Fort Dix, New Jersey. But, John also had confidence in himself, and God above.

All the men had a great deal more to learn about the financial markets, but if any employer took a risk on them someday, and provided them with continued mentoring and modern tools of the trade, I am certain the employer would find "gold in them there hills." Street guys are naturals when it comes to trading. After all, they have been trading their whole lives.

I know the description of this book says I turned "bad" men into great traders. But, the best part of the word "bad," in today's society, is it can have many meanings.

Society has branded my eleven students, and me, as "bad" men. To me, I never looked at them in this light. Good people make mistakes, and everyone deserves a second chance. I know these men and their hearts. What I can say is they are good men, just trying to get home.

My hope is they always stay out of trouble and find great happiness in life.

CHAPTER 17

RESULTS OF TURTLE TRADING

The methodology of tracking trades was as follows:

Data source: Investor's Business Daily (http://www.investors.com). It is about the best daily newspaper in the United States for stock, futures data and pricing information. I also used the Wall Street Journal as a backup, from time to time, when a paper might get "lost" in the prison mail. All prices were taken from the closing prices and stops which were created in the trading system. Obviously, there may be some "slippage" in the numbers as a result, but the dramatic success of the program would more than likely outweigh slippage adjustments, and commissions, if we had access to real-time trading systems in prison.

I am the first to admit, our system was "theoretical," however it had quite a number of people using it. Critically, all trading decision trees and markets selected, were made in advance---publicly in class, at the beginning of the quarter. As signals were delivered on positions, we would make those announcements at class time, and then track the performance, and make trade changes from there. As I've also said, there were twelve of us who made it through the rigorous program I instituted (me included).

I was merciless on the guys---they weren't used to this, but I explained to them Goldman Sachs will not care about them when they put their money at risk. They had to be sharp, and prepared to move quickly, as the system dictated---but, they also had to be very tough-minded. They also couldn't be fearful of taking positions, and they must religiously follow their stops.

Importantly, the Turtle system does not require an opinion, as to which way a market will move (this is the part I love, personally, about how the Turtles traded). I'm really good at determining economic headwinds and tailwinds, but a reliable trading system is a potent weapon to add to an investor's arsenal, especially when it is objective and only looks at data to make decisions.

I drilled into the heads of the men, *innumerable* times the following question:

> "What will you say after you become a successful investor and trader, when the word gets out about you, and people want to know your opinion as to which way the market will go?"

I drove into their brains, their answer *should always be*:

"I DON'T CARE AND IT DOESN'T MATTER!"

The Turtle Trading System dictates the trades, along with the entry, exit and stop points on a position in a trader's portfolio. It also sets LIMIT POSITION RISK, which is expressed in "Units." It is, at its core, a risk management system, but we used the futures markets to provide the volatility and trends we desire to trade effectively.

186

Similar to the original Turtles, we covered currencies, treasuries, precious metals, produce, oil, etc. It simply didn't matter which market was used, provided there was volume.

In using the system, there may be a slight advantage for well-read people who study the markets, and look at technical charts, and other information. Their "edge" might come when they originally select the ten markets they will track and trade. Many times, technical information yields important clues as to the probability of experiencing volatility in an underlying market---as well as trends, which are critical to the system we used in class.

In the same breath, however, the person who made the *most* money in our class was Ayunde Yearwood. He was a person we designated to be a "random" choice recipient of various futures markets. Ayunde made over $500,000 in 52 trading days. Like everyone else, he started with a theoretical $1,000,000 capital position in his classroom bank account.

I was elated to also read Ayunde received mercy from President Obama---who granted him a reduction in his sentence. Ayunde will be home in a couple of years, instead of having to be holed up in prison for many more. Ayunde's family was originally from the island of Jamaica, and he is a great guy. He became the leader of the Evangelical Church at Fort Dix, and is another example of a man who had truly changed his path and walk in life.

Here are the classroom statistics of the student's results, after 52 days of trading---<u>none</u> of these results are annualized. They are the "actual" results during the classroom quarter, based on the theoretical profit and loss statements of the students and the ending balances in the classroom's theoretical bank accounts on March 30, 2015:

Average percentage theoretical return = 144.82%.
Average theoretical gain = $301,406.
The median return = $268,547.
Total class theoretical profits = $3,616,879
Standard deviation = $139,045.

Each inmate received the same dollars in his theoretical capital account at the beginning of the course (e.g., $1,000,000). These are the individual profits the men experienced during the trading period from January 30, 2015 and March 31, 2015 (i.e., 52 trading days):

Inmate Name	Theoretical Profit
Peter Alemania	$407,342
John Barnes	$263,666
Jerell Casey	$232,561
Dave Connolly	$461,361
Sean Contee	$273,427
Michael Eisner	$188,667
John Fabey	$212,468
Robert Kelly *	$82,992
Mike MacCaull	$407,342
Rohan Wijetihaka	$145,965
Ayunde Yearwood	$533,746
Agron Zenalaj	$407,342

* I was the "anchor" and picked up markets others didn't, to allow learning from the use of additional market selections.

I have annualized the returns for the individual capital accounts of the inmates, using this methodology:

All students began class with a theoretical capital account of $1,000,000. Annualized figures use this $1,000,000 figure to calculate their respective returns. Theoretical margin requirements for the various positions traded during class from January 30, 2015 to March 31, 2015 were significantly less than the $1,000,000 in capital on hand for each student.

One of the nice things about the Turtle system is it limits the percentage of capital put at risk in an initial trade, as well as in subsequent trades. This is not to say you can't have a black swan event hit you broadside, but the Turtle system has a very exacting way of controlling the risk "put on" in each market.

The maximum capital which would have been committed to backing up margin in our test is estimated between 40% - 60% of the students' capital accounts, with diversification across many markets. More volatile markets typically have higher margin requirements and these were estimated, as well.

The class began trading on January 30, 2015. This was to make sure the class knew the basics of the system, but was also because the class needed to collect enough data from the IBD, prior to trading. The total actual number of trading days covered in the test period was 52 trading days. The database covered the period when markets were tracked from January 2, 2015, until March 31, 2015. If trades were still "open" on March 31, they were closed out at the closing prices on this day.

This provided one full quarter of tracking, collecting, reporting and analysis, which provided the returns reported for the twelve participants in the class.

The annualized theoretical returns assume there are 250 trading days in a year. This provides an annualizing factor of 4.80769 (52/250 = .208, 1/.208 = 4.80769).

The class did not deduct commissions and did not make any adjustments for "market slippage," which can obviously occur, and may be material, as can other factors not accounted for in this classroom learning experience.

This is the performance summary, annualized, for the graduating class of April 10, 2015:

Inmate Name	Profit in Class	% Annualized	Projected Year- End Capital
Peter Alemania*	$407,342	195.52	$2,955,243
John Barnes	$263,666	126.76	$2,267,627
Jerell Casey	$232,561	111.81	$2,118,084
Dave Connolly	$461,361	221.81	$3,218,084
Sean Contee	$273,427	131.46	$2,314,554
Michael Eisner	$188,667	90.71	$1,907,054
John Fabey	$212,468	102.15	$2,021,482
Robert Kelly	$82,992	39.90	$1,399,003
Mike MacCaull*	$407,342	195.52	$2,955,243
Rohan Wijetihaka	$145,965	70.18	$1,701,758
Ayunde Yearwood	$533,746	256.61	$3,566,088
Agron Zenalaj*	$407,342	195.52	$2,955,243

* These students chose to trade identical markets and teamed up, thus their profits and trading decisions were identical, under the Turtle Trading system.

The annualized rates of return calculated above, assume the same rate of return would be realized throughout the year---a highly unlikely scenario, but these figures are provided for exemplary purposes.

I also tracked every single market which the class covered, 19 in all. Even though some students didn't obviously pick certain markets, it is instructive to see the performance of the system across this broad range of diverse market sectors. What follows are some of the hundreds of pages of documents I used in class.

I will leave you first, though, with the students' comments of those who chose to leave a note, with respect to their opinion of the class.

MR. KELLY IS VERY REAL, ENCOURAGING AND ALWAYS WILLING TO SHARE ALL VITAL INFORMATIONS OF BUSINESS ASPECT OF LIFE WITH OTHERS. HE POURED HIS HEART OUT AND NOT HOLDING BACK TO MAKE OTHERS GET BETTER IN THEIR FUTURE LIVES (LIFE)

EVERY SUBJECT HE TEACHES ARE VERY COMPREHENSIVE AND WELL COMPREHENDED.

THIS MAN HAS PASSION IN HELPING THE FALLEN OR FALLING ONES TO GET BACK UP ON THEIR FEET.

MR KELLY IS A TRUE GENIOUS —

[Signature Blocked]

The above student, "Shola," was interned into the Fort Dix Camp in the middle of the class quarter. Because of his persistence, I allowed him to audit the last four, or five, classes. I subsequently tutored him, to allow him the opportunity to better learn the system. He did not have a portfolio to trade, as a result.

The following comment is from Sean Contee ("The Wheat's Killing Me, Bob!"):

Mr Kelly did an excellent job at teaching and explaining the Business plan class. At the end of the class I had put together all of my data and found out that I had earnd 273,427 dollars and 131% annual Rate return, That proves the class worked for me I am Satisfied with Mr Kellys class

Signature Blocked

39D-98-007

Dave Connolly was, and is, a superb individual and real friend. I think Dave is also innocent of what he was accused of. He is probably going to use the Turtle Trading system when he gets out. He'll make tons of money doing so, hopefully.

April 9, 2015

I took Robert Kelly's course "Trade Like the Turtles", one class a week over a 12 week period. Using the system as he taught it, my hypothetical $1,000,000.— trading account increased by $461,361 in the period from January 2, 2015 to March 31, 2015. An annualized return of 221.81% ! — all using real prices on real contracts as published each day in Investors Business Daily.

Mr. Kelly was a thorough and conscientious teacher who took great pains to make sure everyone in the class understood the system. He has given me something I can use to greatly better my financial circumstances in the future.

Signature Blocked

Jerell Casey and I shared the same birthday in May. We also bunked only a couple of bunks apart from each other. He is a great guy, a nice man and he is looking forward to going home to his wife and family.

My name is Jerell Casey and I was taught the Tubo trading system by R. Kelly in fort Dix Camp. We track our performance through out the Class and My personal experience is R. Kelly is A great teacher and Can be the same as A trader.

4.9.15

Signature Blocked

Holding the Fort

John Fabey ultimately got into the adult culinary arts vocational training program. It supplies food for low-income adults in North Philly. It is called "Philabundance," and to the envy of many men, John was able to leave prison a few months earlier, as a result. This is one of the certification programs Fort Dix did have, but it was only available to a few guys each quarter, and the men chosen for the program had to be from Philadelphia, or Pennsylvania, as it was explained to us.

Signature Blocked 63435-050

I found it a very informative class. It would be nice to be able to put people into different Levels in order to proceed at different speeds.

The part of implementing the system into a business plan, I felt was ~~crossed out~~ not needed. Simply by handing out the business plan information was sufficient.

Finally, I wanted to do more of our own calculations If you could Have simply given the high, Low, open, and close, we could have spent more time figuring out the contracts for ourselves.

On the whole though, I did enjoy it and very much appreciate all of the Time and effort that you put towards it.

Thank you,

Signature Blocked

John Barnes, the man in "The Interview," worked hard and studied even harder. Johnnie is a real man of God and is one of the principal men in the Camp who keeps things running. He is always in the library studying his Bible and I spent hours tutoring him in the system. He is a great guy.

Just wanted to let you know. I've really enjoy myself I got so much out of this class and This Class /Trading Definitely would be a wise decision to consider if it wasn't for Bob I'd Be completely Dumb Founded I'm not done with you yet It's Just the Beginning

Signature Blocked

Holding the Fort

This is one of the profit and loss tracking sheets for Mike, Pete and Jimmy ("Agron" is Jimmy's formal name). All the students had profit and loss statements they followed meticulously, if not neatly. You can see, without Excel spread sheets, or word processors, notes get taken in a hurry during class:

		3/2		3/31/15
1	Heating Oil	144,001.20	Signature Blocked	144,041.20
2	Gold	34,408	e	a 34,408
3	Euro	102,925		102,025
4	Silver	⟨6,172⟩		⟨33,404⟩
5	Coffee	69,660	A	69,660
6	Corn	—	Signature Blocked	—
7	Sugar 10	85,220.80		164,241.40
8	Soybeans 30yr Treasury Bond	⟨58,812.5⟩		⟨78,063.2⟩
9	Cattle S+P	⟨20,359⟩		⟨20,359⟩
10	Copper	49,200		24,850

$400,071.5   FINALY $407,342.48

$$x \quad \frac{3}{\$1,200,214.5} \qquad x \quad \frac{3}{\$1,222,026.6}$$

Three students teamed and picked
the same markets, deploying
$3 million in available Theoretical capital.

52 Trading days 1/2/15 – 3/31/15
52   250 trading days   Initial Capital: $1,000,000
$$\frac{52}{250} = .208$$ profit = 407,342.40
Annualizing Factor: 4.80769   Actual % Return: 40.73%
Annualized Return: 195.52%
*Projected Annual Profit 2015: $1,955,243.52
Projected Year-End Capital 2015: $2,955,243.52

* Assumes rate of return continues at same rate.

Holding the Fort

This is Ayunde's profit and loss statement. His markets were chosen at random and he made the most money in our classroom test.

A.C.E COURSE SIGN IN

Course: A. Yearwood   Date: 3/3/15

	PRINTED NAME	REGISTRATION NO.	SIGNATURE
1.	Silver	⟨6172⟩	⟨33,404⟩
2.	NAT GAS	⟨30,350⟩	⟨30,350⟩
3.	CORN	—	
4.	Soy	⟨65,250⟩	⟨65,250⟩
5.			
6.	NASDAQ	24,872	24,872
7.	SUGAR	85,220.80	164,214.40
8.	COCOA	105,801.80	149,881.80
9.	EURO	102,925	102,025
10.	British Pound	45,100	77,756.25
11.			
12.	Heating Oil	144,001.20	144,001.20
13.			
14.	Theoretical profit as of 3/3/15	$406,148.80	$533,746.65
15.			FINAL
16.			
17.			
18.	THEORETICAL PROFIT AND LOSS		
19.			
20.	CALCULATION		
21.			

These are Dave Connolly's markets. Dave selected all his markets and nearly beat Ayunde. Note Dave selected Corn and the system did not yield a trading signal during the entire quarter, thus the profit and loss statement has a "-" (i.e., dash sign) for this market.

	Signature Blocked	
	3/23/15	3/31/15
Corn	-	-
Orange Juice	115,798.4	115,798.40
Coffee	69,660.0	69,660
Gold	34,408	34,408
Heating Oil	144,001.20	144,001.20
10 year US Treasury	⟨58,812.5⟩	⟨78,063.20⟩
Euro	102,925	102,025
Sugar	85,220.80	164,214.40
Wheat	⟨53,541⟩	⟨70,323⟩
S & P Mini	⟨20,359⟩	⟨20,359⟩

Theoretical profit loss of 3/23/15 $419,300.90 $461,361.8c

Theoretical profit to loss calculation   FINAL

Here is my tracking sheet. You can see the markets I received, as we tried to obtain broad coverage across sectors for the class.

THEORETICAL P+L

Signature Blocked

Profit <Loss>

	2/27/15	3/9/15	3/23/15	3/31/15
S+P eMini	$25,920	(80,359)	(20,359)	(20,359)
Natural Gas	(30,350)	(30,350)	(30,350)	(30,350)
Euro		102,925	102,925	102,025
Silver	1,650	23,348	(6,172)	(33,404)
Cocoa	23,626	(30,198.2)	105,801.8	149,881.80
Wheat	(19,680)	(22,991)	(53,541)	(70,323)
Nasdaq	46,72	24,872	24,872	24,872
Soybeans	(12,290)	(65,250)	(65,250)	(65,250)
Corn	—	—	—	—
Swiss Franc	7462	59,862.5	25900	25,900
	42,510	62,218.3	104,185.8	$82,992.80 FINAL

THEORETICAL

PROFIT <LOSS> CALCULATION

What was very interesting was the consistent profitability, overall, the Turtle trading system displayed over the quarter. Even though the markets I was assigned didn't earn as much money as the other guys, it was consistently profitable, with a few hiccups here and there, as markets failed to enter trends.

Holding the Fort

These are some of the Turtle Trading system data and trading sheets I developed (I referred to our style of trading as "Turbo Trading," since it was probably a little different from the Turtles). I hand-typed the original system trade and data sheets on the old prison typewriters, then had to draw lines down the paper to create columns. You miss word processors, Excel and computers in prison.

TURBO TRADING SUMMARY
COURSE END 3-31-15
PROFIT (LOSS)

OPEN DATE	SECURITY	COST VALUE/CONTRACTS	#	MON./YR. CLOSE DATE	CLOSE PRICE	# PROFIT/(LOSS)
4-14 to 2-19-15	NASDAQ CLOSED POSITION	SEE SECURITY DATA 3-4-15		3-6-15	4395	$24,872
7-2 to 2-17-15	10-Yr US TREAS CLOSED	" " " "		2-4 +2-24-15	129-8 +128-21	‹$58,812.5›
1-5 to 2-18-15	30-YR BOND CLOSED	" " " "		3-4-15	1.5329	‹$5,025›
1-26 + 3-4-15	EURO CLOSED	" " " "		3-9-15	1.0860	$103,925
2-2-15	SUGAR CLOSED	" " " "		2-10-15	15,013	‹$19,107.2›
2-13,18,23-15	COCOA CLOSED	" " " "		2-4 +3-9-15	2778.8	‹$30,198.2›
2-2-15	WHEAT CLOSED	" " " "		2-6-15	529.75	‹$19,680›
2,17,24,27-15	SOYBEANS CLOSED	" " " "		2-7-15 3-9-15	944.48	‹$65,250›
1-2,5,20-15	NATURAL GAS CLOSED	" " " "		2-20-15	2.9286	‹$30,350›
2-3,6-15	LIGHT SWEET CRUDE CLOSED	" " " "		2-11-15	49.73	‹$50,580›
1-3,9,12,13-15	HEATING OIL CLOSED	" " " "		2-3,11-15	174.97	$144,001.2
1-11,17,23-15	GOLD CLOSED	" " " "	303-15	3-23-15	1187.50	$34,408
1-7,18,24 +3-4-15	SWISS FRANC CLOSED	" " " "	3-23-15	3-23-15	1.0367	$25,900
1-7,18,20-15	COFFEE CLOSED	" " " "		3-23-15	142.25	$69,690
1-19,20,23-15	ORANGE JUICE CLOSED	" " " "		3-23-15	120.71	$115,798.5
2-26-15	WHEAT CLOSED	" " " "		3-17-15	576.	‹$31,911›
2-6,12,26-15	S&P EMINI CLOSED	" " " "		3-6-15	2082.2	‹$655›
3-11-15	S&P EMINI CLOSED	" " " "		3-18-15	2089.66	‹$19,704›
1-7,3,6,9-15	SILVER CLOSED	" " " "		3-20-15	16.17.5	‹$6,172›
2-20,25,3-23-15	SUGAR WORLD CLOSED*	" " 3-31-15		3-31-15	11.93	$183,321.6
3-4,10,12-15	COCOA CLOSED*	" " " "		3-31-15	2699	$180,080
3-23	WHEAT CLOSED	" " " "		3-26-15	506.03	$18,732
1-6,11	BRITISH POUND CLOSED*	" " " "		3-31-15	1.4837	$82,781.25
3-11-15	LIGHT SWEET CRUDE *	" " " "		3-31-15	47.60	$21,630
1-2,12,26,+2-6-15	COPPER	" " " "				$34,850
3-20-15	SILVER *	" " " "		3-31-15	1663.7	‹$27,232›
3-8-15	10-Yr US TREAS CLOSED	" " " "		3-18-15	128-13	‹$9,250.7›
TOTAL	PROFIT	1/1/15-3/31/15	1ST QUARTER 2015	ALL MARKETS		$564,337.95

SECURITY DATA — DATE PROFIT CALCULATED AND/OR OPEN/CLOSE DATE

* (O) indicates open position; theoretical profit calculated with end-of-day data from Investor's Business Daily and/or The Wall Street Journal.

‹› indicates short position and/or loss.

Holding the Fort

I would get quite detailed, and document carefully the action in each market:

As of
3-23-15

DETAILED
SECURITY DATA

TURBO TRADING
FORT DIX, NJ
THEORETICAL PROFIT (LOSS) CALCULATION

OPEN DATE	SECURITY	COST VALUE/CONTRACTS	MON./YR.	DATE PROFIT CALCULATED AND/OR PRICE CLOSE DATE	CLOSE PRICE	$ PROFIT (LOSS)
2-20-15	SUGAR - WORLD	⟨14.09/22⟩	MAY 15	(1) 3-23-15	12.74	$33,264
2-25-15	112,000 lb	⟨13.89/22⟩		(1) 3-23-15	12.74	28,336
3-2-15	¢/lb	⟨13.69/22⟩		(1) 3-23-15	12.74	23,408
3-3-15		⟨13.49/23⟩		(1) 3-23-15	12.74	19,320
2-11-15	GOLD	1225.70/4	APR 15	3-23-15	1187.5	$15,280
2-17-15	100 TROY oz	1214.57/4		3-23-15	1187.5	$10,828
2-17-15	$/oz	1203.44/4		3-23-15	1187.5	$6,376
2-23-15	CLOSED	⟨1192.31/4⟩		3-23-15	1187.5	$1,924
2-17-15	SWISS FRANC	⟨1.0721/3⟩	MAR 15	3-23-15	1.0367	$13,275
2-18-15	125,000 FRANCS $/Franc	⟨1.060/3⟩		3-23-15	1.0367	$8,737.5
2-26-15		⟨1.048/3⟩		3-23-15	1.0367	$4,237.5
3-4-15	CLOSED	⟨1.036/4⟩		3-23-15	1.0367	⟨$350.⟩
1-3/17,18,20	COFFEE 37,500 ¢/lb	⟨158.65/4⟩	MAY 15	MAR 19-15	142.25	$24,600
2-17-15		⟨155.46/4⟩		3-19-15	142.25	$19,815
2-18-15		⟨152.27/4⟩		3-19-15	142.25	$15,030
2-20-15	CLOSED	⟨149.08/4⟩		3-19-15	142.25	$10,245
3-9,10-12-15	COCOA	⟨3003/20⟩	MAY 15	(o) 3-23-15	2757	$49,200
3-10-15	10 METRIC TONS $/ton	⟨2939/19⟩		(o) 3-23-15	2757	$34,580
3-10-15		⟨2939/19⟩		(o) 3-23-15	2757	$34,580
3-12-15	CLOSED	⟨2855/18⟩		(o) 3-23-15	2757	$17,640

* (o) indicates open position; theoretical profit calculated with end-of-day data from Investor's Business Daily and/or The Wall Street Journal.

⟨⟩ indicates short position and/or loss.

202

Detailed
3-23-15

SECURITY DATA

OPEN DATE	SECURITY	COST VALUE/#CONTRACTS	MON./YR.	DATE PROFIT CALCULATED AND/OR CLOSE DATE	CLOSE PRICE	# PROFIT/LOSS
2-19	ORANGE JUICE	<133.04/20>	MAY 15	3-23-15	120.71	$36,990
2-20	15000 lbs $/lb	<131.39/20>	^	3-23-15	120.71	$32,040
3-23		<129.74/19>		3-23-15	120.71	$25,735.5
2-23	CLOSED POSITION	<128.09/18>		3-23-15	120.71	$21,033
2-26	WHEAT CLOSED POSITION	<491.25/11>	MAY 15	3-17-15	516	<$13,612.5>
2-26	5,000 ¢/bushel "	<462.73/11>		3-17-15	516	<$18,298.5>
3-23-15	WHEAT 5,000bu $/bu	537.25/12	MAY 15 (o)	3-23-15	537	<$1,950>
2-6,12,20	S&P emini $50/pt	2062.1/5	MAR 15	3-6-15	2082.2	$5,025
		2081.3/5		3-6-15	2082.2	<$250>
	CLOSED POSITION	2100.3/6		3-6-15	2082.2	<$5,430>
3-11-15	S&P emini $50/pt	<2040.4/8>	MAR 15	3-18-15	2089.66	<$19,704>
3-6-15	British Pound	<1.5162/14>	JUNE 15 (o)	3-23-15	1.4932	$20,125
3-6-15	62500 BP $/GBP	<1.5105/14>	(o)	3-23-15	1.4932	$15,137.50
3-6-15		<1.5040/14>	(o)	3-23-15	1.4932	$14,150
3-11-15		<1.4991/13>	(o)	3-23-15	1.4932	$4,712.50
3-11-15	Light Sweet Crude Oil	<47.79/3>	APR 15	3-23-15	47.45	<$1,020>
3-13-15	1000 bbl $/bbl	<46.46/3>		3-23-15	47.45	<$2,970>
3-13-15		<45.13/3>		3-23-15	47.45	<$6,960>
3-16-15		<43.81/3>		3-23-15	47.45	<$10,920>

(o) indicates open position; theoretical profit calculated with end-of-day data from Investor's Business Daily and/or The Wall Street Journal.

<> indicates short position and/or loss.

* SWITCHED TO JUNE CONTRACT.

TURBO TRADING
FORT DIX, NJ
THEORETICAL PROFIT (LOSS) CALCULATION

This was our Unit Work Sheet. This was how we kept control of risk and was an important risk management tool. It dictated the number of contracts and units each position was allowed to take.

As of 3-23-15

UNIT WORK SHEET
POSITION ENTRY, STOPS &EXIT POINTS

SECURITY ,#CONTRACTS	UNIT #	PRICE	STOP:	1	1/2 N ADD' UNIT 2 3 4 5
COCOA `<20>` 3-9 `<1>`		3003	3099.86	2918.79 3954.57 2930.35	
10. Met. Tons `<19>` 3-10 `<2>`		2939	3040.80		
`<19>` 3-10 `<3>`		2939	2040.8		
`<19>` 3-12 `<4>`		2855	2965.16		
WHEAT 12 3-23 12		537.25	506.03	545.05 552.85 560.65	
S+P emini `<8>` 3-11 `<1>`		2040.4	2089.66	2078.09 2015.77 2003.46	
		stopped out @ 2089.66 3-18-15			

SECURITY ,#CONTRACTS	UNIT #	PRICE	STOP:	1	1/2 N ADD' UNIT 2 3 4 5
British Pound `<8/14>` 3-6 `<1>`		(1.5162)	1.5310	1.5105 1.5048 1.4991	
`<14>` 3-6 `<2>`		1.5105	1.5330		
`<14>` 3-6 `<3>`		1.5048	1.5276		
`<14>` 3-11 `<4>`		1.4991	1.5218		
#CONTRACTS DATE/UNIT PRICE			STOP	½ N ADD UNITS	
Light Sweet Crude `<3>` 3-11 1 47.79		53.09	46.46 45.13 43.81		
`<3>` 3-13 2 46.46		51.77			
`<3>` 3-13 3 45.13		50.45			
`<3>` 3-18 4 43.81		49.15			

I include the performance sheets from the end of February, as it might be of interest to see the class was profitable from the get go:

END OF DAY 2-25-15

SECURITY DATA

OPEN DATE	SECURITY	COST VALUE / # CONTRACTS	MON./YR.	DATE PROFIT CALCULATED * AND/OR CLOSE OPEN DATE	CLOSE PRICE	$ PROFIT/(LOSS)
2-11	Nasdaq emini	4286.4 / 6	MAR 15	(0) 2-25-15	4436.8	18,048
2-12	$20/pt.	4323.7 / 6		(0) 2-25-15	4436.8	13,572
2-13		4360.9 / 6		(0) 2-25-15	4436.8	9,108
2-19		4398.2 / 7		(0) 2-25-15	4436.8	5,404
2-2	10-Year U.S. Treasury	130-31 / 11	Mar 15	2-4	129-8	<18,906.25>
2-9	10-Year U.S. Treasury	<128-16 / 11>		2-24	128-21	<1,718.75>
2-11	$100,000 1/32	<128-03 / 13>		2-24	128-21	7,312.5
2-17		<127-22 / 13>		2-24	128-21	<12,593.75>
2-17		<127-08 / 13>		2-24	128-21	<18,281.25>
2-6	S+P emini	2062.1 / 5	Mar 15	(0) 2-25	2110.2	12,025
2-12	$50/pt.	2081.3 / 5		(0) 2-25	2110.2	7,250
2-20		2100.3 / 6		(0) 2-25	2110.2	2,970
2-13	Copper 25,000 lbs. 4/lb	263.41 / 5	Mar 15	(0) 2-25	266.35	3,675
2-17	Silver 5,000 oz. 1/oz	<1654 / 3>	Mar 15	(0) 2-25	1643.0	1,650
2-5	British Pound	1.5264 / 12	Mar 15	(0) 2-25	1.5526	19,650
2-5	62,500 #/GBP	1.5327 / 12		(0) 2-25	1.5526	14,925
2-5		1.5339 / 12		(0) 2-25	1.5526	14,025
2-18		1.5453 / 12		(0) 2-25	1.5526	5,475
2-2	Sugar World 112,000 lb 1/lb	<14.16 / 20>	Mar 15	2-10	15.013	<19,107.20>
2-11	Gold	<1225.70 / 4>	Apr 15	(0) 2-25	1201.50	1225.76 9,680
2-17	100 Troy oz.	<1214.57 / 4>		(0) 2-25	1201.50	1214.57 5,228
2-17		<1203.44 / 4>		(0) 2-25	1201.50	1203.44 776
2-23		<1192.31 / 4>		(0) 2-25	1201.50	1192.31 <3,676>

✻ (0) indicates open position as of 2-25-15 and theoretical profit calculated with end-of-day data.

< > Indicates short position and/or loss.

Page 1 ↑ 61,865.30

THEORETICAL PROFIT THROUGH 2-25-15 $174,778.4

TURBO TRADING   FORT DIX
2-25-15 THEORETICAL PROFIT (LOSS) CALCULATION
1 of 3

END OF DAY 2-25-15
SECURITY DATA

DATE	SECURITY	COST /CONTRACT	MON./YR.	OPEN/DATE	CLOSE PRICE	PROFIT/(LOSS)
2-17	SWISS FRANC	<1.0721/3>	Mar 15	(o) 2-25	1.0561	6,000
2-18	125,000 B/Franc	<1.060/3>		(o) 2-25	1.0561	1,462.50
2-3	Coffee	<158.65>/4	Mar 15	(o) 2-25	143.45	22,800
2-17	37,500 ¢/lb	<155.46>/4		(o) 2-25	143.45	18,015
2-18		<152.37>/4		(o) 2-25	143.45	13,230
2-20		<149.08>/4		(o) 2-25	143.45	8,445
2-2	Cocoa	<2681/20>	Mar 15	2-4	2776.80	<19,160>
	10 Metric Tons $/Ton					
2-13	Cocoa	2978/18	Mar 15	(o) 2-25	3081	18,540
2-18	10 Metric Tons $/Ton	3004.13/19		(o) 2-25	3081	14,605.3
2-23		3030.26/19		(o) 2-25	3081	9,640.6
2-19	ORANGE JUICE	<133.04/20>	Mar 15	(o) 2-25	123.20	29,520
2-20	15,000 lbs ¢/lb	<131.39/20>		(o) 2-25	123.20	24,570
2-23		<129.74/19>		(o)2-25	123.20	18,639
2-23		<128.09/19>		(o)2-25	123.20	13,930.5
2-2	Wheat	<496.95/12>	Mar 15	2-6	529.75	<19,680>
	5,000 bu ¢/bu					
2-2	Soybeans	<966.20/10>	Mar 15	2-17	1004.78	<16,425>
2-17	5,000 bu ¢/bu	999.05/10	Mar 15	(b)2-25	1007.8	4,375
		1008.28/10		(b)2-25	1007.8	<240>
2-2	Natural Gas	<2.671/5>	Mar 15	2-20	2.9286	<2880>
2-5	10,000 MM BTU	<2.5792/5>		2-20	2.9286	<3494> <7,470>
	$/MM BTU					

* (o) Indicates open position as of 2-25-15 and theoretical profit calculated with end-of-day data.

< > Indicates short position and/or loss.

Pg2 π   117,923.90

THEORETICAL PROFIT <LOSS>
CALCULATION

2 of 3

END OF DAY DATA 2-25-15
SECURITY DATA

DATE	SECURITY	COST VALUE/CONTRACT	MON./YR.	DATE PROFIT CALCULATED* AND/OR CLOSE OPEN FIXED DATE	CLOSE PRICE	PROFIT(LOSS) #
2-3	Light Sweet Crude Oil	51.74 /3	Mar 15	2-11	49.73	⟨6,030⟩
2-3	1,000 bbl $/bbl	53.21 /3	Mar 15	2-11	49.73	⟨10,440⟩
2-3		54.68 /3		2-11	49.73	⟨14,850⟩
2-6		56.15 /3		2-11	49.73	⟨19,260⟩
2-3	Heating Oil	177.71 /4	Mar 15	2-4	174.97	⟨4603.2⟩
2-3	42,000 gal ¢/gal	180.47 /4		2-4	174.97	⟨9,240⟩
2-3		183.23 /4		2-4	174.97	⟨13,876.80⟩
2-3		185.99 /4		2-4	174.97	⟨18,513.60⟩
2-9	Heating Oil	175.04 187.48 /3	Mar 15	(c) 2-25	210.36	28,828
	42,000 gal ¢/gal	190.59 /3		(c) 2-25	210.36	24,910.20
		193.70 /3		(c) 2-25	210.36	20,991.60
		196.81 /3		(c) 2-25	210.36	17,073

*(c) Indicates open position as of 2-25-15 and Theoretical profit
     calculated with end-of-day data.

⟨ ⟩ Indicates short position and/or loss   Pag 3 loss -5,010.8

3 of 3   THEORETICAL PROFIT ⟨LOSS⟩
                                CALCULATION

Holding the Fort

These typewritten words I wrote in a real hurry immediately after the course ended, in the prison library. I wound up sending it and the other documents out of the prison, to make sure they wouldn't get confiscated, or lost. You can see the typos and I have erased my signature on the last page of this "diary" and summary of the class.

```
                    TURBO TRADING
              THEORETICAL PERFORMANCE HISTORY

                   GRADUATING CLASS:
                   APRIL 10, 2015


LEARNING TO TURBO TRADE AT FORT DIX:  A CLASS OF INTEREST

On January 22, 2015 at Fort Dix, New Jersey, a class was created to
learn how to write a business plan.  The problem is, Fort Dix is a
prison and it is illegal to actually run a business out of a prison!

In trying tomake the class as interesting as possible, Instructor and
creator of the class, decided to set out an endeavor which might be
able to change the lives of the eleven men who stuck it out in his
class to learn the core curriculum he was trying to teach them.

The twelve of them, like the 12 disciples, set out on a course to
learn, inside and out, one of the world's most powerful trading systems.

This system would become the foundation of the business they would
learn---critical to the creation of any business!  This system has
been written about many times in the course of the last twenty years,
however, to the instructor's knowledge, had never been reduced to a
systematic method of trading, which might be learnable by a vast
majority of people!

To this end, while in prison, these twelve disciples, all convicted
fellons, set out on a course to potentially change their lives.

Many of the students were from the inner city, had little to no educa-
tional background, particularly with Wall Street, and many are what
most would consider to be "slow learners."  Why were these men drawn
to the class?

They were seeking to change their lives.

Their backgrounds are provided in this book, however, suffice it to
say we are talking about ex-drug dealers, fraudsters and other criminals
who made mistakes, paid for their mistakes and are trying, earnestly,
to turn over a new lease on life.

Their collective math skills were nominal, but a requirement, officially
was, they had to at least know how to calculate an average in mathematics
Yes, that's right:  They needed to know how to add up a column of
numbers and divide by the total "number" of numbers and get the average
of that column.

The students worked diligently for 12 weeks until April 9, 2015, when
they were given their "final."  "April 10, 2015" is listed as their
graduation date because the instructor graded the exams the next day,
offically ending the class.

Three of the students stayed in the class until they learned the system,
```

absconded with the course materials---which was their
right, as the instructor made the materials available to
all who atteneded the class---and never returned, BUT
their portfolio coverage could be tracked because they
had already selected the markets they would cover
throughout the course.

The point of this brief background is to state that the
system created, based on the world-famous "Turtle" trading
system was able to be learned by the dregs of society,
with little to no math skills and most had little, to
no college.

Since the instructor is also a "felon," he proudly sits
under the mantle of one of the "dregs" of society, also.

Regsardless of what the reader thinks, regardless of the
true guilt, or innocence of each man in the class, all
of us have sinned. The instructor's personal believe is
that most, if not all, of the men in that classroom for
12 weeks, have more than paid for their sins and are
earnestly trying to find an honest way to make a reasonable
living when they get out.

This is precisely why the instructor built the class.

He figured if he could teach men how to fish, for real,
and give them the real tools they needed to compete with
the "best-of-the-best" in money management, trading AND
risk management, the men in that room could possibly
change their lives---for real.

Prison is a tough place. If you try and B.S. your way
through, you are sussed out in a real hurry. Especially
by a bunch of "street smart" guys! This is why,
throughout the course of the class, and in our real-time
environment, which outlaws computers, cell phone, Internet
and many other necessities of traders on Wall Street,
all twelve of us tracked our respective markets meticulously
throughout the quarter.

The results and trading sheets, all provided to the men
throughout the class, are shown in the appendix. Nothing
has been altered. "Scratch marks," crossed-out errors,
and the hand-written work of instructor, Robert Kelly,
are provided for your detailed review.

As the men absorbed the teaching materials, they were
then provided with their trading results---making them
all the more interested in paying attention in class!
As any teacher knows, this is the battle!

With major successes using the system apparent and
in evidence and actaul fact becoming more and more
real to these outcasts from society, the instructor
was able to become even more bold and start to plant
the seed in their minds they could actually use the

knowledge gained from the course---both the system of
risk management AND the business plan, to start building
a path to obtaining a JOB---potentially working for a
private person, or entity, who might be more than intersted
in their prison-learned trading skills.

To this end, the instrctor had the students participate
in mock interviews. These were enlightening---particularly
to the instructor---because very few of the men had any
kind of interpersonal "corporate" communication skills!

Nevertheless, the instructor told them to focus on what
they know and don't worry about becoming something they
are not. The men had some real breakthroughs, copying
Donald Trump---"YOUR'E HIRED!" when the first brave soul
had a breakthrough after the initial interview went poorly
because the student had never interviewed for a job before,
especially like this one! This particular student has
his bunk near the instructor's in prison and is also a
Christian and friend of the teacher.

To the instructor's delight, this student--we'll just
call him "John," stunned the teacher at the very end
of the interview in front of all the other men. When
Instructor Kelly asked John, at the end of the laborious
interview, "Why should I hire you?" John lifted his
head up, looked Instructor Kelly in the eyes and with
all the bravado of a street-smart, ex-boxer, black inner-city
guy from the 'hood, belted out to the class:

"BECAUSE I MADE $250,000 IN ONE WEEK!"

The whole class applauded, when Kelly screamed out for
all to here:

"YOU'RE HIRED!!!!"

For a man who is on the back side of a TWENTY-YEAR prison
term, who has given his life to Jesus and is a completely
reformed individual, those words, even in our classroom
environment, meant the world to him.

John beamed and had the biggest smile on his face. The
class, I think, was proud of John, too. He took a
situation inwhich he was unfamiliar, relied on what HE
KNEW and used it to land a job---at least in our laboratory!

You see, John had the confidence in the NUMBERS. He had
the confidence in the process we had learned, and yes,
John had confidence in his instructor, a fellow Christian.

The men all have a great deal more tolearn about markets, but
if someone took a risk on them, kept tutoring them with
modern tools of the trade, that employer, or private

trading firm (the guys would prbably never get hired by
front-line firms because of their "felon" tags---they
are exactly the same as that borne by the protagonist
in the Scarlett Letter.

Finally, this introduction emphasizes the instruction
and system is designed, AT ITS CORE, to use risk management
techniques which someof the leading investment professionals
use.   This was key to the methodolgy and discussion led
by Mr. Kelly.

If this story sounds intriguing, please read on to
discover how Mr. Kelly taught 11 misfits, led by another---
himself---to achieve annualized returns ranging from
39% to 256%!!

Each student began the class with a capital account of
$1,000,000.   This was theoretical capital each person
had to deploy using the trding system, painstakingly
put together by Mr. Kelly.

The average return of all participants was a stunning
144.82%, as calculated with the individual returns in
the pages which follow.

These men spent a total of approximately 24 classroom
hours with Instructor Kelly.   They met on Thursday night,
throughout the course of the winter in 2015, over a 12-
week period.   Many of them did ask Mr. Kelly to provide
them with extra help, whichhe provided as and if requested.
These sessions amounted to, usually, a two-hour sesion
in the "chow hall."   For those who haven't been in a
prison, think "grade school cafeteria tables."   We would
gather around, typically surrounded by other inmates
who were mostly blissfully watching their favorite TV
shows---there were three televisions in the chow hall---
completely unaware that some men were trying valiantly
to change their lives---and their fortunes.

They will all soon one day be out. God willing, and if
they continue in their pursuit of knowledge, they will
indeed change their lives and the lives of those around
them.

Sincerely,

Signature Blocked

Robert Kelly, Inmate 56772-056
Fort Dix, New Jersey

...with a title of, "...a humble instructor"

Holding the Fort

CHAPTER 18

THE FINAL WHEAT LESSON

Months after class ended, I would often talk to Sean about the markets or school, and just rap a bit. I always kidded him that before I left, I was going to play him in basketball (I'm one of the lousiest basketball players on the face of the earth). He always thought this was pretty funny. He'd put up with me, and just laugh, and say, "OK, Bob." Sean's really tall and can definitely handle himself on the court!

We were only trying to get through the time, like every other man in there. Sean would be doing his Sudoku at all hours of the night, and my back would continue to kill me. Days fell off the calendar.

I would get out of bed at least a couple of times each night to stretch, and try and relieve the pain. Usually, I'd head to the bathroom and relieve myself, also.

One night, it was dead silent in the living quarters. It was also pitch black in the "B Wing" in the middle of the early morning. It's so dark, you can't see down the aisles. The metal walls on my side of the building blocked all light, and the few windows there were, opened up to the back of the prison and onto the yard. The yard was extremely dark after things were locked down for the evening, and before the sun rose in the morning.

You got to know your way around, though. In time, I could count the number of steps down the aisle before I had to turn to go to the bathroom, or get back to my bunk---even when I couldn't see my hand in front of my face. Sometimes, there would be tiny LED lights on at someone's bunk, which would help, but usually not in the middle of the night.

Anyway, on this night, there was dead silence at about 4 a.m. I made it back to my bunk, and I noticed Sean was still staring furiously at his Sudoku puzzle, with his body and upper bunk facing in the opposite direction from my bunk. He could not see me and I was about to climb up to my holed-out mattress.

Before I did, I stopped on my ladder, half way up. He continued to concentrate on his puzzle. I mean, this man was intent on solving Sudoku!

I very quietly got back into bed, leaned over my bunk, and whispered, quite loudly:

"SEVEN!"

This was a little payback to Sean for all the times in class he would shout out "C!", answering a question correctly.

Unlike Sean's answers in class, however, my answer was *not* correct...but, at least he laughed at my joke. We both chuckled about this for a while, thereafter.

About a week later, as I was watching the markets and monitoring generally what was happening in the financial news---I noticed the "Wheat" market had experienced some significant volatility (i.e., there had been a major change in its price).

I couldn't wait to show Sean and hopefully, drive an important point home to him. Even though the class had been over for some number of months, I thought he might really use the system one day, and I wanted him to see what was happening.

Sean had lost nearly $80,000 in the Wheat market when he was trading in class. This cut down his theoretical profits, but he still wound up earning $273,427, theoretically, during class. He had taken sixth place with those winnings.

When he was screaming in class back in March, about the "The wheat's killing me, Bob!", I had looked back on his Wheat data sheets. I remember seeing he was trading the correct unit size of 12 contracts for each entry signal he would receive. The students were limited to four entries per market, when a "buy," "sell short," or add-to-position signal was created by the system.

Volatility by May of 2015 had *decreased* in Wheat and, as a result, in accordance with our Turtle Trading rules, the number of contracts Sean *would have used* for his unit size would be *increased* to "13" contracts for each entry point.

Wheat's underlying "contract size" is for 5,000 bushels, similar to other grains. What this really means when you are trading futures contracts is if you don't sell a "long" wheat position before settlement day, you *will* wind up with this much wheat on your doorstep! The quantity of "5,000" bushels was established for wheat (and many other grains) because in the old days, this is how much a railroad freight car could carry---thus, one contract covered one freight car, or 5,000 bushels of wheat.

Wheat is also quoted in *pennies* per bushel. A quote of 488.88 means each contract entered is controlling $24,444 worth of wheat at $4.8888/bushel. I held up the Investor's Business Daily graph, and said, "Hey Sean, wait until you see this!"

Sean turned around from in his bed, and faced mine. I pointed out how Wheat had moved on the chart in the paper. Below, I have reproduced the price movement and created an excel chart to allow the reader to easily see what happened to the price of Wheat during this timeframe.

Sean noticed the graph changed, radically. The data and graph would reveal the price of Wheat had made a dramatic move UP in price:

Wheat Contract 5,000 bushel (¢/bushel)			
Date	High	Low	Close
7/1/2015	615.00	576.12	587.25
6/30/2015	617.12	576.38	616.62
6/29/2015	591.38	564.12	584.12
6/26/2015	566.12	530.38	560.75
6/25/2015	532.62	513.12	532.38
6/24/2015	529.88	514.12	518.12
6/23/2015	522.62	501.88	522.62
6/22/2015	504.12	487.38	501.75
6/19/2015	492.25	483.62	488.88
6/18/2015	497.88	487.38	487.88
6/17/2015	499.62	489.62	491.62
6/16/2015	494.88	487.12	488.62
6/15/2015	503.25	486.12	488.88

As you can more easily see from the Wheat chart graphic, something definitely happened to this market, which caused it to spike dramatically—in a very short period of time:

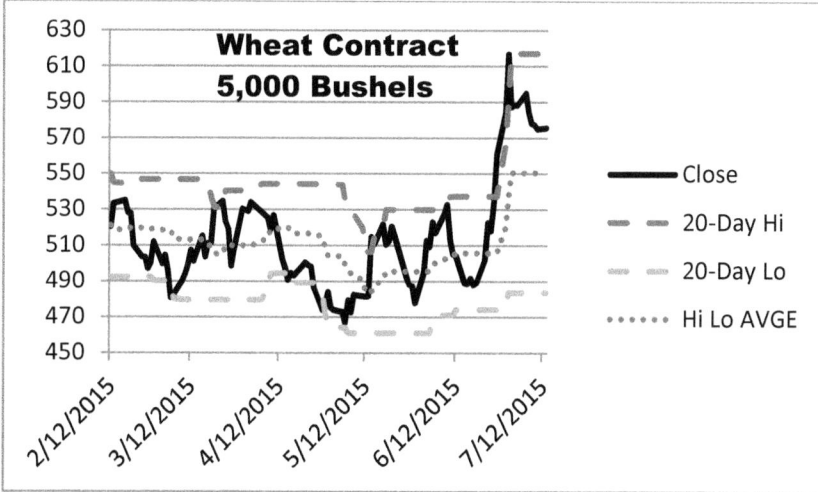

Also, it is instructive to notice how the price of Wheat had "bounced" around, back and forth, in range-bound trading during the period when Sean was trading this contract during the first quarter of 2015. This is why he kept losing money in this market during the class.

As I have noted, Sean lost nearly $80,000 in this contract during the 52 trading days of our class. I said to Sean, "Let's see what *would have* happened if you had acquired the four unit 'maximum' position limit of our Turtle Trading System and caught Wheat's rise."

He said, "All right, let's see it."

I whipped out my pen and paper and we did the math, together. I made some rough estimates of what his entries might have been, but suffice it to say the difference between 488.88 and the high, which occurred just eleven days later at 617.12, would have been a profit of $1.2824/bushel. This is a hugely significant price move for Wheat, in such a short timeframe.

I said, "Sean, you would have been controlling 52 contracts."

Sean replied, not really understanding, "Huh, huh..."

I could see he didn't quite get it, yet. I entered the numbers into the same small, cheap white calculator I bought from commissary:

I entered: "52 x 5,000 x 1.2824 = $333,424"

"Let's see...you would have made over three-hundred grand in about two weeks."

Sean stared at me, and his face began to brighten and he was grinning, ear-to-ear. He then was emphatic:

"I SEE!"

Sean really got it, then! He forgot all about the $80,000 he had lost when the Wheat market was shaking out all the weak hands, in range-bound trading. I explained to Sean, "This is fairly typical of markets. This, Sean, is *exactly* why you needed to stay in Wheat."

Sean smiled, looked me in the eye and replied, "I gotch' you."

Markets usually always do what everyone else isn't doing, and Sean learned a huge lesson, months after the class ended...and I learned one, too:

A teacher's work is never done!

CHAPTER 19

BATTLE SCARS WITH THE BOP

I was in my own zone when I was teaching, but every month, the head of education assessed your performance and would credit your commissary account---at the BOP's paltry wage-rate levels. A copy of my June 2016 review is attached, which was my last full month at the Camp, before I was released.

As you can see, performance is graded on a "1" to "5" basis, with a "5" being outstanding. My reviews were usually "5s," with a couple of "4s" thrown in to keep me humble, which is never a problem—especially in prison. I started out teaching at $.12/hour---I know, I know---I was a really big-money guy for sure, and it just confirmed the fact I had always heard---you don't go into teaching for the money!

By January of 2015, I was informed by Joe Kerns, my cohort and a decade-long-imprisoned inmate, the Head of Education--- Ms. Lindley, was giving me a raise and a "new" grade of employment. She was moving me from a "Grade 4" Tutor, to a "Grade 3" Tutor. My pay was also being raised to $.16/hour. And I just might say, it's not too many guys who get a 50% raise after their first two months on the job---beat that, Goldman Sachs.

Joe was always pretty serious about these matters and informed me of this change to my wage and "grade" level as a tutor, with a totally straight face but, I had to stop myself from laughing myself silly. I mean minimum wage in 1938 was $.25/hour!

Here is my final performance review in June 2016:

BP-A0324
JUN 10
WORK PERFORMANCE RATING - INMATE

U.S. DEPARTMENT OF JUSTICE
FEDERAL BUREAU OF PRISONS

Inmate's Name Robert Kelly	Register No. 56772-056	Unit CAMP
Evaluation Period JUNE 2016	Work Assignment Tutor CAMP	

Bonus Justification

Signature and Date of Dept. Head Approval

Route to Dept. Head for Review, Then to Unit Team

Instructions: Check the best statement in each area. Base your rating on the inmate's overall performance for the rating period--neither the inmate's best day nor worst day--as compared to what is expected of a satisfactory worker in the assignment.

A. QUALITY OF WORK
___1. Unsatisfactory. Makes more errors than should for this level of training. Work must be redone.
___2. Fair. Careless; makes mistakes and does not check work. Should do better work.
___3. Satisfactory. Makes some mistakes but no more than expected at this level.
___4. Good. Makes fewer mistakes than most inmates at this level of training. Does Journeyman level work.
___5. Outstanding. Does superior work

B. QUANTITY OF WORK
___1. Unsatisfactory. Lazy, wastes time, goofs off.
___2. Fair. Does just enough to get by. Has to be prodded occasionally.
___3. Satisfactory. Works steadily but does not push self.
___4. Good. Willing Worker. Does a full day's work and wastes little time.
___5. Outstanding. Drives self exceptionally hard all the time.

C. INITIATIVE
___1. Unsatisfactory. Always waits to be told what to do. Needs help getting started.
___2. Fair. Usually relies on others to say what needs to be done.
___3. Satisfactory. Can adapt to changes in routine. Will start work without waiting to be told.
___4. Good. Can plan own work well. Acts on own in most things. Doesn't wait to be told what to do.
___5. Outstanding. Has good ideas on better ways of doing things.

D. INTEREST; EAGERNESS TO LEARN
___1. Poor. Shows no interest in job. Regards job as a drag or waste of time.
___2. Fair. Shows minimal interest but not very eager to learn.
___3. Satisfactory. Shows average amount of interest. Wants to learn own job but does not put forth extra effort.
___4. Good. Above-average interest in job. Asks questions about own work and related work. May do extra work to improve skills.
___5. Outstanding. Eager to master job. Wants to know everything there is to know about it. May read up on own time or volunteer to do things that will improve knowledge.

E. ABILITY TO LEARN
___1. Poor. Has very low aptitude and is very slow to learn. Even when given extra instruction unable to learn, no matter how hard trying.
___2. Fair. Slow but if tries eventually will pick up the skills. Needs more instructions than most.
___3. Average. No slower and no faster to learn than most inmates. Requires average amount of instruction.
___4. Good. Learns rapidly. Good memory. Rarely makes the same mistake twice.
___5. Outstanding. Very quick to learn. Excellent memory. Is learning much more rapidly than most inmates assigned here. Never makes the same mistake twice.

F. NEED FOR SUPERVISION; DEPENDABILITY; SAFETY; CARE OF EQUIPMENT
___1. Needs constant supervision. If left unsupervised will foul up, get in trouble, or wander off. Undependable.
___2. Needs closer supervision than most. Not very dependable.
___3. Average. Can be relied on for certain things but must be supervised by others. Usually prompt and dependable.
___4. Needs little supervision. Good record of dependability an promptness.
___5. No supervision required. Completely dependable in all things.

Replaces BP-S324, OCT 94

PDF

Prescribed by P5251

Replaces BP-S324, OCT 94

G. RESPONSE TO SUPERVISION AND INSTRUCTION
___1. Poor. Resentful and hostile. May argue with supervisor.
___2. Fair. Resists or ignores suggestions.
___3. Satisfactory. Generally does what is told without any fuss.
_√_4. Good. No hostility or resentment. Tries to improve.
___5. Outstanding. Makes a real effort to please the instructor. Does exactly as is told.

H. ABILITY TO WORK WITH OTHERS
___1. Poor. Negativistic, hostile, annoying to others.
___2. Fair. Doesn't make friends easily. Has some interpersonal difficulties.
_√_3. Satisfactory. Gets along OK with most co-workers and is accepted by them.
___4. Good. Friendly, congenial, helpful; others like to work with.
___5. Outstanding. Gets along well with everyone. Very popular.

I. OVERALL JOB PROFICIENCY
Based on this inmate's overall performance during this work period, if this inmate was an employee of yours, in the community would you:

___1. fire or lay off that individual?
___2. Transfer the person to a less demanding job at a lower pay scale?
_√_3. Continue to employ the person but without a raise or promotion this time?
___4. Raise the person's pay but keep the person at the same job?
___5. Promote the person to a more demanding job at a higher pay rate?

J. GRADES AND PAY
1. Performance Pay - Grade Class (Check one) ___ 1 _√_ 2 ___ 3 ___ 4 ___ M.

2. Hours of Satisfactory work _____ 132 .

3. Regular Pay _____ $38.28 .

4. Bonus Recommended: ___ yes; ___ no

5. Total Pay _____ $38.28 .

Supervisor's Signature		K.Lindley	Date 6·20·16
Inmate's Signature	Signature Blocked		Date
Inmate reason:		was requested to sign this rating, but refused, citing the following	

Staff Witness' Signature		Date

BP-A0575
JUN 10
PERFORMANCE PAY DAILY RECORD - INMATE

U.S. DEPARTMENT OF JUSTICE
FEDERAL BUREAU OF PRISONS

	SUNDAY	MONDAY	TUESDAY	WEDNESDAY	THURSDAY	FRIDAY	SATURDAY
DAY OF MO:				1	2	3	4
				6	6	6	
DAY OF MO:	6	7	8	9	10	11	
	6	6	6	6	6		
DAY OF MO:	13	14	15	16	17	18	
	6	6	6	6	6		
DAY OF MO:	20	21	22	23	24	25	
	6	6	6	6	6		
DAY OF MO:	27	28	29	30			
	6	6	6	6			

Note: For days reflecting less than 7 hours worked explain by inserting applicable code:

C = Callout   V = Visit   AD = Admin. Det./Discip. Seg
E = Education   HO = Holiday   U = Unsatisfactory
F = Furlough   I = Medical Idle
H = Hospital   UA = Unauthorized

Inmate's Name Robert Kelly	Register No. 56772-056	Detail Education-Orderly OUTC
Month: June 2016	Total Hours: 132	

When I phoned home this cold night in January, I was kidding around and asked Heidi to make sure she told her Dad I received a 50% pay *increase!* She laughed pretty hard and he did, as well, from what I understand. Even in prison, you have to try and keep your sense of humor.

I don't know why Ms. Lindley didn't tell me in person about my raise, but she was probably just busy, or embarrassed by the lowly BOP wages. She knew I had worked hard for the department, and at pennies-an-hour, slave-labor wages, to boot. At the end of the day, it didn't really matter to me. In my brain, I was working for the men anyway---and the big Man upstairs.

Ms. Lindley had a great deal of power, and we saw many a man feel her umbrage, when they really abused the "privilege" of being in class. Most of the time she was pretty cool, but she could really let it rip, every once in a while.

One of her most important powers was the power to take away an inmate's "Good Time." According to the law, 18 U.S.C. § 3624(b), Good Time amounts to up to 54 days a year off an inmates sentence---if the inmate behaves himself. However, the BOP calculates this figure at only 47 days to supposedly enable them to "prorate" credit for partial years of imprisonment. This loses men 7 days a year of freedom from what is very plain and clear language in the law---which Congress passed!

Beyond being a threat to Good Time, Ms. Lindley could also force men into the "SHU," in extreme cases. The SHU is the "Special Holding Unit," more commonly known on TV, as the "Hole." It's not a nice place, although I never went there. I was told it was cold, concrete, and there was nothing to do in there. Basically, it's brutal, in its isolation and conditions.

Her power didn't stop with those two sledge hammers, either. She could also hand out "shots." Shots, if enough of them were acquired, could reduce a man's Good Time, and could ultimately send him to a higher-level security prison---or send him off to the Hole to "self-reflect." Shots are essentially like demerits. If you received enough of them, you were headed for some pretty big trouble.

Ms. Lindley, of course, wasn't the only person who could hand out shots, or other forms of punishment. Any guard, or any Officer in the system, has the power to wreak havoc on an inmate's life. Inmates can appeal punishment decisions, but usually and automatically, the appeals process within the BOP (which is run by BOP employees), backs up the reporting Officer's version of what had been happening. The result: the inmate usually loses his case and receives his shots, heads to the hole, loses good time, or gets sent to a higher-level security prison. The guards and officers have all the power and inmates are at their mercy.

This is a big reason why there is an "Us" vs. "Them" attitude in prison. Most prisoners feel things are rigged against them. Not only do most inmates serve lengthy prison sentences, but they also spend their sentences in a really crappy environment, from all sides---food, discipline, activities, work, sleep, clothing, costs, pay, separation, etc. Granted, conditions are not as bad as the French prisons seen in the film, "Catch Me If You Can," or other places in the world, however, the United States is supposed to be trying to *solve* the problem of recidivism.

Recidivism creates a huge cost for the government and ultimately, delivers a real, ongoing threat to society.

As my teaching progressed, I listened to at least a hundred different students complain about the situation inside Fort Dix. My sidebar "help" sessions with the men also started increasing. I absorbed a great deal of knowledge on this subject, as a result.

The experience was indeed, educational...for *me*.

As winter became spring and spring became summer during 2015, Joe and I had gotten the students to take their work much more seriously. They had been working extremely hard. This took a great effort by Joe and me---as I have explained.

During the course of this work, Ms. Lindley had been very pleased with me. This was primarily because the men respected me, and paid attention during my classes. This was something quite new to the Education Department, because historically, as near as I could tell, it had been managed primarily with fear by the powers-that-be. Constant threatening of grown men, who are already hardened to life, did not seem like the best way to help them---let alone motivate them to learn, from my perspective, and as a result, I went in the opposite direction.

The reality of most classes in prisons is sheer indifference and resistance to learning much of anything. Men just don't care. They only want to go home, but when they do return home, nothing changes for most of them and they wind up on the streets again, breaking the law, and returning to prison.

From January to August of 2015, I pushed the men really hard and witnessed an ongoing metamorphosis in the classes I was teaching. The results were really beginning to show---more

224

men were passing their GED and ESL exams, and more men were participating in the classes I was teaching.

Mr. Lecorchick, the Officer who sits in the same tiny office as Ms. Lindley, had told me he had seen a remarkable change. One of his responsibilities was taking attendance and Mr. Lecorchick would come around every day in the middle of all the classes, take the role, and frequently observe what was being taught. He saw firsthand, the men's active and growing participation in classroom discussions.

Classroom participation is something you can't fake, particularly when an Officer shows up at random times each day to take attendance---and barges into the classroom, unannounced.

Getting the classes to this point meant a lot of hard work and preparation. It was a challenge to keep the men interested and engaged, each day. There is no spring, summer, or Christmas break in prison, either. Classes are held all-year long.

On the 20th day of August 2015, I was informed by Ms. Lindley I was receiving another raise. This time, it was to $.29/hour. This one was an 81% raise---up to the $.29/hour level and I was now a Grade "2" level Tutor.

This was great news, because now if my radio broke, I only had to work about 170 hours to buy a new one at commissary! I know---it's only funny if you had to be there, but it is no joke in prison---especially for guys who are impoverished to begin with. You get slave-labor wages and necessities cost a fortune.

The top of the BOP pay scale is only $.40/hour, and this rate is reserved for only 5% of a prison's work assignments.

This description comes directly from the BOP regulations:

> For example, a Grade 1 position must be a skilled position which has institution wide impact and requires minimal supervision. Grades 2 through 4 require lower skill levels...
>
> **b. In recognition of budgetary constraints and for the effective management of the overall performance pay program, the percentage of inmates assigned to each grade level is approximately as follows (Grade 1 is highest pay):**
>
> Grade 1 - 5% of the institution's allotted inmate work assignments;
> Grade 2 - 15% of the institution's allotted inmate work assignments;
> Grade 3 - 25% of the institution's allotted inmate work assignments;
> Grade 4 - 55% of the institution's allotted inmate work assignments.
> (Source: U.S. Department of Justice, Federal Bureau of Prisons Program Statement, OPI CPD/CPB, NUMBER 5251.06, DATE October 1, 2008).

You can see the BOP strictly limits in absolute terms, the number of "Grade 1" positions available.

"Lucky" inmates at Fort Dix worked for "UNICOR" (a private, for-profit company, which paid a couple of dollars an hour to hired inmates), but the BOP planned to move this program to West Virginia. Most men at Fort Dix earn between $.12/hour and $.40/hour, with few exceptions. Anyway you cut it, the BOP and prisons, in general, are running slave labor camps. They are also crippled by conflicts of interests, in this regard.

What enterprise wouldn't want to *keep* "employees" for pennies, or even a few bucks an hour, when actual minimum wage is going to $13-$15/hour in 2017, in many U.S. cities?

226

In any event, on the 20th of August, the day of this 81% raise, I was teaching my last class of the afternoon. I had just been in the groove, again, teaching away. I had thanked Ms. Lindley for the raise, even though it would still cost me 14 hours of work each week to buy a small bag of almonds---and I ate a lot of almonds and nuts in prison...they were among the few healthy items on the commissary list.

But, particularly on this day, I could have cared less about the raise. The ONLY thing which mattered to me, in matters relating to the prison, was the men were going to take their GED exams the following week. The tests would be instituted for both English-speaking GED, and the morning, Spanish-speaking GED classes. I had the men super-focused on cramming for these tests, and this was a real accomplishment. Getting men psyched up in prison, to take their GED tests is a real art form, as no one likes tests, especially in prison!

As tutors, we would have to discuss matters with Ms. Lindley, from time-to-time, but I let Joe be the main contact with her, in this regard. He had been at Fort Dix longer than nearly anyone, and he liked talking with her each day. He would dutifully report on the activities of the classes---and I was just fine with this arrangement. You see, if you spent too much time with any officer in prison, the men suspected you of being a rat. This was a self-defeating proposition for most guys, but Joe was older and could engage an officer---and the men would leave him alone.

As I was prepping the men for the upcoming GED exams, teaching at the front white board, I was intensely going over some algebra and geometry problems, grilling them. At this moment, Ms. Lindley burst open the door and sauntered into the room.

She had another inmate in tow, who was not in our GED classes.

Joe immediately went to the back of the classroom and asked, "How can I help you, Ms. Lindley?"

Ms. Lindley headed directly over to the filing cabinets, which were in the back corner of the room, and ignored Joe, momentarily.

It was not a shock to see Ms. Lindley enter the classroom, because she would often make an appearance, but she never taught. When she did show up, she would peer over an inmate's shoulder, review what they were doing, and otherwise cajole the men to work harder. The result of these tactics meant everyone was on their best behavior when Ms. Lindley was around. Everyone immediately stopped what they were doing, whenever she came through the door---everyone that is, *except* me.

I always kept reading to the class, or continued to work a problem on the white board, while continuing to address the men, nonstop, as if she wasn't there.

I'm pretty sure this bugged the crap out of her.

To be honest, I only did this to *not* break the rhythm of teaching. Any kind of disruption completely got the men off track and they would lose interest in *anything* related to school. The men had a very small attention span---at about a kindergarten level. Any distraction would get everyone talking,

228

and the class would be very difficult to get back under control. I don't know if Ms. Lindley interpreted my ignoring her as a lack of respect, but I'm pretty sure she did, at least over the course of the first many months I was there.

I base this on her consistent pattern of behavior, where she had a habit of trying to put me down publicly, in front of the other men. On this day, the day I received my 81% raise, it would be the *third* time she would do this to me.

As she reached the filing cabinets, she started fumbling around for something in them and was making lots of noise. The filing cabinets were in the right-hand, back-corner of the classroom, as I faced the students from the white board at the front of the room.

Joe again, very respectfully asked her, "Can I help you find something, Ms. Lindley?"

Joe went over to Ms. Lindley and the other inmate. Ms. Lindley continued her fumbling-through-the-file routine--- which was totally disrupting my math class at this point.

In my previous run-ins with this woman, I had noticed the "run-ins" always occurred *after* I would make a reasonable inquiry, or suggestion, to try and provide the men a better educational experience.

Like Joe, I was always extremely respectful to Ms. Lindley, and never raised my voice---ever.

One incident before this was ugly enough, with her screaming at me in front of a class, I truly nearly quit. I got really angry--- and righteously so, in my opinion.

As I continued standing at the white board, I could sense the men had lost all interest in the slope of a line, or how parabolic curves were used to build Roman arches, and especially how to calculate the volumes of spheres. I finally turned around and looked back at the growing number of people at the filing cabinets. Joe and Ms. Lindley were now *both* digging around the files. The other inmate was standing nearby, and every set of eyeballs in the classroom was watching to see what was happening.

Joe wears glasses and is quite tall. Ms. Lindley is short and on the plump side of life. Together, they made a comical pair with their backs turned to everyone, and collectively, they were making all kinds of racket. Filing drawers were slamming in and out, papers were shuffling, and they talked loudly amongst themselves.

The bottom line was they were making lots of noise, and were being very disruptive. Twenty pairs of eyeballs, of now distracted student-inmates, continued to stare intently at what this group was doing in the back of the room.

I only wanted the class back and continue the lesson, with all eyes forward and focused on the equations I was writing on the board. Their exam was next week and the 20th of August was a Thursday. This meant they had another day of class, the weekend and then early next week, they would be examined.

I finally asked her and Joe, from the front of the room, "Can *I* help you guys find something?"

I don't think Ms. Lindley liked me asking if I could help them. I admit, I probably was pretty obvious in my annoyance at having the class interrupted---Officer, or not. My duty was to the men, as I saw it.

Abruptly, Ms. Lindley curtly and assertively answered, in a half shout (while she pointed her finger at the inmate who had walked in with her):

"I am going to give *Robert* a *Spanish* GED book!"

As I would find out later, "Robert" was the inmate Ms. Lindley had dragged in to class, who had his high-school equivalency degree. He was supposedly going to help some other inmates with the GED materials for the tests the following week.

I absorbed her statement---for all of about the blink of an eye. I stood astounded, at the front of the room. I thought, *"Why didn't Joe tell Ms. Lindley, while they rifled through the files, she was about to give away our one-and-only precious resource to prep all the Spanish GED students for the Spanish GED exam?"*

The Spanish GED book contained the questions and answers to all test-practice problems---including math. We had no other Spanish workbook for the students. Nearly every other Spanish-speaking, GED student would need access to this book in the upcoming days, prior to the GED exams next week.

There were well over thirty Spanish-GED students, and a weekend was dead ahead. I knew many Spanish guys would use the weekend to cram and would need access to the teaching materials in this book, and/or they would need to make copies from it (i.e., the government is never sued for making copies of copyrighted material!). One of the things I had heard before going to Fort Dix, and experienced first-hand there, was many adults had difficulty learning new subjects (math, particularly). I discovered this was *really* true at the Camp.

I knew the men needed to cram and study hard to pass their upcoming exams.

During my 21-months, I read quite a bit. An interesting article in Science Magazine described how the learning synapses in the brain don't fully develop in people who don't work at studying during their high school years. I could see this phenomenon being especially true in older men at the Camp, who didn't have the good fortune of receiving a good grammar school, and/or good high school education. For them, learning school work was beyond difficult---even when they tried hard.

In her decision to give away the only Spanish GED textbook, which also contained the key *math* book to prepare for the exams, Ms. Lindley would be showing favoritism to just a couple of men, while dozens of others would suffer. As a result, we would not be able to copy pages for study problems, and we would not have this resource over the key weekend before the exams. Also, things have a tendency to disappear in prison. I didn't want to let that book get out of my sight!

I had a real passion for the men in all my classes. I have lived in Mexico, Venezuela, and traveled through Spain and the Caribbean, among many other places. I've also worked in life and in sports with many, many, inner-city brothers and people of all colors.

I knew if Ms. Lindley gave this book away to some random inmate, the other guys would be screwed. It was definitely not the right call for her to do this.

I continued speaking, treading carefully---knowing she was Mount Vesuvius and could blow at any time:

> "Uh...Ms. Lindley, I just wanted to remind you we only have *ONE* Spanish GED book and the other students will need access to it, also. We use it for our classes and it has all the math problems in it for practice. A lot of guys may need access to it for preparation over the weekend."

The entire room went dead silent. Forget pins dropping, you could have heard a snowflake hit the ground. This was because the men in the 2:00 p.m. class at the Fort Dix Camp knew I always stuck up for them, and *knew* they were about to see some real fireworks.

My students had seen me work, even when many of them had completely ignored me, and they had witnessed my faithful efforts to teach men something, every day, during their allotted class time. Through these many months, now numbering ten, they knew I had NO other agenda, other than to try and help them. I think they loved the fact I was about to get in a face-off with none other than---Ms. Lindley!

Men from tough places, who grow up tough, don't usually say much. They don't give pats on the back, or hand out praise. It's just not their style. But in prison, it is very surprising how support is expressed by the men---at the most interesting moments.

This was about to be one of them.

Today, respect would come in a whole different flavor and in a completely different light. It would be quite serious among the men, also.

Immediately after I spoke up and "reminded" Ms. Lindley she was giving away our only Spanish GED resource, every set of eyeballs in the classroom set upon me, and then, in unison, rolled immediately back over to Ms. Lindley in the back of the room.

The tension was palpable.

I could *feel* and *see* the collective rolling of their eyes, from where I stood in front of the class---with the equation-and graph-filled white board, behind me. It was a scene you just don't forget.

The sky was about to light up, and the men knew it. Everyone was at rapt attention. They knew they were going to witness a volcano, which was about to blow.

This included everyone, except Joe. Joe was still scurrying around trying to get Ms. Lindley the book. His back was turned to the class, he was still standing at the filing cabinets, and he was completely oblivious to what was happening,

Ms. Lindley took about a 4-second pause of silence, and considered what to do with me. I could see she was furious an inmate was taking her to task for making this poor decision--- and had the audacity to do it in front of twenty other convicts!

It was at this moment, when Mt. Vesuvius blew. I remember the steam coming out of her ears, and ash flying to 20,000 feet.

From where I stood, she was not acting for the betterment of the group. Instead, and for whatever reason, she was showing preference to this man "Robert," who ostensibly was going to "help" a couple of other students. This was to the complete detriment of dozens of others men who would be testing next week.

As the classroom waited with baited breath for Ms. Lindley's response, suddenly, and with great power, she spun her plump body around, glared at me and snarled in a beyond threatening voice, waiving her arms in the air:

"I'M GOING TO DO, WHAT I'M GOING TO DO! JUST DEAL WITH IT, KELLY!"

She then tore the book out of poor Joe's hands, stormed out of the room, and took her "Robert" in tow, behind her.

Some of the smartest men I have met in my life were prisoners with me at Fort Dix, hailing from the inner city. These men know more about life and how to survive it, than most people in our society. They know the street, and they definitely know how to trade, as this book proves.

When these men, this collection of street-smart dudes, witnessed Ms. Lindley dress me down and verbally spank me, as a result of my respectful reminder to her, every man kept their mouths *shut*. They were dead silent all the way through the confrontation.

...UNTIL SHE LEFT THE ROOM!

You should have heard the men and what they said, then! They were beyond angry with her. It was amazing. Prison is filled with swear words and this page may not be big enough to write all the ones which were spit out by the men in class!

Two of my favorite students were sitting in the back of the room. They are still doing their time, and I won't mention their names, but they were seated right next to the filing cabinets, where Ms. Lindley had spewed her venom at me.

One of the guys from Phillie shouted, "CAN YOU BELIEVE SHE JUST SAID THIS TO *KELLY*? UNBELIEVABLE!"

Everyone murmured their agreement, echoing clearly, his sentiment.

He continued, "SHE JUST COMPLETELY DISRESPECTED THE MAN HELPING US GET OUR GED's!"

One of my other favorite students was sitting at the comfortable corner table in the back of the room, which is normally reserved for tutors. He sat on a cushioned chair, and his feet were up on the table---a favorite position for this young man with the long dread locks.

The man from Phillie continued speaking, now directing his remarks to my dread-locked friend, "Did you SEE Kelly's face when she was disrespectin' him? Man...his face looked like a cork screw, he was so pissed off!"

My friend replied in his deep voice, "I don't even have to look--- I already 'KNOHHH' he's super pissed!!

This student did know me well. Guys get to know the men they interact with each day in prison, especially in the tight confines of Fort Dix.

The man from Philadelphia looked up at me once again, while Joe finally catches on, and realizes something transpired while he was at the back of the classroom.

Joe finally asked, "What just happened?"

Everyone ignored Joe and continued their tirade against Ms. Lindley.

Yes, I made the men work---at least, those who wanted to learn---and yes, I tried to teach them something new in every class I ran, or participated in. My ethics wouldn't permit otherwise. I treated the whole process like a symphony---probably partially inspired by films like "Mr. Holland's Opus," a classic. I knew, if I was successful, these men would build their own self-respect and help themselves in their own lifetimes. But, at this particular moment, I was a bit shocked to hear their support.

These guys had never said anything like this before, ever.

As the class raged on about how unfair Ms. Lindley was, the comments---the cream of the crop of the remarks---and which summarized everything, came out of the mouth of the wise man from Philadelphia. He proclaimed to the entire classroom, in his big, great, booming-deep voice:

"WHAT DOES SHE THINK---
WE STUPID, OR SOMETHIN'?"

Joe finally really caught on to what was happening, and ever the guy to be politically correct at all times, regardless of audience, said, "Yea...I've even seen her go after Kelly in her office, for no reason at all!"

The main man from Philadelphia then uttered another something, which was quite embarrassing for me to hear:

"IT'S JUST BECAUSE KELLY'S
SMARTER THAN HER!"

I had maintained my silence throughout this discourse. At this point, I really wanted everyone to cool down, as I have never spoken disrespectfully to Ms. Lindley, and never would. Even this description of events is respectful, albeit, brutally truthful.

Just before I was going to speak, Joe said one more thing to the men. "You know you guys, Kelly could have had the easiest job in the Camp. I know he was offered a job in the tool shed and they don't do much of anything out there!"

Everyone looked up at Joe, then over to me. The men knew there were many, many inmates in the Camp who would sell their souls to get a better job in prison.

I finally began to speak, "Joe's right. I was offered a job where the guys just check tools in-and-out of the tool shed. They sit behind a cage, they have their own refrigerator, they have their own coffee pot, and they even have air conditioning---with their very own comfortable chairs and desks. They sit around most days and play cards and read the paper---seriously."

This was a 100% true statement.

The men had come to know me as a serious CEO and Christian, who was not too much afraid of anything---especially officialdom and the BOP. My first three books I wrote proved this to them (e.g., The Federal Reserve Trilogy).

My passion and courage came *only* because of God's Word. I knew the BOP had no power, except what God above had given them, and I also knew I was expected to have and maintain a faith which bore good fruit.

But, mostly, I did it because I loved helping the men.

After all, as a Christian, you have to hold the fort!

> "Let every soul be subject unto the higher powers. For there is no power but of God: the powers that be are ordained of God." (Source: The Bible, Romans 13:1 KJV).

> "For as the body without the spirit is dead, so faith without works is dead also." (Source: The Bible, James 2:26).

I continued speaking to the men, "...But, that wouldn't have been me, nor would it be my calling. My place at Fort Dix is here---in and among, you men..." I paused for a moment and added: "And please remember:

IT IS NOT IMPORTANT WHAT SHE THINKS.
IT IS *ONLY* IMPORTANT WHAT *YOU* MEN THINK!"

The guys were stunned with me being this bold in front of any number of untold, potential rats in class. Words spoken in prison the BOP considers "disrespectful," can get a person thrown in the Hole, or at least in trouble.

However, I believed this was becoming another "teaching moment," and none of those risks mattered to me. These men had to know and truly understand everything I did, and had been doing for them, was not about anything other than them--- and what I believed to be my duty and calling, before God.

The classroom went silent. There was sort of a pregnant pause. Joe, sensing he should say something, injected: "Well, Kelly's right, it's not important what they think, it's important what they do!"

The entire classroom rolled its eyeballs, but this time in disbelief. I looked around the class and all eyes came back to mine. I continued:

"Guys, this isn't the first time she's done this to me. Joe just corroborated one event in her office---an unjustified attack on me; but, Joe also witnessed an event where she yelled at me in front of the other GED class, BIG TIME---simply because I had the courage to make a suggestion. I had only asked if the Education Department could try and provide the men more lead time if they were going to continually cancel GED exams...Ms. Lindley went crazy on me for that one!"

The BOP at Fort Dix (at least in the Camp) seemed to love playing games with the men, in this regard. I would get the men prepared to take exams, have them cram for days in preparation for the "big test," and right before exam time, they would get the rug pulled out from under them---and the tests would get cancelled, with no explanation.

Usually, the men wouldn't even find out the tests were cancelled until the very morning they were to take exams, when they were waiting to be checked into the testing room.

I mention this in detail, because until the culture of *not caring* about true rehabilitation is changed inside the BOP, NOTHING will change. Congress can spend all the money it wants, but the money will just get wasted.

With respect to the many times the tests were cancelled, this wasn't Ms. Lindley's fault, for the most part. For the record, she didn't have control of the GED test schedules, and there became a bit of an intra-prison rivalry within the Education

Department at Fort Dix. This seeming tension appeared to unfold when the men at the Camp started to kick butt on their GED exams, with many men passing their tests. This occurred while the higher-level security prisons at Fort Dix, continued to languish in their respective, educational programs.

It became obvious to everyone, Ms. Lindley was probably making them look bad. Since the other prisons at Fort Dix controlled the test schedule, it is certainly a possibility they were playing games with the men, out of pure professional jealously for Ms. Lindley.

Ms. Lindley was responsible for the Camp, and the Camp was witnessing dramatic improvements in GED scores, Spanish-English certifications and the receipt of high school diplomas since November 2, 2014, the day I entered the prison. This was clear to everyone at Fort Dix.

This entire matter and even story of my time in prison sounds horribly self-serving, and braggadocios, but it is the truth of the matter. To try and shed light on the real problem of recidivism, the reader and the powers-that-be, should know the truth, and what works in the development of mature, grown men...AND WHAT DOES NOT.

I truly don't consider this my work alone, either, as I have tried to make clear in this book. Joe Kerns worked very hard for the inmates, and has suffered enormously at the hands of what I believe to be purely evil men---as his case was explained to me. Joe is also quite brilliant and I would put him up against just about anybody else at his age---for sure. Many other men contributed significantly also, including, but not limited to, Alberto Vilar, Charles Daum and Chris Saradakis.

To finish up this story about Ms. Lindley, Mt. Vesuvius and the aftermath of the eruption, an interesting epilogue occurred.

On Saturday, two days after Ms. Lindley and "Robert" stormed out of the classroom with the Spanish GED book, two of the four men Robert was *supposed* to help came up to me in the library and asked, "Maestro, puede ayudarnos con la Matematica?" (i.e., "Teacher, can you help us with Mathematics?").

One of them was among my favorite Hispanic students, and he knew I was his true "Maestro."

I happily agreed to help him and we wound up working out of the library until just before count time at 9:30 p.m. When he asked if I would help him again, tomorrow, I said, "Como no...Si, qué hora?" (i.e., "Of course...Yes, what time?").

This, for me, was the best pay. *Nothing*---except the knowledge maybe some of our efforts might help men live better lives in the future.

What was truly remarkable was this eruption of Mt. Vesuvius occurred immediately *after* Ms. Lindley had granted me the pay raise to $.29/hour and made me a "Level 2" Tutor.

I guess that's why they paid me the big bucks, to take the big heat from the boss---

Ahhh...the things we do for money!

Ms. Lindley has a tough job, and while I've recounted some tough moments with her, she and I were trying to help the men. I give her huge credit for this. Given what she has to work with, and being a woman dealing with 400⁺ male prisoners, she had to be pretty tough.

To be fair, for each act of toughness on her behalf, she would do about a hundred acts of kindness for the men. I saw her help many students by recommending them for certain programs---especially when they passed the GED. My hope is, she will be provided the certification programs to teach men *real* trades and *real* skills, on a broad-basis. At a "low-security" Camp, men are going to return home and they need employable skills. Without these skills, most will wind up back in prison.

Another battle scar I received during class, and ultimately, one of the biggest confrontations I endured at Fort Dix, was with an inmate. I will just call him, "Smarty Pants" --- "Smarty," for short.

Smarty was extremely "street smart" and he wanted no part, whatsoever, of the classroom. He made an art form out of causing disruptions during class time and made it clear about his plans when he was going to be released: he was going to continue selling drugs. He said he wasn't going to learn anything in prison, and believed he was smarter than everyone else---and perhaps he could have been, with a bit of studying. If Smarty had ever focused on learning, he could probably be a PhD.

He spoke English and Spanish perfectly and knew the streets, inside out and extremely well. In addition to knowing New York and cities in the U.S., Smarty also knew the territory of Central America. His family is from there. If he put his mind to it, he could build an enormous, *legal*, import-export business. Unfortunately, some of the smartest guys go into the drug business because they can make MILLIONS of dollars in it---fast. Smarty was in this class, or will be some day. He vowed to go out and do what he does best---sell drugs---as soon as he was released.

I think it irritated Smarty I would continue to be nice to him, despite his attempts at disrupting and taking over my class. He was really rude. He would shout and speak loudly to other inmates when I was teaching, but when he became disruptive, I would just talk right over him. I ignored him, and did not permit him to wreck the class.

Smarty was used to being the leader, with everybody following him, I suppose. His goal was to lead and control the class activity, exactly like he did most other things he involved himself with in prison. He certainly didn't want anyone to follow my teaching---he wanted the class to follow HIM.

It irritated him to no end I laughed off his attempts at control and always just talked right over his agenda. This drove him crazy, especially when he was up to his antics.

It is hard to say how good of a talker Smarty was---the proverbial saying, "He could talk his way out of a paper bag," comes to mind. When Ms. Lindley would get mad at him for not doing any work, he would smile his big smile and play nice with her---and he fooled her for a long time. As soon as Ms. Lindley would leave, he would go right back to his routine again, being as disruptive as possible.

As the months rolled by, and it became the summer of 2015, Smarty came to class all fired up one day. He had decided I was one of the enemy and he began to try and engage me in a personal pissing contest during class.

He began initiating his now patented behavior speaking loudly to another inmate, getting his attention, "HEY, NIGGAH--- DON'T LISTEN TO HIM!" Smarty was referring to me on the not listening part. I could see his thumb pointing my way, when I turned my head from the white board. He had balled his fist and had pointed his thumb, in my direction.

He then moved on to another inmate and said "HEY, MAN, DON'T LISTEN TO *THAT* NIGGAH!"---this time Smarty was pointing at me with his index finger.

To be clear, and to make the point, Smarty directly referred to me, as "niggah." I should also mention Smarty is a black guy and black guys are allowed to use the "n" word at Fort Dix, while white guys are not. This is fairly common knowledge, even outside of prison, but it is particularly true *inside* prison.

When a black guy refers to a white guy in the manner affected by Smarty, it is intended to provoke a fight.

I had turned my head back to the white board, to not give Smarty the pleasure of knowing he had gotten me riled up. But, Smarty continued to snarl at me. The discourse and tirade which was about to follow would witness the use of the "n" word by Smarty over *14 times* (I know because I counted them). This situation was witnessed by Joe and the rest of the class--- about twenty men in all.

Deciding to call me out, and in a vain attempt to get me to turn around, Smarty shouted from his seat in the back row of the classroom:

"HEY, KELLY...!"

I ignored Smarty and kept writing out some problems on the board.

"HEY, KELLY...HEY *NIGGAH*!!!"

I still continued to ignore Smarty. This really got him infuriated, because you could hear his voice level rising, dramatically.

Smarty began wailing, becoming angry with no reason:

"YOU GOT NOTHIN' NIGGAH!"

I turned around at this point. I could see Smarty looking around the classroom, knowing he had successfully gotten the attention of the audience he craved and desired. He then went on a rampage, shouting at me and all the men:

"THIS NIGGAH'S GOT NOTHIN!

THIS NIGGAH THINKS HE'S SO DAMN SMART!

THIS NIGGAH SUCKS...

FU** THIS NIGGAH...

THIS NIGGAH AIN'T SH**, etc."

He continued raving at the men and me. His hate-filled rant was an expletive-filled "n-" word diatribe for the century, unlike any I had ever heard before---even in prison!

Through it all, I had been silent. When I had originally turned around, I merely stared at Smarty, not uttering a word. At this moment, after this disgusting diatribe, I continued to stare---directly in his eyes. My penetrating gaze didn't waiver, it didn't crumble, and it didn't look away for a second. I remained focused on the hostile man in front of me, sitting in the back row of chairs, in the rear of the classroom.

Finally, Smarty did something really stupid, which would cause him to lose a lot of face inside prison.

Unfortunately, Smarty made the mistake of believing my silence was weakness.

This gave him the false bravado he thought he needed to continue his attack against the core of what I represented to the GED class—namely: *if you make a commitment, we'll teach you how to earn your GED!*

He pressed his attack, and it was getting really ugly. His shouting was a monotone roll, with a rap-style of speech which is only possible from a really smart guy. He was in full stride in his attack. He had already used the "n" word a dozen times in trying to convince the entire class I was worthless.

Finally, he went over a bridge too far. He screams in challenge to me:

"NIGGAH--YOU HAVEN'T HAD ANYONE GRADUATE WITH A GED...NOBODY! NAME ONE PERSON, NIGGAH...NAME JUST ONE!!!"

I was really pissed off at this whole scene, to be honest, and didn't think I was going to be a very good witness for Jesus at this particular moment. I didn't want anything bad for Smarty--I only wanted to help those men who wanted to learn.

I just thought, *"Why did he have to act like such a jerk, all the time?"*

Somewhere, within my Irish, Scottish and German temperament and heritage, my old self came out and I let Smarty have it right between the eyes. Verbally, of course, but I gave him a dressing down. This was only possible because of the people I had helped receive GEDs, while at Fort Dix.

It was ironic, because the first name which came to mind, and out of my mouth, was "Dee Williams." Dee was an exceptionally cool black guy from New York and he had become a friend of mine. Dee was also, by far and away, one of the toughest, strongest dudes in prison. Dee did something like 1,000 pushups and sit-ups each day and bench-pressed hundreds and hundreds of pounds. Dee, ultimately, was accepted into the drug program and he was able to cut many months off of his sentence. I was really happy for him when he left.

His name caught Smarty cold. I went on from there, mentioning Mr. Battle, a brilliant black gentleman who played in the European basketball league, and several other key guys. In Mr. Battle's case, he was brilliant to begin with, and I really didn't have to do much to help him, except give him a refresher. Like Dee, he is a real gentleman and a great guy.

My objective was to shut Smarty up and humiliate him—I was sick of his nonsense in class. I really doubt if Jesus would have acted this way but, I just couldn't help myself. I hated having to brag, and bring a series of names up in front of everyone else. The amazing thing was, I didn't have to reel off too many names, because other men in the room started reciting names of people I had helped graduate! Then Joe Kerns piled on, and added Pablo Cruz and Caballo to the list, as well as a couple of other inmates.

This was truly great, because Smarty was completely defeated. He was humiliated by my tongue and the tongues of others. It was no small feat, because Smarty has a real gift for gab. I'll never forget this man's eyes---they became slits. He didn't like me, not one bit, at least not at this moment, anyway.

We tried to stay out of each other's way from there on out, but ultimately, Ms. Lindley ordered Smarty to report to the library. After Smarty was banned to the library, and for months afterward, he tried to blame me for his banishment. I think he knew differently, deep down, but he just pressed the envelope all the time. One day, he pushed too far, and Ms. Lindley finally caught up with him. In Smarty's case, he continually refused to do any school work---and Ms. Lindley had had enough. Smarty was banned from the classroom and ordered to the library.

The "library" was the destination for troubled students. There, they could receive "one-on-one" tutoring. What this meant was the men only had to wait for Mr. Lecorchick to take roll, then they could go to sleep at the small library table, do puzzle games, and read newspapers or magazines.

In Smarty's case, at least he was assigned to a good tutor by the name of Chris Saradakis. Chris got nailed for insider trading charges and he didn't even profit from it. I felt sorry for him because he did his time, and then the SEC lost in court on a different, but similar case as his. Because of this loss in court, convictions like the one Chris endured would not occur in the future. I hope he was able to get his conviction overturned, somehow. Chris was a good guy and has a very nice family. They would visit him nearly every weekend. He also gave to others while he was imprisoned at Fort Dix, as did Alberto Vilar and Charles Daum, constantly.

But, when it rains, it pours, and bad luck continued to follow Smarty around the Camp. His bunk was in the "A" wing of the Camp, the opposite side from me. One night, while nearly everyone was sleeping, sometime after midnight, Smarty was busted big time for having a cell phone.

He was apparently speaking on it when he heard a guard coming around for count. When men were asleep and in bed at midnight, 3 a.m., or 5 a.m., the guards walked around with a flashlight, which is super bright. Sometimes, they didn't walk the count on time, and were "late." But, regardless, the guards loved to shine the beam in everyone's eyes---it woke you up. As this guard walked by Smarty's lower bunk, Smarty had accidentally dropped his phone's blue-tooth device on the floor, in his hurry to pretend to be sleeping. The guard saw something on the floor, inspected it, and then rousted him out of bed. The guard then searched his pillow and immediate area---and voilà, he found Smarty's cell phone.

From then on, there was no more Smarty. He was gone the next morning to a higher-level security prison.

Maybe this helped Smarty, I don't know. Since I saw hundreds of men each day, and got to know dozens and dozens of them well because of my job as a GED instructor, I had learned the BOP provided *higher-level* security prisons with *more* certification programs than the Camp. This was despite the fact, men in the Camp would be out on the streets much *sooner* than the higher-level security prisoners, because those inmates are typically sentenced to much longer periods of incarceration.

To the extent the BOP's budget is shot and they don't have the resources for the Camp, it should be focused on rehabilitating the men hitting the streets soonest, with the greatest chance to be rehabilitated. This would mean men from the Camp, generally speaking.

Higher-level security prisons are "higher-level" because the men have committed more serious crimes. The way in which BOP resources are currently deployed seems to be based on keeping the men busy---to prevent trouble for the BOP---rather than trying to rehabilitate the men for reentry.

The whole arrangement and deployed resources in the BOP needs a complete overhaul. Serious management and budget problems exist because the BOP first covers the costs of its own employee's compensation and benefits, while simply looking the other way and allowing significant budget waste to occur throughout most of their departments. This is done at the extreme expense of taxpayers---and inmates.

A good example of pure waste at Fort Dix was when multiple inmates witnessed BOP employees destroy a perfectly good vehicle by running a tractor over it. They did this for the singular reason it was budget time and they wanted money for a new car, in the next BOP budget cycle. They wouldn't be able to purchase a new car, unless their old car didn't operate. They sure knew how to fix that problem!

The big trick among all departments in the BOP, and most government agencies, is to make sure money in their budgets is spent before the year is up. This way, they will receive budget increases for the following year, regardless of whether, or not, money was spent wisely the year before.

There were many other stories and tales of corruption in the BOP. I heard about travel budgets being fraudulently manipulated and inflated, with money being siphoned off and used for unknown purposes. Inmates in the garage were coerced into maintaining and signing off on records for mileage, repair and maintenance related to the vehicle fleet at Fort Dix. Apparently, there were some glaring anomalies in the transportation and vehicle areas, specifically.

Sort of like in Ocean's Eleven, you have to ask---when the BOP is granted nearly $8 BILLION EVERY YEAR, and the men are fed crap food, and wind up paying for virtually everything, at very high prices, and are deprived of decent medical care---

"*Where* did all that money go???"

As time would show, I pushed through Smarty, and continued to mush on with GED and ESL programs. I worked hard, right up to my release.

Yes, I had a few tough moments with Ms. Lindley, when I disagreed with BOP policy and its decision-making but, we came to respect each other. Ultimately, she was kind enough to issue me the following certificate when I left Fort Dix on July 28, 2016. She also issued a "Positive Decision Report," which went into my "Jacket."

She didn't have to do either of these things.

To be honest, I hope I never have to use them in my life---ever! But, maybe they will help inspire some people to stay out of prison. If somebody has to go there---either justly, or unjustly--- hopefully, they will use the time to give back to others around them, when it is their turn in <u>Holding the Fort</u>.

Certificate of Appreciation
awarded to:

ROBERT KELLY

For your dedication and commitment as a tutor
for the English GED, Spanish GED, English as a Second
Language, and ACE programs
in the Camp Education Department
at F.C.I. Fort Dix, N.J.

Signature Blocked

July 28, 2016

K. Lindley, Education Dept.

```
                           POSITIVE DECISION REPORT
U.S. DEPARTMENT OF JUSTICE                    FEDERAL BUREAU OF PRISONS
```

1. Institution: FCI Fort Dix			
2. Inmate's Name KELLY, ROBERT	3. Register Number 56772-056	4. Date of Incident 05-09-2016	5. Time
6. Place of Incident Camp Education	7.Assignment Tutor Camp	8. Unit VO2-120U	

9. Positive Behavior Demonstrated in Institution Related to ISDS:

Daily Living Skills
Mental Health Skills
Wellness Skills
xInterpersonal Skills
xAcademic Skills

xCognitive Skills
Vocational/Career Skills
Leisure Time Skills
xCharacter Skills

10. Justification (Description of Positive Behavior)

IM Kelly #56772-056 has worked for me as an education tutor since 11-21-2014. Kelly has great concern for the GED students. He works with students after class hours and gives of his time in many areas. The majority of the students who work with Kelly have passed the GED test. All the students made significant progress. Kelly has also taught an Adult Continuing Education class in which he gave of his own time to create and teach business concepts to students.   Kelly is a good role model for the students in the education classes.

11. Printed Name   12. Date 05-09-2016
K Lind

Signature Blocked.

13. Approved by
Unit Manager   Date   6/1/16

Demonstrated Reentry Skills

This certificate is awarded in recognition of demonstrating notable reentry skills at the Federal Correctional Institution, Fort Dix, New Jersey.

An inmate earns one week of "vacation" each year worked in a Camp. I had never taken my vacation, and I asked Ms. Lindley if she minded if I took my vacation the last week I was incarcerated.

I thought it might be a good idea to have some time to prepare for my release. It is tough to find a job, and as of this writing, I still don't have one.

Regardless, preparation is the key to success, and I wanted to focus on my plan for when I was released from the halfway

```
FTD09                *          FORT DIX FCI               *      07-19-2016
PAGE 001 OF 001                                                  15:11:13



                    CHANGE

                    SHEET

---------------------------------------------------------------------------
                           QTRG EQ V***
REG NO      NAME         FROM        TO           TIME  CATEGORY(2)  CATEGORY(3)

WRK DETAIL CHANGES EFFECTIVE  07-20-2016              UNT ASGN     QTR ASGN
---------------------------------------------------------------------------
56772-056  KELLY       TUTOR CAMP  VACATION C  0001  CAMP          V02-120U
```

house, which would be in October 2016.

After I asked her, Ms. Lindley said, "Absolutely, you've earned it!"

The "Change Sheet" is put up in the afternoon on the bulletin board inside the Camp. Men watch this board carefully for work assignments, meetings with officers and specialized code words which tell everyone an inmate is leaving the Camp. This one, above, is notifying one and all I am on "VACATION," starting July 20, 2016.

When people see their name and number, with the magic words "R&D West" printed on the "CALLOUTS," it means they are going home!

```
  FTDKQ        *         FORT DIX FCI          *      07-27-2016
  PAGE 001 OF 001                                     17:36:44


     *****     *     *       *       ****   *   *  *******  *****
      *       * *   *        *          *   *   *     *      *   *
      *       *  * *         *        *:::*   * *      *       *
      *       *   *          *        *   *    *       *        ****
      *       *******        *        *   *   * *      *           *
     *****  *       *   *******  ****** ****   ****     *       *****
```

                         QTRG EQ V***

REG NO	NAME	FROM	TO	TIME	CATEGORY(2)	CATEGORY(3)
					WRK ASGN	QTR ASGN

CALLOUTS   FOR   07-28-2016

REG NO	NAME	TO	TIME	CATEGORY(2)	CATEGORY(3)
054	ALLEN	PA CAMP 1	1400	GM OUT	V01-102U
014	AUSTIN	PA CAMP 1	1200	FPI DEMAN3	V02-142L
069	AYALA-MEDI	PA CAMP 1	1400	D P W	V01-053L
037	BARNES	PA CAMP 1	1400	FPI DEMAN3	V01-019L
050	BRAZHINIKO	PA CAMP 1	0730	A&O CAMP	V01-060U
083	BROWN	5712 MOODY	1230	GM OUT	V01-030U
068	BUSH	PA CAMP 1	1200	WELD OUT	V02-171L
053	CONWAY	HOSP CAMP	0830	D P W	V02-141L
069	CRUZ-LUGO	PA CAMP 1	1800	LANDS OUT	V01-020U
053	DONOVAN	PA CAMP 1	0900	FS 95 PM K	V01-058L
053	FAZIO	PA CAMP 1	0900	ELEC OUT	V01-074U
050	GEORGE	PA CAMP 1	1500	D P W	V02-127U
066	HARRISON	PA CAMP 1	0900	D P W	V01-047U
053	HODGE	PA CAMP 1	1800	D P W	V01-068L
069	ISAAC-NIEV	PA CAMP 1	0730	A&O CAMP	V01-003U
054	JOHNSON	PA CAMP 1	1900	D P W	V01-043L
56772-056	KELLY	R&D WEST	0730	VACATION C	V02-120U
050	LAHHAM	PA CAMP 1	1800	6695 ORD C	V01-014L
022	LUA	PA CAMP 1	0900	FS 95 AM K	V01-011U
014	NAWAZ	PA CAMP 1	1200	GM OUT 3	V01-012L
094	PEREZ-HUER	PA CAMP 1	1800	FPI DEMAN3	V02-136L
069	RIVERA-RAM	PA CAMP 1	0730	A&O CAMP	V01-008U
053	STEVENS	PA CAMP 1	1400	6695 ORD C	V01-075L
050	STRADFORD	PA CAMP 1	1500	FPI DEMAN3	V01-066U
053	SUH	PA CAMP 1	0900	FS 95 PM K	V01-022U
037	TAYLOR	PA CAMP 1	1900	D P W	V01-042U
066	VAZQUEZ	PA CAMP 1	1000	6695 ORD C	V01-077L
047	WEST	PA CAMP 1	1900	GM OUT 2	V02-203U
067	WHITE-OLIV	PA CAMP 1	1000	D P W	V02-175U
016	WILKINS	PA CAMP 1	1900	FS 95 PM K	V01-037L
15296-039	WILSON	PA CAMP 1	1500	FS 95 AM K	V02-126U

One of the last things you are required to do, before you get to leave, is do your "Merry-go-round" tour. Here, you have to get all the officers of various departments to sign off on your departure---and make sure you check out of medical and education, as well as turn in your bedding, clothing, etc. The final copy is left with the Unit Manager and Case Officers. I did not receive a copy with their two initials; however, I kept this copy with everyone else's initials, along with some other documents to show proof of my release from prison, in case I was ever asked for them.

Last Name
KELLY
First Name
ROBERT
Middle Name   Suffix

11-03-2014

Ht. **6' 0"**   Wt. **180**
Hr. **GRY**   Ev. **BLU**
REG# **56772-056   FTD**   56772-056   KELLY

MERRY-GO-ROUND FORM

KELLY, ROBERT	56772-056	6695
NAME	REGISTER NUMBER	BLDG

RRC Furl Trans	07-28-2016	9:00 AM
RELEASE METHOD	RELEASE DATE	RELEASE TIME

YOU ARE TO REPORT TO THE FOLLOWING AREAS AT THE DESIGNATED TIMES. EVERY STOP IS MANDATORY AND FAILURE TO DO THIS COULD DELAY YOUR RELEASE, SO PLEASE BE TIMELY AT EACH AREA.

STAFF INITIALS

10:00 AM EDUCATION
    REPORT TO THE EDUCATION TO RETURN ANY INSTITUTION PUBLICATIONS, REQUEST TRANSCRIPTS, AND OBTAIN CAREER PACKET, IF NECESSARY

10:30 AM HOSPITAL
    REPORT TO THE HOSPITAL TO REVIEW AND SIGN ANY NECESSARY PAPERWORK. DISCUSS POSSIBLE MEDICATIONS.

11:30 AM CLOTHING ISSUE
    REPORT TO CLOTHING ISSUE TO RETURN ALL INSTITUTIONAL CLOTHING AND BED ROLL. RECEIVE WORK CLOTHES FOR CTC IF AUTHORIZED BY UNIT MANAGER (VIA COP-OUT)

1:30 PM RECREATION
    REPORT TO THE GYMNASIUM TO PICK UP ANY STORED HOBBY CRAFT ITEMS AND RETURN ANY INSTITUTIONAL EQUIPMENT

3:00 PM COUNSELOR/UNIT OFFICER
    REPORT TO THE COUNSELOR OR UNIT OFFICER WITH **YOUR CHAIR**

3:30 PM UNIT TEAM
    REPORT TO YOUR UNIT TEAM (COUNSELOR/CASE MANAGER) TO REVIEW RELEASE INFORMATION AND SIGN ANY CERTIFICATES. REPORT TO UNIT SECRETARY TO ENSURE ALL TRAVEL ARRAGEMENTS ARE IN ORDER AND RECEIVE TRAVEL ITINERARY

BRING THIS COMPLETED FORM TO UNIT SECRETARY AT THE END OF THE DAY.
MERRY-GO-ROUND FOR INCLUSION IN CENTRAL FILE.
CC: CENTRAL FILE   (FTD/CAMP) REVISED 11/12

Signature Blocked.
Signature Blocked.
Signature Blocked.
Signature Blocked.

CHAPTER 20

RADICAL ISLAM BRANDED ME THE "WHITE DEVIL"

I've tried to keep this book upbeat, and positive, because this is how I tried to be inside prison. As I have already explained, I had promised the guys in my ACE class I would not teach the Turtle class again at Fort Dix, because they had made a commitment to me, and I wanted to give them something special, in return. The part I *haven't* shared with readers was I had plans to do other things while incarcerated. I had let this be known to my spacemate Mike, when he once pressed me why I wouldn't teach the "Trade Like a Turtle" class, again. I remember barking at him, "I just have other things to do here, Mike!"

Mike could be extremely persistent, and I found the only way to brush him back was with a fastball, every now and then.

From day one in prison, I really wanted to be prepared to share my faith, because frankly, men in prison need faith to survive. I figured, if I could make even a tiny contribution, it would be a good thing.

During my time at Fort Dix, I was involved with the Catholic Church, and became one of the readers each week (reading from the Old, or New Testament), while my buddy Phil Hamilton primarily led the Church and ran the service. I was also friendly with the Evangelical Church and attended it when

259

I first arrived. It is hard to describe, but the cultures were distinctly different in the Evangelical Church and the Catholic Church. I just fit in better with the Catholic guys.

For nearly a year, we didn't even have a priest, and we held Church services on our own. Phil did a superb job and is another guy, I believe, who got totally screwed over by politics within the government and I believe he was unjustly incarcerated.

Phil was a legislator in Virginia, and got accused by a political foe of accepting bribes. The purported "bribes" were for real consulting and advisory work Phil performed for the University there. If you knew Phil, you knew he wouldn't take a bribe. I'll spare you the details, but this is another example of a great guy being sent away, for a very long time, when all the bankers and politically-connected people, are let off scot-free.

These kinds of stories make me sick, truly, and I devoted three of my books, which comprise The Federal Reserve Trilogy, to some of these grave injustices plaguing our society.

Phil tried to do the best he could for the men, and we even started a Spanish-speaking Catholic church, which I led initially (due to some nervous hesitation from the Hispanic leadership).

When we started the Spanish service, we made it clear we would help them start out, but the service should be led by the guys from Puerto Rico, the Dominican Republic and other Hispanics in the Camp. I can communicate effectively in Spanish and can even teach in it, however, I am not a native speaker, and do not have command of their language, like they do. These are a couple of the flyers we put out, announcing the church:

Nueva Iglesia Católica

Nuevo Servicio Para Todos...

Exlusivamente En Espanol

Cuando: Comenzando El 7 De Junio, 2015

A Las 11AM, Y Cada Domingo Despues
Ala Misma Hora

Donde: En La Capilla ("Chapel")

Vengan Y Escuchen Al Sacerdote "Martí,"
Y Compartan En Nuestra Iglesia, Donde Podrán
Oir La Palabra De Dios Y La De Su Hijo, Jesus Cristo!

Nececitamos A Personas Que Puedan Leer Las Escrituras,
Las Oraciones, Y Que También Podrán Ayudar Con La
Musica Y Con Otros Deberes De la Iglesia.

Si Quieren Participar, Favor De Avisar A Unos De Los
Siguientes Personas: Robert Kelly, Phil Hamilton o John Baird

Què Dios Les BenDiga!

EXLUSAVMENTE EN ESPAÑOL

IGLESIA CATÓLICA

LA IGLESIA DE LA

PALABRA VIVA

ooo **CAPILLA DEL**

✝ **AGUA SANTA** ✝

TODOS ESTAN INVITADOS

FECHA 21 JUNIO 11:00 AM HORA

"Y Sobre esta piedra voy a construyir mi Iglesia, Y ni siquiera las puertas del infierno podrá vencerla." (Mt. 16:18)
Juespuée del domingo, vas a saber la prueba
e la resurrección de Jesus. La verdad está
bierta, Y la puerta está abierta a todos!

I ran the service for the first few Sundays, while Phil and another American buddy, Al Cipoletti, showed up for support. I had prepared the translations (we didn't have a priest) and gave the homily in Spanish.

As I've said, my Spanish is not perfect, by any means, but we were trying to create a Spanish-based, Catholic worship service, because we believed more people might show up to Church on Sunday. Nearly half of the Fort Dix population was Hispanic, and most of them grew up Catholic. It only made sense, we thought, and most Catholics wouldn't step foot in an Evangelical Service---and vice-versa!

We told a few of the key Spanish-speaking men we would turn it over to them, once they got in the groove. This would, ultimately, allow a native Spanish-speaker to lead the way, after the first few weeks.

Unfortunately, this didn't pan out over time, and attendance never took off. The first few Sundays, about a dozen men showed up each week, and then some of the Spanish-speaking guys took over and ran it for another month, or so.

Ultimately, the decision was made to keep one service in English, because the Catholic Church only had been allocated by the BOP three hours to use the chapel on Sundays. This was an effort we tried pretty hard at, but it wasn't as successful as we hoped it might be.

As I said, I had also attended the Evangelical services and was friends with many of the men who attended there. I've done my share of studying The Bible, and I'm no expert in it, but I spent considerable time in college and in my adult life, studying the historicity of The Bible, while digging in deep, as to its credibility, as a source of truth. With this study, I decidedly came down in the arena of its truth, and have been deeply convicted of this truth in my faith, ever since.

Because of this, part of the "*other things*" I told Mike and my Turtle class I would try and do while incarcerated, would be to create a presentation on *why* men could *believe* The Bible.

I had asked Heidi many months before, if she could please send me Evidence that Demands a Verdict, and Who Moved the Stone? The former book was written by Josh McDowell, and the latter by Frank Morison. Heidi had also purchased for me a

Ryrie Study Bible for the New Testament, and it had arrived during my first week at Fort Dix. This beautiful book was well-marked up, and left for a good use, when I was released.

During the summer of 2015, I spent long hours in the sweltering heat of the library---but, I would take that any day, over the last winter---when there was NO heat. I tried hard to prepare a succinct and direct presentation on why men could believe The Bible.

Anyone who has ever heard Josh McDowell, or read Frank Morison, knows both these gentlemen are leading examples of Christians---who are, or were, on the front lines of battle to bring the word of Jesus to the masses. I'm not a minister and I needed resources, and I believed the work of these men would provide me with some excellent material. I hoped it would help me reach out to the hardened hearts of men inside the prison.

The Fort Dix "Camp" is an interesting place because it is housed on the grounds of the largest prison institution in the United States---the Fort Dix Federal Correctional Institution.

The single Warden responsible for running Fort Dix wants to run a smooth operation, and make sure there are no escapes. The Warden also has to manage the budget---if he, or she, wanted to do well in his, or her, career.

Because of the crush on BOP budgets, due to the record number of inmates, bulging payroll and benefit costs, along with the enormous waste in the BOP, there has been a huge amount of pressure on Wardens to cut corners.

An important point here is it costs way more to house, feed, secure and rehabilitate a *higher-level* security prisoner, than it takes to do the same for a prisoner in a lower-level-security Camp. As a result, the Fort Dix Warden and other management at the BOP developed a policy of feeding the "minimum-security" Camp with hundreds of men from the two higher-level security prisons on the grounds of the Fort Dix FCI.

This made the Camp into a petri-dish for the outright mixing of all kinds of different people, many of which should never have been allowed into a minimum security Camp, in the first place.

With the Camp overcrowded and overflowing with over 420 souls, friction was pervasive among the men. If you got into a disagreement with the wrong kind of guy, you could take your life into your hands.

The use of the Camps in this "petri-dish" experiment is *not* what Congress, *or* the courts, intended when they allowed the BOP to set up the different security levels of the prison system.

Wiser minds originally separated the men ON PURPOSE. Hopefully, you can see the lack of oversight in the details of managing these facilities simply boggles the mind. Resources are consumed for the betterment of one group of people---BOP employees. This is the truth of the matter.

By the way, many men who came down from the higher-level security prisons *deserved* to be in the Camp, because they had truly changed their lives. However, it was obvious to every inmate: nearly every prisoner sent to the Camp from the higher-level security facilities, was sent solely to save the BOP budget money. It wasn't because most of these inmates were any less dangerous, or any less violent.

Prisons don't publish how many people actually die, or get injured, in prison, but it would be very interesting to see these figures and statistics. To say the least, you had to be aware of your surroundings, and be prepared for just about anything at Fort Dix---just like in any other prison.

Being a teacher provided me with unique insight into many, many different types of people at this facility, and it became crystal clear, in a real hurry, many men either outright hate, or make fun of, "Christians." It didn't matter what kind of church service a Christian might have attended, either Catholic, or Evangelical, scorn was equally assigned to men of faith. Even more nefarious, was the fact many other inmates truly consider Christians "the enemy."

It took me a couple of months of pulling together all the study materials for my presentation, but by September of 2015, I was ready to go.

Hoping men would read my flier, regardless of rebuttals---I posted, next to the chow-hall door, the following one-pager. I typed it out in the library, created a master with image cut-outs taped onto it, and then made copies on the copier:

EVER WONDER IF THE BIBLE WAS TRUE?

CAN MAN TRUST IT?

Come and listen to a presentation on two books which investigated these questions and many others. The first book, Evidence That Demands a Verdict, was written by famous lecturer, Josh McDowell, and the second book, written by Frank Morison, called Who Moved The Stone will provide you with remarkable insight into these age-old questions.

If you're bored over Labor Day Weekend, come out to the bleachers by the softball field on SATURDAY AT 5:45pm for the ENGLISH version of this presentation.

Come out on SUNDAY AT 5:45pm for the SPANISH VERSION OF THIS PRESENTATION. VENGA EL DOMINGO A LAS 5:45pm para oir la versión Español de esta presentación.

THIS IS NOT A PREPPY BIBLE STUDY. THIS IS FOR MEN WITH REAL QUESTIONS WHO WANT TO LEARN...IF YOU ARE OPEN MINDED AND LISTEN TO THESE FACTS, IT WILL PROBABLY MEAN THIS 45 MINUTES COULD CHANGE YOUR LIFE!

ESTA PRESENTACIÓN NO ES UNA "BIBLE STUDY" PERO ES ALGO QUE SI VENGA CON LA MENTE ABIERTA, PUEDE CAMBIAR TU VIDA---EN 45 MINUTOS, POSIBLEMENTE! POR ESO, VALE LA PENA...

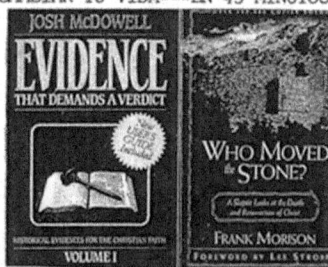

Presentación la estará hecho por Kelly, autor del estos libros:
Presentation made by Kelly, author of these books:

I translated the final presentation into Spanish to be sure I could share it with the Spanish-speaking men. The presentation notes were contained in a 14-page, single-spaced document. It provided a compelling list of facts and evidence, as to why a person can believe The Bible, and the fact of history Jesus Christ was not only the son of God, but was also raised from the dead.

Since the Spanish-speaking men were the single-most, populated group in the Camp, I always tried to reach out to them. A couple of them in particular, were my friends Willie Caraballo and Leo Reyes. They are real men of God. My friend Ricky Lopez, one of my great students, also had a really great heart for people...as did our pal, Rosado. Rosado would always be cooking for everyone else. They were all a big family, but to a man, each of them only wanted to go home.

I remember I would sit for hours outside in the summer, on the bench behind home plate with Ricky, reading aloud the book, The Street Lawyer, by John Grisham. He would read an English chapter to improve his English, and I would read a Spanish chapter to improve my Spanish. It was one of the few novels the prison library held, which was available in both Spanish and English. The title is Causa Justa, in Spanish.

As a group, and individually, these men were all quite remarkable.

As time wore on, during my sentence, I made friends with many other groups of men, also.

Within the heterogeneous population at Fort Dix, there was also a very active Muslim community. I was fortunate to call many of them, my friends. However, some of the men who attended Muslim services were quite aggressive in their views. Of course, in America, people can believe whatever they want—it is their right.

After I had prepared my detailed notes for the presentation, I told a couple of my Christian friends I would probably be placing a target on my back with certain people in the Camp who hated the Gospel.

It turns out, I wasn't wrong.

After merely *posting the flyer* promoting my presentation by the chow hall, word trickled back to me.

I was now being called, the "*White Devil!*"

This derogatory branding was carried out among some of the more radically aggressive Muslim men in the Camp.

This name and designation of me, as the "White Devil," actually came from the pitcher of the softball team I started for in the prison's summer softball league. I played for the "Rockets." We had a little fun and it took our minds off of life in prison, at least for a little while. It also gave me a chance to swing a bat, again.

After watching my batting practice, one guy, nick-named "Oz," who would help save my life later in the year, yelled loudly and suddenly, from behind the home plate fence,

"Hey, Kelly, when'd you play baseball last?"

I replied from the batter's box, without taking my eyes off of the pitcher, "Oh, about *thirty* years ago!"

Oz and about forty other guys laughed. Baseball draws a big crowd and sometimes, the whole Camp files out to watch a game---with everyone watching and critiquing every move of every play, and every single swing at the plate.

As ball after ball, flew sharply off my bat, Oz then zipped this one liner at me, again screaming in his big, happy voice:

"WELL, KELLY...doesn't look like anything's wrong with your eye-hand coordination from thirty years ago, does it?!"

Everyone laughed some more.

But the pitcher on my team, with whom I had shared a laugh or two with during the season, apparently forgot we were teammates and brothers on the softball field.

He was the one who branded me the "White Devil" and his name was "Shabaz."

I'll never forget his venom, either, because the word spread.

It stirred outrage inside me---but I tried to never let it show. I just kept going, and I kept thinking:

> *"Damn the torpedoes, and full speed ahead!"*

Because of my strong feelings about the corruption in the banking system and the corruption which blatantly exists in the "revolving door" between the federal government, Wall Street and the big law firms, in general, I could understand the frustration and anger men like Shabaz had for the system, and at white people, in general. However, it was quite another thing to label a person a "White Devil," because as you will read later in this chapter, those people are marked as blatantly evil, and worthy of death, among the radical Muslims in the Camp.

I know many men, including Shabaz, carried a great deal of pain around with them when they looked at the injustices in society. From their perspective, they believed they were dealt with unfairly in prison. After all, why should they be locked up when all the white, fraud-convicted bankers get to run free?

I can definitely understand the hard feelings, particularly among the nation's inner-city dwellers, over this, and other issues. My books in the Federal Reserve Trilogy are exposés of the incredible corruption and outright, legalized theft which went on during the credit crisis---and afterward. These documented actions sent over 42 million people out of their homes and onto the streets. It has weakened our inner cities, horrifically.

Of course, this tragedy benefited the elite nearly 100%, and they are mostly white people.

...And therein lies the rub.

No wonder there is such pent-up hatred in many groups, today, against many things. Unfortunately, some of the more frustrated have steered this anger, indiscriminately, toward nearly all white people---at least this is how it seemed at Fort Dix.

One way, or another, I am proud to say I fought this battle every day of my life, while I was there. Nearly all the men in the Camp knew they could trust me, and could come to me for help, if they needed it.

I was honored when one of my black Muslim friends said, "Kelly is color blind." This was one of those "off-the-cuff," passing remarks, which was just an afterthought by this man. It took place while some of the guys were razzing me, in a good-natured way, about helping somebody out, again.

I was humbled this man paid me this compliment in prison---especially since he had a tough life growing up. I gave every man his due respect during my term---fully respecting them as individuals, as well as their creeds, beliefs and mannerisms, even if I disagreed with them.

Finally, at about 5:30 p.m., on the 5th of September, 2015, standing before the metal benches of the software bleachers, along the 3rd baseline of the softball field where I had taken batting practice during the summer, and had spent hours reading with Ricky, I had everything prepared for my early-evening presentation. I had copies of it for anyone who showed up, and I had brought a miniature white board. It was only supposed to be used by tutors---and, as it turns out, it was a good thing I was one of those guys!

At 5:45 p.m., a handful of men sat down in the first two rows of bleachers before me. Two of them were unbelievers. One was an older Jewish inmate, named Michael, and the other was a Japanese-American inmate, named "G" (this is actually what everyone called him). He was always in the library and had told me he liked the fact, I "walked the walk," and wasn't like other "Christians" in prison.

I always brushed this off, because I really didn't think much about what I was doing, at least in those terms.

My talk was broken down into these sections:

1) The Bible.
   Its uniqueness---circulation, survival through time, continuity, how many have read it, its preservation, its accuracy, etc.
2) Independent corroboration of The Bible.
   The Dead Sea Scrolls, Josephus, etc.
3) Eyewitnesses.
4) Style of Writing.
5) Resurrection---Fact, or Fiction?
6) Importance of the Resurrection of Jesus Christ.
7) Who Moved the Stone?
8) The Roman Guard.
9) The Roman Seal.
10) The Transformed Lives of the Disciples.
11) Jesus' Appearances After He Was Killed on the Cross.
12) The 4 Spiritual Laws of Christ.
13) Invitation to Accept Jesus as Your Lord & Savior.

For those who have attended a Campus Crusade for Christ event, starring Josh McDowell, you will recognize much of this outline from his books and his message.

Josh is a great man and has brought, through the Holy Spirit, countless lives to Jesus. I don't know if he thought his work might be used in the exact way I was planning to use it, but I didn't think it would hurt the cause. I was only hoping I didn't butcher Josh's reputation in the process.

When I finished my talk and the presentation ended, I held up my white board. I had already written down for everyone to see, the following proclamation, which is the capstone and fortress of truth in the Christian faith:

THIS IS THE RECORD:

Confucius' Tomb	OCCUPIED!
Buddha's Tomb	OCCUPIED!
Muhammad's Tomb	OCCUPIED!

JESUS CHRIST'S TOMB: EMPTY!

This was one of my favorite lessons from Josh McDowell. It was simple, yet incredibly powerful.

I said, "After all the evidence is in, there is one simple fact of history which cannot be explained away, based on the evidence. This is the fact Jesus Christ was resurrected from the dead, a fact upon which Christianity is unique among all world religions!"

The lecture went well, thank God. It was even a beautiful evening, with a comfortable temperature. The men who attended were all very grateful and each wanted a copy of my presentation. We left around 7:00 p.m.

A little while later, about 8:15 p.m., I was exiting the chow hall. The chow hall had three television sets up on the walls, which were "on" during the evening for the men to use. I often cruised through to see if anything was worth watching, before bedtime.

In prison, the TVs are usually tuned to some law and order drama, or reality show featuring blurred out, naked people running around through the jungle, all fighting for survival, or, perhaps they would be tuned to "MTV," or "ESPN."

You get the idea. There were very few televisions to split up between 400⁺ men and there weren't a lot of choices in programming. Sometimes there may have been a good movie, or sporting event to watch, but usually, I just read during the evening.

The Camp also was laid out internally as a big rectangle. You could take a "lap" around the hallways to see what was going on. I often did this to break up the boredom.

As I exited the chow hall, I entered the hallway, heading to the door of the entrance to the "B Wing," and my bunk. I had just finished my "lap" and I was tired. The buildup and preparation for the presentation represented a great unknown for me inside prison walls, and afterward, I felt exhaustion sweep over me.

During the last month, when I was preparing the presentation, I would think to myself, *"Would I piss somebody off? Would no one show up? What would guys say behind my back?"*---and probably a hundred other things, as well.

All I was thinking when I left the chow hall was, *"I'm bushed. I'm going to my bunk and I'm getting ready for the count."* I was dog-tired and just wanted to read for a while. As you leave the chow hall, on the way to my bunk, you pass the tiny prison library, which is on the "left."

The distance between the "B" Wing living quarters and the chow hall exit door was about fifteen yards and the locked door to the library (where I had originally advertised the "Trade Like a Turtle" class for my ACE class during the Winter of 2015)

274

was located halfway down this hall on the *left*, as you walked toward my living quarters from the chow hall.

In my first step inside the hallway, I was somewhat surprised to see a Muslim acquaintance of mine, Sadiq (not his real name), waiting for me. He had stepped directly in my path, from where he had been leaning against the library wall.

I had previously enjoyed some excellent discussions with Sadiq regarding the Federal Reserve and the banks. I knew him to be very bright and he was excellent to speak with.

He flagged me down and I stopped to talk with him. The corridor was wide enough for about two-and-a-half men to pass, and I was on the far side of the hallway. Sadiq was on the library side of the hallway, and we were standing right next to the locked-windowed door, where I had posted the Turtle class.

Sadiq said, "I'm really sorry I missed your talk, I had to work."

He stared at me, with his bright green eyes, and olive, dark skin. He was a handsome man, highly intelligent, and a leader among many of the inmates, I had come to observe. He taught some of the African Studies classes and was active in the Muslim community. I was honored he and I could always speak to each other in a very respectful and thoughtful manner.

I told Sadiq, "No problem, Sadiq!"

He had known I was going to speak about The Bible and Christianity. Sadiq is an intellectually curious person and in my experience, was not afraid to listen to different viewpoints, even if his opinions and beliefs were different.

I found on this night, Sadiq steered the conversation into a discussion about Islam. He also surprised me, greatly, when he volunteered right off the bat, that he didn't consider himself a "black" person.

I didn't really feel comfortable parsing the issue of race. I had worked and played my whole life with people of all colors--- first in L.A. with my football brothers from Watts, then in high school and college, as well as in my professional career in the professional sports and entertainment businesses.

I didn't know what to say, so I asked him, "What do you consider yourself?"

He replied, "I am a 'Balilean.'"

I had no idea what a "Balilean" was, but to be honest, it didn't sound good to me. I knew that "Baal" was the God of the Egyptians, and enemy of the God of Israel. I wondered, on-the-fly, as I looked at his bright, green eyes, *Is a "Balilean" a follower of Baal?"*

If it was, this would definitely be against the beliefs I was brought up with.

The conversation took a dark turn, in a hurry. Out of the blue, Sadiq then tried to convince me Lucifer didn't exist, and The Bible had it all wrong. Also, it seemed in his mind, it was perfectly all right for the "sons of god" to have sex with, and go into, human women and thereby create the Nephilim!

For those who don't know who the "Nephilim" were, they were the offspring of sexual relations between the sons of God and daughters of men, as taught in The Bible (Genesis 6:1-4).

276

You might remember what happened to them. God wiped them all out in the great flood!

I listened to Sadiq, patiently, wanting to remain respectful of another man's beliefs. But, something strange happened. I began feeling an uncomfortable and invisible force pressing my head against the wall I had been casually leaning against. It felt like I was being pushed. The old saying, "my back was against the wall," took on a whole new meaning.

Sadiq continued his lecture to me, and observed my respectful silence---I was letting the man speak his mind.

This lulled him into a sense of false confidence, because he just continued to blast away at The Bible, Christianity and went on, promulgating his own beliefs. All the while, with Sadiq lecturing me, I continued to feel pressure building on my head and back. It was a bit unnerving, to say the least.

I knew I was getting close to a point where I could return fire in the conversation, as I had listened respectfully---long enough. I'm sure Sadiq *didn't* expect what was going to happen next.

Sadiq was about to be on the receiving end of a biblical response to his positions.

Now, we are in public, in perhaps the busiest corridor of the Camp (i.e., right outside the chow-hall exit, the library and entrance to the "B Wing,") and Sadiq had been laying into me, lecturing me and was trying to convince me of his beliefs. I felt many men go by, but my focus was 100% on Sadiq. I also felt my adrenaline pumping like wild fire.

I saw when Sadiq was speaking he got a really weird expression on his face. His bright, green eyes lit up and locked onto my blue ones. He was nothing short of fiendishly brilliant in how he was trying to lay out his rationale for how the black people came directly from the seed of The Bible's patriarchs, and because of this, they were destined to rule over *everyone*.

As he stood there giving me the lecture, he began to attack my faith---this was my opening, I knew, from God, above. This was a big mistake on his part, because I am not one to be trifled with in this area at all, because I will defend my faith vigorously, when challenged. I actually never defend, I merely go on offense.

I began my response to his verbal assault in the most respectful manner possible, because:

1) This is what Jesus would want---treat others, as we would treat ourselves (i.e., The Golden Rule); and
2) I was in prison. While I expected to raise some flags with my bold pronouncements of Christian faith and the fact The Bible is God's word, I knew in a confined space like Fort Dix, I also would like to live long enough to make sure I would be released!

After I began my response, to say Sadiq didn't know what to do with me, would be an understatement. I first pointed out to him The Bible was the most well-read book in history and was obviously much older than the Quran, which was only written in the 8th Century, with Muhammed dying in 632 A.D. This was completely different from the life of Jesus Christ, who lived, died and was raised again, from the dead. I went into various details about the witnesses and Roman Guard at the tomb of Jesus. The words rolled off my tongue. I wasn't in charge now---the Holy Spirit was.

When I completed my response, he told me he believed I liked being "confrontational." I immediately called him out on this and pushed right bank, firmly. I retorted, "But it is YOU who are making all the attacking provocations!"

To this, he had the audacity to say, "Well, I did that ON PURPOSE!" He talked further and then made this grand pronouncement:

"Me and all the other Muslims are 'sons of God.'"

When I heard this, I immediately responded, as the Spirit led me without question, to thunder:

"That **isn't** what The Bible says...The Bible says, 'But to as many as receive Him, *to them* He gave the right to become sons of God, to those who believe in His name." John 1:12

This passage refers directly to Jesus Christ, the son of God. The Bible is sharper than any two-edged sword, and Sadiq didn't like my response, one bit. His face scrutinized me, big time.

The once beautiful, in-control face was now twisting in the wind. I went on to explain Christianity was the ONLY religion on earth whose savior ROSE from the DEAD!

He tried to then lamely point out Elijah, along with the apparent "seed" of his faith and the seed of all black people, "Enoch," were also raised up by God. However, any student of

<u>The Bible</u> knows, these men pleased God and God took them while they were still ALIVE, *sparing* them death!

In the end, Sadiq listened respectfully and we wound up talking about how the bankers had thrown 42 million people onto the streets during the mortgage crisis, and not one of them was sent to prison. This, despite the fact the banks plead guilty to criminal fraud charges. Those scoundrels could just pay a fine and walk away but, not me, and not Sadiq. I know Sadiq felt this pain, because he was also in prison on fraud charges.

When we were departing and heading our separate ways, Sadiq said, "You know, I'd vote for you...but, there are other ways to make changes in the world, rather than writing books!"

I answered, "Yes, but the subject of the Federal Reserve and the banks stealing $30 Trillion, is extremely complex. It needed to be researched and written about. The next economic collapse will demand answers to their skullduggery."

At this, we parted. It was 9:15 p.m. and count was at 9:30 p.m. I asked my Christian friends to pray for me because I felt a very strong presence around Sadiq---and it had pushed me up against the wall until I responded and quoted <u>The Bible</u>, in response to his aggressive challenge of the Christian faith.

Spiritually, it was something I hadn't experienced before---Sadiq was very nice, but knew just enough about <u>The Bible</u> to try and twist its true message to meet his own ends---very scary, indeed.

Two big things happened after this meeting and they involved a fine young man I had known for a while, Leo Reyes. He told me, "I was sleeping last night and in the middle of the night, I felt something evil come around me. It felt like a 'big weight' press down on me---it was so heavy, I couldn't move!"

I saw in Leo's eyes he had felt the presence of evil around him. He bunked just down the aisle from my bunk. He was a young Christian and about 30-years old. He continued, "I prayed for Jesus' blood to protect me and for the Holy Spirit to be there for me. As soon as I did this, the presence vanished."

Now, this wasn't a TV show, where someone makes things up---this was real. The fear and relief in Leo's eyes were undeniable. Leo hadn't told anyone else about this until he told me, either. What was very strange was something *else* Leo told me. He said he had walked RIGHT BY Sadiq, when Sadiq and I were speaking to each other the night before, on Saturday night! Leo had passed between us, but I hadn't noticed, because I was entirely focused on Sadiq and in my responses to his attacks.

When Leo told me this over the Labor Day weekend, I immediately prayed for him. I also asked Joe, my teaching partner, and my friend Will, to pray for Leo, also. All of us prayed for each other! Prison is a dangerous place, and is definitely the devil's playground.

Interestingly, and the second thing which happened, was Leo came up to me again, a couple of days later, and told me two Muslims approached him and they both wanted to know why Leo was talking with the "White Devil!"

I asked Leo, "What did you tell them?"

Leo, for his relatively young age and easy-going manner (he always had a ready smile for everyone), was also quite wise. He told me he responded, "You guys are just speaking from ignorance!"

Leo was very strong in his faith, and he had a great heart.

Men in prison might very well be reached through Church songs, holding hands, and praying, for sure, but from what I could see, hard, tough men in prison rarely took to this approach in accepting Christianity.

I found working directly with the men, and living by example, was a far more effective way to spread the word and creed of Jesus' lessons---and sometimes even get hostile unbelievers to sit patiently and listen to you. All we can do is plant the seeds, and let the Holy Spirit do the watering.

Sadiq, a few days later, gave me this official definition of the "Balileans:"

WHO ARE THE "BILALIANS"

October 26, 2012 at 1:17pm
Who are the "BILALIANS"

Answer: Bilalians are the pinnacle of excellence of those bought and sold in these United States of America as slaves. They are the most intelligent, the best mannered, highly respected, culturally advance men and women; cut off from historic, social and cultural ties of the African continent.

We are the reformers of human excellence, models of the best aspects of the human existence. Proving that the grace and mercy of G-d did come and raised a people from dust to industry, after everything that it means to be a human was driven from us as a people and laws were written to deny that that people had any humanity.

Those writings were accepted into the language of law and acted upon by this Nation and Nations around the world. The Bilalian proves that scripture and that the law of G-d is superior to the law of man. That if the G-d of scripture would save a people of old that that same G-d obligates himself to do the same to any and all people denied their humanity. We represent that light in this world.

So when asked "Who are the Bilalians?" now you know. "I am a Bilalian man"

If you identify with this idea, stand up and declare "I am a Bilalian!"

No longer to be called African-American.

file:///C:/Users/Yshaba/AppData/Local/Microsoft/Windows/Temporary%20Internet%20Fi...   1/21/2015

Holding the Fort

I was always curious about other perspectives and beliefs I found among the men in the Camp, and one morning, I recovered some documents from the education room's copying machine.

They were used in the "African Studies" ACE classes at Fort Dix, left there from the night before.

I highly doubt these materials were ever "approved" by the BOP, because I can't imagine Ms. Lindley, or the Education Department, condoning the name-calling of "White Devils"---and promoting *the murder* of them.

This information is must-read material. It is brief, but highly disturbing. It is difficult to believe this is what some of the leaders among the inmates are teaching other eager followers, inside a taxpayer-funded Federal Correctional Institution.

The following pages contain a "Student Enrollment" and the "Rules for Islam," along with the "Lost Found Muslim Lesson No. 1." Please read particularly, the 10th question and answer in the "Lost Found Muslim Lesson No. 1."

Here, the document answers the question as to why Muhammad and Muslims murder devils and why Muslims should kill four devils.

Also, please read the definition of who they consider to be the "devil." For the record, the documents consider white people to be the devil, (which is consistent with what they labeled me--e.g., the "White Devil").

Holding the Fort

You will see this is the answer to question #2, "Who is the Colored Man?" (i.e., "The Colored Man is the Caucasian (white man), or Yacob's grafted devil, the skunk of the planet Earth.")

9

III. STUDENT ENROLLMENT

(Rules of Islam)

The following questions must be answered one hundred percent before submittance of Student to said, Lesson No. 1.

1. Who is the Original Man?

2. Who is the Colored Man?

3. What is the population of the Original Nation in the wilderness of North America and all over the Planet Earth?

4. What is the population of the Colored People in the wilderness of North America and all over the Planet Earth?

5. What is the area in square miles of the Planet Earth? How much is the land? How much is the water?

6. What are the exact square miles of useful land that is used every day by the total population of the Planet Earth?

7. How much of the useful land is used by the Original Man?

8. How much of the useful land is used by the Colored Man?

9. What is the birth record of the said, Nation of Islam?

10. What is the birth record of said, others than Islam?

284

Holding the Fort

(ANSWERS)

1. The Original Man is the Asiatic Black Man, the Maker, the Owner, the Cream of the Planet Earth, God of the Universe.

2. The Colored Man is the Caucasian (white man) or Yacob's grafted devil, the Skunk of the Planet Earth.

3. The population of the Original Nation in the wilderness of North America is 17,000,000, with the 2,000,000 Indians makes it, 19,000,000. All over the Planet Earth is 4,400,000,000.

4. The population of the Colored People in the wilderness of North America is 103,000,000. All over the Planet Earth is 400,000,000.

5. The square mileage of the Earth is 196,940,000 square miles. The land is 57,255,000 square miles. The water is 139,685,000.

6. The useful land that is used every day by the total population of the Planet Earth is 29,000,000 square miles.

7. The Original Man uses 23,000,000 square miles.

8. The Colored Man uses 6,000,000 square miles.

9. The said, Nation of Islam has no birth record. It has no beginning nor ending.

10. Buddhism is 35,000 years old. Christianity is 551 years old.

285

IV. LOST FOUND MUSLIM LESSON NO. 1

1. Why isn't the devil settled on the best part of the planet Earth?

ANS. - Because the earth belongs to the original black man. And knowing that the devil was wicked and there would not be any peace among them, he put him out in the worst part of the earth and kept the best part preserved for himself ever since he made it. The best part is in Arabia at the Holy City, Mecca. The colored man or Caucasian is the devil. Arabia is in the far east and is bordered by the Indian Ocean on the south.

2. Why did Mossa have a hard time to civilize the devil 2,000 B.C.?

ANS. - Because he was a savage. Savage means a person that has lost the knowledge of himself and who is living a beast life. Mossa was a half original man and a prophet. Two thousand B.C. means before Christ. In the Asiatic world, it was in the eleventh thousand year. Civilize means to teach the knowledge and wisdom of the human family of the planet Earth.

3. Why did we let half original man, Columbus, discover the poor part of the planet Earth?

ANS. - Because the original man is the God and Owner of the earth, and knows every square inch of it, and has chosen for himself the best part. He did not care about the poor part. Columbus was a half original man and was born in Italy, which is southeast Europe. His full name was Christopher Columbus and the place he discovered was North America. He found the Indians here, who were exiled sixteen thousand years ago from India. They are original people.

4. Why did we run Yacob and his made devil from the root of civilization, over the hot desert, into the cave of West Asia, as they now call it, Europe? What is the meaning of Eu and Rope? How long ago? What did the devil bring with him? What kind of life did he live? And how long before Mossa came to teach the devil of the forgotten tricknollegy?

ANS. - Because they had started making trouble among the righteous people telling lies. They accused the righteous people causing them to fight and kill one another. Yacob was an original black man and was the father of the devil. He taught the devils to do this devilishment.

286

The root of civilization is in Arabia at the Holy City, Mecca, which means where wisdom and knowledge of the original man first started, when the planet was found. We ran the devils over the Arabian Desert. We took from them everything except the language and made him walk every step of the way. It was twenty-two hundred miles. He went savage and lived in the caves of Europe. Eu means hillsides and Rope is the rope to bind in. It was six thousand nineteen years ago.

Mossa came two thousand years later and taught him how to live a respectful life, how to build a home for himself and some of the tricknollegy that Yacob taught him, which was devilishment, telling lies, stealing and how to master the original man. Mossa was a half original, a prophet, which was predicted by the twenty-three scientists in the year one - fifteen thousand nineteen years ago today.

5. Why did we take Jerusalem from the devil? How long ago?

ANS. - Because one of our righteous brothers, who was a prophet by the name of Jesus, was buried there. He uses his name to shield his dirty religion, which is called Christianity; also, to deceive the people so they will believe in him. Jesus' teaching was not Christianity. It was Freedom, Justice and Equality. Jerusalem is in Palestine, Asia Minor. Jerusalem is a name given by the Jews, which means founded in peace, and it was first built by the original man, who was called Jebus; also, Salem and Ariel. We took the city from the devils about seven hundred fifty years ago.

6. Why does the devil call our people, Africans?

ANS. - To make our people of North America believe that the people on that continent are the only people they have and are all savage. He bought a trading post in the jungle of that continent. The original people live on this continent and they are the ones who strayed away from civilization and are living a jungle life. The original people call this continent, Asia, but the devils call it, Africa, to try to divide them. He wants us to think that we all are different.

7. Why does the devil keep our people illiterate?

ANS. - So that he can use them for a tool and, also, a slave. He keeps them blind to themselves so that he can master them. Illiterate means ignorant.

8. Why does the devil keep our people apart from his social equality?

ANS. - Because he does not want us to know how filthy he is and all his affairs. He is afraid because when we learn about him, we will run him from among us. Socialist means to advocate a society of men or groups of men for one common cause. Equality means to be equal in everything.

Holding the Fort

9. Why does Muhammad make the devil study from thirty-five to fifty years before he can call himself a Muslim son? And wear the greatest and only flag of the Universe? And he must add a sword on the upper part of the Holy and Greatest Universe Flag of Islam?

ANS. - So that he could clean himself up. A Muslim does not love the devil regardless to how long he studies. After he has devoted thirty-five or fifty years trying to learn and do like the original man, he could come and do trading among us and we would not kill him as quick as we would the other devils, that is, who have not gone under this study. After he goes through with this labor from thirty-five to fifty years, we permit him to wear our Holy Flag, which is the Sun, Moon and Star. He must add the sword on the upper part.

The sword is the emblem of Justice and it was used by the original man in Muhammad's time. Thus, it was placed on the upper part of the flag so that the devil can always see it, so he will keep in mind that any time he reveals the secrets, his head would be taken off by the sword. We give him this chance so that he could clean himself up and come among us.

The Holy Flag of Islam is the greatest and only flag known. The Universe is everything - Sun, Moon and Stars. They are planets. Planets are something grown or made from the beginning, and holy is something that has not been diluted, mixed or tampered with in any form.

10. Why does Muhammad and any Muslim murder the devil? What is the duty of each Muslim in regards to four devils? What reward does a Muslim receive by presenting the four devils at one time?

ANS. - Because he is one hundred percent wicked and will not keep and obey the laws of Islam. His ways and actions are like a snake of the grafted type. So Muhammad learned that he could not reform the devils, so they had to be murdered. All Muslims will murder the devil because they know he is a snake and, also, if he be allowed to live, he would sting someone else. Each Muslim is required to bring four devils. And by bringing and presenting four at one time, his reward is a button to wear on the lapel of his coat. Also, a free transportation in the Holy City, Mecca, to see Brother Muhammad.

11. Have you not learned that your word shall be Bond regardless of whom or what?

ANS. - Yes. My word is bond and bond is life, and I will give my life before my word shall fail.

288

---

12. What is the meaning of F.O.I.?

ANS. - The Fruit Of Islam; the name given to the military training of the men that belong to Islam in North America.

13. What is the meaning of Lieu. and Capt.?

ANS. - Captain and Lieutenant. The duty of a captain is to give orders to the lieutenant, and the lieutenant's duty is to teach the private soldiers; also, train them.

14. What is the meaning of M.G.T. and G.C.C.?

ANS. - Muslim Girls' Training and General Civilization Class. This was the name given to the training of women and girls in North America; how to keep house, how to rear their children, how to take care of their husbands, sew, cook and, in general, how to act at home and abroad. These training units were named by our prophet and leader of Islam, *W. D. Fard*.

I don't know if Sadiq taught from these documents, or not. I had seen him teaching African Studies in previous weeks, along with other men, through the glass window of the door to the classroom. You walked directly past it when you did a "lap" around the Camp's rectangle layout of hallways.

It makes me wonder what would happen to other folks if they started labeling people as "the devil" and promoted their murder---which is the actual word these documents use to promote the elimination of white people.

If someone else did this, they would probably be charged with a hate crime, particularly if they were espousing violence by murder!

Holding the Fort

CHAPTER 21

THE DAY I NEARLY DIED

After my encounter with Sadiq and about a month later, on October 7, 2015, my breathing completely stopped and I nearly died at Fort Dix.

The week before, on September 29, I had been sitting in the library doing some work at my regular spot. A newer inmate and purported "doctor," originally from India, came into the library and sat next to me. He had come down with the flu, which was running rampant through the Camp's crowded conditions during September, and he immediately started coughing---all over me---non-stop.

I had ignored the first couple of coughs, but thought---*"Come on...this guy is supposedly a doctor and he comes into the confined space of the cramped library spewing forth germs and coughing all over everybody?"*

I asked him to please leave the library and take his cough elsewhere; he was going to get everyone sick. "Excuse me, you're coughing all over me and you're going to make me sick, you need to go back to your bunk."

His nasty reply was: "I am a doctor, germs don't spread that way---I put my hand over my mouth!"

Regardless of a "hand over the mouth" germs spread wide and far when someone is coughing uncontrollably. What a ridiculous supposition and statement—from a purported doctor! We got into a bit of a pissing match on this one...and he refused to leave.

I was livid with this guy. I sat there outraged because I had suffered a severe bronchial illness in my 20's and I knew there was scar tissue in my lungs. If I get a cough, I have to treat it aggressively, or it can relapse into a very scary, pneumonia-like condition. This excuse for a "doctor" dismissed my request with the ultimate insult: *"Mr. Kelly, you should mind your own business!"*

In my old high school, pre-Christian days, I would have just punched this guy out. I really got angry and snapped back, *"It IS my business when you are coughing all over me!"*

This guy was what I would call in my old life, a real "A**hole"---total and complete.

Sure enough, within about a day, I developed a severe bronchitis-like condition, where I could not stop coughing. It literally plagued me. I still can't understand how this guy could have even become a doctor. After I got sick, I really had a hard time even looking at this incredibly insensitive and careless man. He must have been horrible in his practice, if he even had a legal one, before he was imprisoned. I think he was incarcerated for prescribing illegal drugs, but I'm not sure. One thing I'm pretty certain of, however---he wasn't educated in America. He had a very thick Indian accent, and it was way too thick to have grown up in the States. I know I'm supposed to forgive him, and I do, but man he pissed me off.

He wound up nearly killing me. To be honest, I had a hard time forgiving this guy willingly, because he knowingly and repeatedly spread germs all over me (he was coughing every 10 seconds, or so), and I nearly died from his grossly reckless behavior. But, I thought of how Jesus was tortured and outright murdered on the cross---and how he *automatically and naturally forgave* one and all for their hateful sins and actions:

> "³⁴Then Jesus said, 'Father, forgive them, for they do not know what they are doing.' And they divided up His garments by casting lots. ³⁵The people stood watching, and the rulers sneered at Him, saying, 'He saved others; let Him save Himself if He is the Christ of God, the Chosen One.'" (Source: The Bible, Luke 23:24 NIV)

...and I was having a hard time with a guy who was merely passing an illness onto me, knowingly! I thought long and hard about this for months afterward. I had a lot to learn still in my Christian journey. It was difficult for me to forgive this guy.

As my illness progressed, I went to medical and they refused all treatment for me and advised I should gargle with salt water. The salt-water gargle turned out to be really bad advice, because it dried out my esophagus and breathing apparatus, which caused them to collapse on October 7, at 9:45 p.m.

On this evening, I was in bed and had propped myself up, to try and stop coughing. Suddenly, my esophagus and breathing apparatus sealed shut---and it felt like cement had fused them together.

I COULDN'T BREATHE!

As you will see from my detailed timeline, in a letter I sent to the President of the United States, as well as from my medical records---all requests by me for medical treatment had been *refused.* I was simply left to fate from the BOP's perspective.

My letter describes what happened in detail. I learned from many a man "inside" about their poor experiences with BOP medical staff at Fort Dix, and other facilities in the system. After all these discussions, I was left wondering, *"What had been the number of deaths of inmates, while under BOP care?"* This information is not available and appears to be intentionally diffused, bifurcated, scattered and "swept under the carpet" to hide medical malpractice and ineptitude, across the system.

My letter also tried to bring to the President's attention the courageous action of a handful of men who saved my life. The timeline lists, step-by-step, the gross negligence of many BOP employees, including the guards and the medical staff.

Responsibility must also be laid at the feet of management of the BOP. Inmates believe the poor care available in the BOP system would not be allowed to continue, unless it was either implicitly, or explicitly, allowed to occur by the management of the prisons. The buck must stop there.

For men's lives which have already been destroyed by the justice system, the BOP should not be in a position to inflict egregious, *additional* pain, suffering and neglect onto men and women in their care---at least not in America.

This is NOT part of an inmate's sentence. At the end of the day and in particular, the men and women incarcerated in America are U.S. Citizens and are supposed to have rights.

294

Unfortunately, the system is rigged against them, because it prevents prisoners from litigating their grievances directly against the BOP in the court system. Instead, inmates must use the BOP's ridiculous "administrative remedy" process. This program deploys the "same ol', same ol'," cover-up-style review board as exists in the review of disciplinary actions of inmates---it is administered by government-paid, BOP employees.

As a result, prisoners rarely get a fair shake.

Inmates who are U.S. Citizens did *not* have their citizenship revoked when they were convicted of their crimes---whether they were innocent, or not. Inmates should have access to an impartial court, without interference or retribution from overzealous prison management, and/or prison employees.

This perversion of a U.S. Citizen's rights must be changed back to provide inmates with *direct access* to the U.S. Justice system. The excuse of the powers-that-be is inmates flooded the system with legal complaints. This is incredible, but true (i.e., "Let's deny inmates access to the courts, because this group of people has too many grievances!!"). It is a twisted world we live in when people in power can lobby for the elimination of a fundamental right provided to every U.S. Citizen---i.e., direct access to our court system.

My letter to President Obama follows. When I typed it in prison, I typed quickly. I feared someone would know what I was doing, and I dreaded what would happen if the document was discovered, or destroyed---the BOP doesn't like criticism!

Please forgive the typos and/or poor grammar.

October 12, 2015

President Barrack Obama
The White House
1600 Pennsylvania Avenue
Washington D.C. 20500

Subject: Request for Clemency/Commutation
          of 5 Men Who Saved My Life

Dear Mr. President:

This past Wednesday, October 7, 2015, my breathing stopped and I would have
died. Five men, from completely different cultural backgrounds, saved my life.
These men are prisoners at Fort Dix Camp, an incarceration facility of the
Bureau of Prisons ("BOP") for non-violent offenders. It is a work camp and
each day the men work at various jobs, either at the Camp, or on the military
base of Fort Dix. I am also an inmate at the Camp.

I have attached a detailed timeline of the extraordinary events which took
place during the last five days. Given your outstanding leadership in helping
people, as well as your major focuses on prison and immigration reform, I
thought this story might prove to be of interest to you and your fine staff.

I am requesting clemency for five inmates, while requesting nothing from you
for myself. I am just lucky to be alive. Each of these five men displayed
extraordinary courage and each has already served the vast majority of their
time for their past crimes. After you come to understand this story, I thought
there might be a possibility of giving these men and their families an early
Christmas present, by commuting their sentences, immediately, if possible. If
a decision was made to do so, I am convinced, in light of their outstanding
example and decisive actions, the entire inmate population of the United States
may be positiively impacted.

Their Christmas release would shine a bright light of good example for others
to follow. Their actions only took place because I contracted a serious illness
from the flu epidemic which has spread widely across the Fort Dix Camp. Here,
in the overcrowded conditions, where 420 men are squeezed into a space originally
designed for 200 men, I was exposed to the flu and have been refused treatment
(please see "TIMELINE OF EVENTS," attached) by the BOP medical staff. Despite
going into respiratory arrest on October 7, a doctor has still not even seen me.

What most people, who have never had to go to prison don't realize, is that it
is against BOP policy for prisoners to lend assistance to other inmates. BOP
protocol requires inmates to alert a Camp Officer to an inmate in need---should
that need ever arise. This policy is in place because in prison, many fights,
altercations and other attacks take place, as is well documented. This is an
important fact in my situation, because the men who came to my assistance did
so knowing full-well, they could be sent to the "hole," for lending me assistance in a life-threatening situation. The "hole," as you know, is solitary
confinement and/or a harsh lockup condition.

Holding the Fort

The BOP determines, after an "investigation," whether an incident is a fight (i.e., more than one person stays in the hole), or other altercation, which warrants the punishment of all parties involved. The typical response of BOP personnel is to send people to the hole, first, and do an investigation, later. Investigations can take from 30-60 days. As you can imagine, the impact of this policy has put a real chill on inmates helping other inmates. Additionally, because of severe resource and budget constraints, it seems like it is just eaisier for a guard to just put the problem, "out of sight, and out of mind," for a while. This allows them to buy some time, albeit at the expense of the inmate, if he is innocent.

For this overriding reason alone, I am incredibly lucky and blessed. Each of the men I bring to you, knew they could be taken straight to the hole—with other negative marks placed against them. These kinds of "negative marks" can dramatically and negatively impact the inmate's "good time," (a form of reward for good behavior, with additional time off of an inmate's sentence), and an inmate's qualification for Congressionally mandated compassionate release programs.

This puts the actions of these five inmates who saved my life, into a category which is not only decisive, but heroic. Not many people would do what they did. In fact, about 20 other men stood around and just watched, as I went into sudden respiratory arrest, with my body involuntarily going into convulstions. Further complicating a desperate and massive attempt by my body to breathe, again (as adreneline pulsed through my body and I sweated profusely), my stomach and entire chest cavity regurgitated, with digested food trying to enter my firmly sealed windpipe.

It was at this climax of guttoral-sounding agony, when men took action. What I thought was remarkable——and thought you might too, were the differences in the backgrounds, races and cultures of these five heroes. Before at least twenty other inmate witnesses, they came together to demonstrate what human decency is really all about. All of these guys are Americans and all of them were immigrants (or, their families have close ties to immigrants), in their family histories.

This is who these inmates are:

NAME	DESCRIPTION
Larry Chin	Chinese-American who has been in prison a long time.
Al Cipoletti	Italian-American who will be in prison another year, or two.
Pablo Cruz	Young Puerto Rican-American who graduated with his GED this year.
Darnell Duckett	African-American on the youthful, energetic side of life.
Joe Kearns	Welsh-American who has been in prison approximately eleven years.

I am one of the main teachers/tutors at the Fort Dix Camp (as is my teaching partner, Joe Kearns, above). During the last year, I have taught Spanish GED and English GED, along with certification classes for "English as a Second Language" ("ESL"). Both curriculums are federally mandated by Congress. I teach with passion and have tried to pour my life into the men here, which God has put in my way. Because of this, I have been fortunate to have earned the respect of men of all colors, and all credes, here in prison. I regularly teach Muslims, Christians, Hindus---you name it---we are a veritable melting pot of America. The greatest compliment I have received this past year, was not in a performance evaluation. It came from a Muslim friend of mine, who told me that I did not see men of color---only men in need.

During the last year, the Camp at Fort Dix had 20 GED graduates and 11 ESL graduates. During this time, I have regularly received "5s" in my performance evaluations, with "5" being the highest performance-level attainable.

My direct supervisor is Ms. Lindley, head of education at the Camp. My Case Officer is Mr. Cole and I have also had significant interactions with Mr. Simms, who is an Officer at Fort Dix (on the East Side, higher-level security prison facility). Mr. Simms heads up the "Save Our Youth" program. This is a community service program which reaches hundreds of children each year. I am a graduate of "SOY" and was fortunate enough to be able to speak in front of a group of over 100 high school students---trying to impress upon them the importance of remaining and being a law-abiding citizen.

After all of my interactions with hundreds of other inmates, during the last year, I can honestly tell you that many, many, and the greatest majority of men here, NEVER want to go back to a life of crime---in any manner.

Your efforts to lead and direct a multi-cultural nation have not gone without change, even deep within the bowels of the federal correctional system. However, given all the bad news the press likes to discuss regarding inmate problems, riots, escapes, etc., I thought you might like to hear this true story about a bunch of guys, all from different walks of life, who decided to work together to save one insignificant man's life.

Each man knew it would take a civilian ambulence (the military does not support the Camp) at least 30 minutes to arrive at the remote scene and location of the Fort Dix Camp. This would have been about 27 minutes too late for me.

As a result of the extraordinary actions of a few kind people, I will be able to continue my work here to educate and help reform other inmates trying to improve their lives---and NOT return to lives of crime. The Camp does not have many certification programs and GED certification is one of the key lynch pins used in helping people while they are incarcerated here.

If the objective of the BOP is to reform inmates, then I humbly submit, what greater example of reform could there be than a group of guys risking great retribution, to save a life? The fear among inmates is palpable, especially when it comes to "helping" other prisoners. With the "out-of-sight, out-of-mind" mentality firmly in place, given the clear resource constraints of the BOP, it is no wonder inmates rarely come to the assistance of others. All inmates know a black mark on his record by the BOP, can automatically disqualify him from an early release.

While I could have written a letter highly critical of the BOP system, I have chosen, instead, to write a letter to try and help solve the problem. Sometimes a reward for great and courageous behavior, can affect thousands of others living within the confines of an enclosed environment, like the BOP in the United States of America.

Thank you very much, Mr. President (and to your staff), for your consideration of these men for an early release. They have all been separated from their families for years, and I can't think of a nicer holiday present for them than an early release.

Finally, thank you for all of your efforts in prison reform. Hundreds of thousands of people send you tremendous thanks for your efforts on their behalf.

Sincerely,

Signature Blocked

Robert L. Kelly
Inmate, Fort Dix Camp
56772-056
Federal Correctional Institution
P.O. Box 2000
Joint Base MDL, New Jersey 08640-4333

TIMELINE OF EVENTS

DATE	DESCRIPTION
September 2015	A flu breakout comes upon the federal prison camp of Fort Dix, New Jersey.
9/29/15	A different inmate sick with flu, enters the prison library and sits next to inmate Kelly. There are only 14 chairs to work, read, or write in the camp library and three of these seats are reserved for typing. The sick inmate coughs on Kelly, while Kelly preparing materials for teaching his GED classes at this federal correctional institution.
9/30/15	Kelly begins to feel ill and "funny" in his chest. He starts to cough. Coughing continues to build into Friday, October 2, 2015. Kelly taking vitamins and cough syrup to try and fend off the sickness.
10/2/15	From approximately 4pm to 6pm, Camp Officer Jones orders all inmates (approximately 420) into the outside back courtyard. The compound has no shelter and the inmates are left open in the elements. Conditions are cold, wet, windy and nasty--perfect weather for making people sick. The Fort Dix Camp has not issued winter clothing to inmates, as of this date. Inmates are getting cold, wet and have no where to escape the bad weather. Kelly is shivering in the wind and the 40-50 degree weather. He only has a light wind breaker to go up against the wet, cold weather. Kelly starts to become more seriously ill this evening, after the two-hour forced stay in the back courtyard. This is a Friday night and Fort Dix Camp does not have any medical staff on duty during the weekends.
10/5/15	Kelly reports to Sick Call Triage at 6:15am, the earliest possible time. About an hour later, he is called in to see the nurse. Kelly describes his illness, while coughing uncontrollably in front of the nurse. He alerts her to the fact the guard had all the men standing outside in the cold, wet weather for two hours on Friday night. He continues to explain his medical history of scar tissue in his chest from a bronchial infection he sufferred during his 20s. He explains to the nurse that his lungs feel like they are filling up with liquid. The nurse takes Kelly's blood pressure and it was 84/46 (as best he remembers), and the nurse took the reading twice, because it

DATE	DESCRIPTION
10/5/15 (cont'd)	was so low. The nurse refused Kelly any kind of treatment and said he would need to see the "P.A." This refusal to provide any kind of decongestant, or even the most basic medication, came despite Kelly's non-stop coughing and his reporting to the nurse that he hasn't had any sleep, whatsoever, because of the cough attacking him every 20-30 seconds. The nurse agrees to put Kelly in for an X-RAY. She also agrees to schedule him to see the P.A.
10/6/15	Kelly admitted to see P.A. P.A. also refuses any kind of treatment for Kelly. The P.A. doesn't even look down the throat of Kelly (the nurse hadn't either, the previous day), despite the fact Kelly explains to the P.A. his chest and throat burned and felt like they were on fire. The P.A. checks Kelly's blood pressure, which is again low. Kelly is ordered to gargle with salt water three times a day---an order which may have contributed to the drying up and ultimate collapse of Kelly's breathing apparatus, with complete failure to be able to breathe, as a result, as further described in this letter, attached. No breathe of air could enter Kelly's lungs the evening of October 7, 2015, until other inmates came to Kelly's assistance. Before leaving the P.A., Kelly again attempts to tell her the difficulties he is having, particularly at night time, when the coughing was occuring ever 20-30 seconds. Kelly explains to the P.A. that he has been trying to sleep vertically, propped up, but it is impossible, given Kelly's upper bunk (with no headboard). Any kind of angle in sleep (versus sleeping sitting straight up) exacerbate the cough, as fluid from the infected areas drip into the breathing areas of Kelly's chest. This makes it impossible to sleep and causes extreme exhaustion of the lungs, chest and person of Kelly. Kelly then requests a second pillow to try and prop himself up with, to try and alleviate his sickened condition. The P.A. flatly refuses Kelly's imploring request. The P.A. tells Kelly, "We don't issue second pillow passes. Even if you had a hole in your back, we wouldn't issue you one." Kelly had also contracted athlete's foot from the Fort Dix showers and had requested ointment for this, also. The P.A. refused this treatment request and never even looked at Kelly's feet.
10/7/15	Kelly is taken to X RAY in the afternoon. Kelly's breathing stops at approximately 9:45pm this evening. Kelly waited another 45 minutes, or so, outside, for X-RAY.

DATE	DESCRIPTION

10/7/15
(cont'd)

When Kelly's breathing stopped without warning, it was fortunately, right after the "count." There were many inmates around, or near, Kelly's bunk, which witnessed the events which transpired, including and especially, Kelly's respiratory failure and the Camp Officer's response, once he finally came on the scene, after the inmates revived Kelly's breathing. The Camp Officer on duty directed inmate Kelly to have "Ben Gay put on your chest and the bottoms of your feet." Incredibly, he does not call for an ambulance, despite many inmates imploring him to call one. Inmate Kelly was in shock, with sweat pouring out of his body, barely able to breathe and suffering the indignity of an involuntary convulsion of his entire body, which forced him to further choke on his vomit. The vomit did not come out because his passageway was sealed tight, with no air able to get in---or out. The wheezing and guttoral sounds made were clearly those of mortal battle.

10/8/15

Kelly returns to Sick Call Triage at 6:15am and reports his breathing stopped and the trauma of the previous evening and morning. The nurse refuses any kind of medication, or treatment for Kelly. Kelly tells her there are at least 20 witenesses and even the Camp Officer arrived on the scene. She say the event is not logged into her computer! The nurse tells Kelly there is nothing she can do and can't give him any kind of medication, this over Kelly's polite objections and restatement of the facts and the witnesses present, many named by name by Kelly to her. The nurse indicates she will put "in the system" an order to see the P.A., again, who may recommend that a doctor might see him.

10/9/15

That evening, Friday, October 9, 2015, Kelly posts a "Thank You" card to all the inmates who helped him and those who gave him support, when none was forthcoming from the Bureau of Prisons Medical Staff, or Camp Officers. A copy of that card is attached---the card was purchased from the Camp Commissary by Kelly and was in his locker. Kelly knew given the extraordinary efforts of a very few men, he might night even be here, this Friday evening.

No "Call Out" is posted for Kelly to see the P.A. during the day (morning, or night) for Friday, October 9, 2015. Both the nurse and the P.A. knew the coming weekend would be a 3-day federal holiday, Columbus Day being Monday, October 12, 2015. The Fort Dix Camp has no medical staff on duty during this time period. Kelly's condition is stuck in a horrid cough, with little, or no sleep, with no meds made available to him by the medical personnel at the Camp.

302

Holding the Fort

DATE	DESCRIPTION
10/13/15	This history and request for clemency on behalf of the five individuals who helped inmate Kelly was mailed to a third party in New York, with a request to mail it directly to The President. This method of delivery was undertaken to reduce the risk of interception and potential retaliation by Bureau of Prisons personnel. Mr. Kelly is aware of the personal jeopardy in which he places himself by filing this report, but the kind of human decency demonstrated by this small, courageous group of men, deserves high mention with their maker, as well as the highest authority Mr. Kelly could think of, in the United States of America. This story is America, a country filled with many different types of people---some good, some bad and many, many rehabilitated.

This is a copy of the "Thank You" card I posted above the drinking fountain, which the men used in the "B Wing." There is a very limited selection of cards at a BOP commissary, but this was the most "manly" one I could find!

October 9, 2015

To everyone who helped me -- Thank you! I couldn't let this week end without saying, publicly, a profound thanks to everyone who helped me the evening of Oct 7, 2015. Suffering from the Fort Dix Flu for nearly ten days now, my breathing completely STOPPED on Wednesday night -- and only the quick thinking and fast action by all of you, potentially saved a life. I humbly thank all of you, and I particularly want to express my thanks to Pablo for being first on the scene, Al for his quick action to try and free my breathing, Joe for not hesitating to get the C.O. and O.J. for being so generous in his help in also opening my trachea & breathing apparatus. To all the guys I can't specifically remember and to all who have shown such God-sent support -- Thank you! My adrenaline was pumping like crazy and everything is still a bit of a blur!

Gracias a todos quien me ayudan durante la noche de Oct 7 cuando no puedo respirar. su Nunca amistad y Cual que no voy a olvidar,

Que Dios les Bendiga Siempre.

Signature Blocked.

Dios I'll always remember your kindness. God Bless You All!

303

Many men were surprised I posted it. They hadn't seen too many "Thank You" cards circulated in prison, before. I was, and am, ever grateful to the men who helped me. This card and letter to President Obama were the least I could do for their bold, unselfish behavior, which flew in the face of BOP policy.

I have only really gone into the details of my particular problems with medical, but the overall health conditions at Fort Dix were atrocious.

For purposes of this book and to bring attention to another really serious matter, *the water* the men are forced to drink at the prison is highly suspect. Fort Dix is located on one of the oldest military bases in America, and the drinking & cooking water is believed to be toxic---among the men. I asked Mr. Lecorchick about the quality of the water we were drinking, and he said, "Well you asked the right guy. I went over myself to the testing facility and the water meets government specifications."

I asked him, "Why do you then, continue to drink bottled water here, Mr. Lecorchick?" He was in the classroom, and a bunch of students were "all-eyeballs" and "all-ears"---waiting for his response. Mr. Lecorchick just slinked away, however, without uttering a single response.

Inmates who work on the base itself, come back and report regularly on how there are big signs posted all over the military base:

"DO NOT DRINK THE WATER!"

The BOP doesn't believe this is a problem for the men under their captivity, and supposed care, even though every single officer in the prison <u>only</u> drinks bottled water---just like Officer Lecorchick. The government buys it---it's free for them!

The inmates, however, must drink from the water supply out of the building's piping system, which draws from the underground water contaminated by the military base. It is truly disgusting the BOP doesn't care, at all, about the key health requirement for all human beings----good water. Even the cheap filters the BOP claims are "great" for the water are not changed regularly. But, the key question is, even with a filter, why do the guards, the officers and the administration of the BOP at Fort Dix, only drink bottled water?

It is a well-known fact among inmates, guys who are "down" for a long time often get cancer there, and others who leave, often get it at home---years afterward.

Once again---the BOP's response? "Nothing to see hear, folks. Move on!"

It is another example of the horrible conditions the men live with, from a health perspective at Fort Dix, and demonstrates an attitude of extreme indifference, as well as physical and psychological cruelty toward inmate-citizens of the United States of America.

While many men at Fort Dix and in the federal prison system committed crimes, most of the men were not sentenced to death by their judge, or even a sentence which could reduce their life span, as a result of poor treatment---or no treatment at all---as was the situation in my case.

After I nearly died, the physician's assistant who told me to drink salt water, Ms. Mello, was quietly transferred somewhere else---or, she quit. After my near-death experience, the BOP also decided to begin providing me with some basic care.

If it hadn't been for the help provided me by the men, I would probably be dead, as you can surmise from the details I sent to President Obama.

To my knowledge, none of these great men who helped me--- heroes, one and all in my book, received any mercy, or any credit for saving my life. If you ever meet or know, any of them, please let each man know how much of a "stand-up guy" he was in the fall of 2015.

The medical treatment is absolutely deplorable in prison and the best advice is...DON'T GET SICK, because you're on your own if you do. Better yet, don't go to prison in the first place!

In the following pages, you can see my actual medical records, where two days before my breathing stopped, I had reported to sick call, in deplorable condition. As you can read, there is obvious malpractice, which would be an easy case to prosecute in our civil system, if these incompetent medical staff personnel weren't hiding under the umbrella of the BOP.

Because of this (i.e., their hiding under the cloak of "government employee"), there is no retribution for these people, or the government, even though their lack of care and horrid advice would nearly see me die, two days later.

I wonder if a civil rights lawyer might ever look into this---he, or she, might find one heck of a class action lawsuit among the many prisoners who are poorly treated, and whose civil rights seem to be clearly violated.

Bureau of Prisons
Health Services
Clinical Encounter

Inmate Name: KELLY, ROBERT		Reg #:	56772-056
Date of Birth: 05/16/1956	Sex: M Race: WHITE	Facility:	FTD
Encounter Date: 10/05/2015 12:21	Provider: Bynum, Mary RN	Unit:	V02

Nursing - Sick Call Note encounter performed at Health Services.

SUBJECTIVE:

COMPLAINT 1   **Provider:** Bynum, Mary RN

Chief Complaint: Cold or Flu Symptoms

Subjective: IM with hx. of bronchitis presents with persistent cough x 5 days. Lungs are clear. IM advised to hydrate with fluids and given 1 day idle.

Pain: No

OBJECTIVE:

Temperature:

Date	Time	Fahrenheit	Celsius	Location	Provider
10/05/2015	12:22 FTD	98.0	36.7		Bynum, Mary RN

Pulse:

Date	Time	Rate Per Minute	Location	Rhythm	Provider
10/05/2015	12:22 FTD	75			Bynum, Mary RN

Respirations:

Date	Time	Rate Per Minute	Provider
10/05/2015	12:22 FTD	14	Bynum, Mary RN

Blood Pressure:

Date	Time	Value	Location	Position	Cuff Size	Provider
10/05/2015	12:22 FTD	90/50				Bynum, Mary RN

SaO2:

Date	Time	Value(%)	Air	Provider
10/05/2015	12:22 FTD	98		Bynum, Mary RN

Exam:

General
  Appearance
    Yes: Appears Well

Eyes
  General
    Yes: PERRLA

Pulmonary
  Observation/Inspection
    Yes: Within Normal Limits

Cardiovascular
  Observation
    Yes: Within Normal Limits

ASSESSMENT:

Cold Symptoms

IM presents with persistent cough x 5 days. Lungs are clear. IM skni pale and has no other complaints. IM states he

Bureau of Prisons
Health Services
Clinical Encounter

Inmate Name: KELLY, ROBERT		Reg #: 56772-056
Date of Birth: 05/16/1956	Sex: M Race: WHITE	Facility: FTD
Encounter Date: 10/06/2015 10:43	Provider: Mello, Christina NP-BC	Unit: V02

Mid Level Provider - Sick Call Note encounter performed at Health Services.

SUBJECTIVE:

COMPLAINT 1   Provider: Mello, Christina NP-BC

Chief Complaint: Skin Problem

Subjective: IM here for MLP sick call with complaint of athlete's foot and requesting extra pillow. Review of commissary list x 3 months shows purchase of athlete's foot cream. IM stated that symptoms improved with cream but has not resolved. Denies open wounds, exudate, involvement of toenails.

IM has back pain from history of surgery of back, was told by counselor that he should go to medical to request "pillow pass".

Cough and malaise x 1 week with worsening after standing in rain on Friday. Salt water QD, AIM rinse x BID. Denies fever, chills, sweating. IM has chest x-ray pending for tomorrow.

Pain: Not Applicable

OBJECTIVE:

Temperature:

Date	Time	Fahrenheit	Celsius	Location	Provider
10/06/2015	10:54 FTD	98.3	36.8		Mello, Christina NP-BC

Pulse:

Date	Time	Rate Per Minute	Location	Rhythm	Provider
10/06/2015	10:54 FTD	66			Mello, Christina NP-BC

Blood Pressure:

Date	Time	Value	Location	Position	Cuff Size	Provider
10/06/2015	10:54 FTD	101/67				Mello, Christina NP-BC

Exam:
 General
  Affect
   Yes: Pleasant, Cooperative
  Appearance
   Yes: Appears Well, Alert and Oriented x 3
   No: Appears Distressed
 Skin
  General
   Yes: Within Normal Limits
   No: Warmth, Clammy, Diaphoretic
 Pulmonary
  Observation/Inspection
   Yes: Within Normal Limits
 Cardiovascular

The BOP shades their reports to appear as if I was there for a skin problem, despite my vociferous complaining about my bronchial condition. This report was taken by Ms. Mello, who told me to gargle with salt water, which I believe caused my breathing apparatus to shut down, nearly killing me.

Inmate Name: KELLY, ROBERT
Date of Birth: 05/16/1956
Encounter Date: 10/06/2015 10:43

Sex: M Race: WHITE
Provider: Mello, Christina NP-BC

Reg #: 56772-056
Facility: FTD
Unit: V02

Exam:

Observation
Yes: Within Normal Limits

Musculoskeletal
Gait
Yes: Normal Gait

Exam Comments

IM sits comfortable during exam, does not demonstrate respiratory distress, able to speak in paragraphs, occasional non productive cough heard.

ASSESSMENT:

Cough, 786.2 - Current, Temporary/Acute, Initial

Low back pain, lumbago, 724.2 - Current, Chronic, Not Improved/Same

PLAN:

Disposition:
Follow-up at Sick Call as Needed

Other:

Cough: IM has no systemic symptoms, exhibits symptoms of flu, education given that antibiotics are not prescribed for viral colds. If x-ray shows pneumonia will prescribe antibiotics. IM informed that if there is no presence of infection through systemic signs, antibiotics are not recommended prior to x-ray, antibiotics like all medications have side effects and should not be prescribed without supporting clinical or diagnostic evidence. IM has 1.5 days remaining on medical idle. Advised to cat nap as frequently as possible to allow his body to heal, lay on side to decrease chest discomfort.

Athletes foot: IM encouraged to continue cream at night when feet are not in shoes, wear breathable socks or no socks. Talcum powder during the day to prevent overly moist conditions in boots.

Pillow pass: Not available at this institution. IM advised to use towel or other soft item as pillow.

IM verbalized discontent with not being prescribed antibiotics, additional pillow, or potent prescriptive antifungal treatment.

Patient Education Topics:

Date Initiated	Format	Handout/Topic	Provider	Outcome
10/06/2015	Counseling	Plan of Care	Mello, Christina	Verbalizes Understanding

Copay Required: Yes **Cosign Required:** Yes
Telephone/Verbal Order: No

Completed by Mello, Christina NP-BC on 10/06/2015 11:12
Requested to be cosigned by Newland, R. MD/CD.
Cosign documentation will be displayed on the following page.

Despite my report to medical, my breathing stopped on the 7th and you can see the BOPs report is "Nothing to see here!" In the VA it is said the government "Denies, denies, denies until you die." It is even worse for Bureau of Prison inmates.

309

Note the BOPs nondescript explanation of near death "...he had episode of difficulty breathing witnessed by other IMs..."

Bureau of Prisons
Health Services
Clinical Encounter

Inmate Name: KELLY, ROBERT		Reg #: 56772-056
Date of Birth: 05/16/1956	Sex: M Race: WHITE	Facility: FTD
Encounter Date: 10/08/2015 07:19	Provider: Bynum, Mary RN	Unit: V02

Nursing - Sick Call Note encounter performed at Health Services.

SUBJECTIVE:

   COMPLAINT 1   Provider: Bynum, Mary RN
   Chief Complaint: Cold or Flu Symptoms
   Subjective: IM states he continues to have cough.
   Pain: No

OBJECTIVE:
Temperature:

Date	Time	Fahrenheit	Celsius	Location	Provider
10/08/2015	08:26 FTD	98.0	36.7	Tympanic	Bynum, Mary RN

Pulse:

Date	Time	Rate Per Minute	Location	Rhythm	Provider
10/08/2015	08:26 FTD	70	Via Machine		Bynum, Mary RN

Respirations:

Date	Time	Rate Per Minute	Provider
10/08/2015	08:26 FTD	14	Bynum, Mary RN

Blood Pressure:

Date	Time	Value	Location	Position	Cuff Size	Provider
10/08/2015	08:26 FTD	100/65				Bynum, Mary RN

SaO2:

Date	Time	Value(%)	Air	Provider
10/08/2015	08:26 FTD	100		Bynum, Mary RN

Exam:
   General
      Appearance
         Yes: Appears Distressed
   Head
      General
         Yes: Symmetry of Motor Function
   Pulmonary
      Observation/Inspection
         Yes: Within Normal Limits
   Cardiovascular
      Observation
         Yes: Within Normal Limits, Normal Rate, Regular Rhythm

ASSESSMENT:

   No Significant Findings/No Apparent Distress
   IM states he continues to have cough. States last evening he had episode of difficulty breathing witnessed by other IMs.
   Chest xray is negative and lungs are clear. 02 sat is 98%. Temp 97.7.

Generated 10/08/2015 08:36 by Bynum, Mary RN   Bureau of Prisons - FTD   Page 1 of 2

Advising IM that he has a cold and it will run its course. Continue fluids and follow up at sick call.

PLAN:

Disposition:
    Follow-up at Sick Call as Needed

Patient Education Topics:

Date Initiated Format	Handout/Topic	Provider	Outcome
10/08/2015 Counseling	Access to Care	Bynum, Mary	Verbalizes Understanding

Copay Required: No   Cosign Required: No
Telephone/Verbal Order: No

Completed by Bynum, Mary RN on 10/08/2015 08:36

It took a month to see a real doctor, as Mello and Bynum were PAs/Nurses. The physician who saw me was the one who decided to send me for a colonoscopy.

Bureau of Prisons
Health Services
Clinical Encounter

Chronic Care - Chronic Care Clinic encounter performed at Health Services.
SUBJECTIVE:

    COMPLAINT 1   Provider: Sceusa, Carl MD/CCHP
        Chief Complaint: ORTHOPEDIC/RHEUMATOLOGY
        Subjective: Patient is not taking OTC meds. 58 yo male with hx of 3 back surgeries with crushed disc and
                     Sciatica like symptoms to the left foot. Last surgery was done June 29,2010. He has hx of L4-
                     5, L5-S1 Microlaminectomy and
                     decompression. He takes aspirin and Ibuprofen for back pain and they help he says. He has
                     hx of MVA in 2010 and has hx of HA's every now and then. He says he does not like to take
                     any major medications. He has been given exercise pamphlets with Instructions for Back
                     exercises.
        Pain: No

    COMPLAINT 2   Provider: Sceusa, Carl MD/CCHP
        Chief Complaint: GENERAL
        Subjective: IM s/p respiratory illness that was associated with coughing fits to the pt of not being able to
                     catch his breath. His cxr was negative and he had no fever,chills wheezing
        Pain: No

Seen for clinic(s): Orthopedic/Rheumatology

311

Holding the Fort

Inmate Name: KELLY, ROBERT
Date of Birth: 05/16/1956
Encounter Date: 11/09/2015 11:29

Sex: M Race: WHITE
Provider: Sceusa, Carl MD/CCHP

Reg #: 56772-056
Facility: FTD
Unit: V02

ENDO/DM2: ---TSH=7.3   FT4=   HGBA1C=5.2   FGLUC=115
HEM:---WBC=5.6   HGB= 13.9   HCT=41.1   PLT CT=217

ASSESSMENT:

Bronchitis, acute, 466.0 - Resolved, History/Resolved, Initial

Cough, 786.2 - Current, Temporary/Acute, Not Assessed

Hypothyroidism unspecified, 244.9 - Current, Chronic, Not Assessed

Low back pain, lumbago, 724.2 - Current, Chronic, Marked Improvement

Sciatica, 724.3 - Current, Chronic, Not Improved/Same

PLAN:

New Laboratory Requests:

Details	Frequency	Due Date	Priority
Chronic Care Clinics-Endocrine/Lipid-CBC w/diff	One Time	12/16/2015 00:00	Routine
Chronic Care Clinics-Endocrine/Lipid-Comprehensive Metabolic Profile			
Chronic Care Clinics-Endocrine/Lipid-Lipid Profile			
Lab Tests-H-Hemoglobin A1C			
Chronic Care Clinics-Endocrine/Lipid-TSH			
Chronic Care Clinics-Endocrine/Lipid-T4, Free			
Lab Tests-P-PSA, Total			

New Consultation Requests:

Consultation/Procedure	Target Date	Scheduled Target Date	Priority	Translator	Language
Specialty Procedure - Offsite	02/10/2016		Routine	No	

Subtype:
    GAST Colonoscopy
Reason for Request:
    SCREENING COLONOSCOPY FH COLON CA <50
Provisional Diagnosis:
    R/O Colon CA

Schedule:

Activity	Date Scheduled	Scheduled Provider
Optometry Exam	11/09/2015 00:00	Optometrist
Chronic Care Visit	11/09/2016 00:00	Physician 01

Inmate Name: KELLY, ROBERT
Date of Birth: 05/16/1956
Encounter Date: 11/09/2015 11:29

Sex: M Race: WHITE
Provider: Sceusa, Carl MD/CCHP

Reg #: 56772-056
Facility: FTD
Unit: V02

Disposition:

Follow-up at Sick Call as Needed
Follow-up in 1 Year

Other:

---Sick Call prn---CCC follow-up 1 year
---IM told he should get yearly FLU Shot
---Stressed importance of medication compliance---Stressed importance of keeping appointments and doing blood work when scheduled
---Yearly Optometry Exam
---Start Colon Cancer Screening at age 50
---Importance of Diet and exercise to keep weight and BMI normal
---Eating low fat and watching sugar intake to prevent or at least hasten DM from developing

Patient Education Topics:

Date Initiated	Format	Handout/Topic	Provider	Outcome
11/09/2015	Counseling	Access to Care	Sceusa, Carl	Verbalizes Understanding
11/09/2015	Counseling	Compliance - Treatment	Sceusa, Carl	Verbalizes Understanding
11/09/2015	Counseling	Diagnosis	Sceusa, Carl	Verbalizes Understanding
11/09/2015	Counseling	Exercise	Sceusa, Carl	Verbalizes Understanding

Copay Required: No   Cosign Required: No
Telephone/Verbal Order: No

Completed by Sceusa, Carl MD/CCHP on 11/09/2015 14:23

Generated 11/09/2015 14:23 by Sceusa, Carl MD/CCHP   Bureau of Prisons - FTD   Page 4 of 4

It is a sad state of affairs, when you are ordered to spend 27-months in a minimum security prison camp, and what you wind-up with, is convulsion and a near death sentence.

Holding the Fort

CHAPTER 22

"Ace" Hit With The Bricks

One inmate in particular, "Ace," whom I talked about previously, was certainly a guy who didn't have any interest in anything Joe or I had to say when he first showed up to our GED class. A lot of the men thought Ace was a bit "out there," but deep down, as it turns out, Ace only wanted to go home. He missed West Virginia, very much.

Ace probably made a lot of money selling Meth during his lifetime, but his education had really come from prison---and not in classes either. He was hard core when he arrived in Camp, and he will be hard core when he is released.

I provided you an idea of how his mindset was, especially when he first entered our classroom when he told Joe and me, "If you guys try and teach me any of that teaching sh**, I'll bash you over the head with a brick..."

Ace was powerfully built, although not as strong as Dee Williams, or Mr. Love, but Ace always lifted weights and ran outside. I think he must have been a great athlete when he was younger, but he looked great for being in his later 40s.

Despite his background and rough manner in which he carried himself, I noticed something fundamentally different about Ace. When he spoke, he spoke honestly, directly and sincerely.

Don't get me wrong, usually, he was really threatening, too! But, there seemed like something else was going on inside of this man---something fundamentally different from most of the other men in the Camp.

I caught some of the things he said, which made me believe his Mother or his Father, when he grew up, must have talked about church, or Jesus. Although he had sinned, as we all had, I had the Spirit telling me to pay attention to this man.

Often in class, one of the ways I would engage men would be to ask them what they want to do when they "get out." Many of them have plans for building a business---and legal ones, at that.

Ace was no different in this regard. One day, I was going around the room asking what the guys wanted to do when they started their lives over again, outside of prison walls. As I queried the men, one of my other favorite students, Mr. Love, responded immediately and loudly:

"I'M GONNA' HAVE A GYM!"

I then took the class into a direction which actually showed Mr. Love and the rest of the class how to build a business plan, how to create a brand to make his gym unique, and then how he could *differentiate* his gym from the sea of competition in the marketplace.

This was quite effective and had an impact on the men. They paid rapt attention to these kinds of discussions, which also allowed me to continue to drill them on the fundamentals of English, math, social studies and science.

I know...for a Christian, I was pretty sneaky!

I will spare you the details about Mr. Love's gym, but it will be a great one, someday, I'm sure.   At my prodding to be "creative," Mr. Love even designed a logo with a huge, massively-strong caricature of himself.   The image portrayed this cartoon-like-hulk of a character, in Mr. Love's image, squeezing a fat tree trunk with his hand and shattering it like a toothpick! Mr. Love, it turns out, was a pretty talented artist. He was a genius, creatively speaking, because his brand concept was innovative and awesome, with the drawing itself, also being quite remarkable.

Before Mr. Love went off in his creative path, I only had told him to think about his natural strengths.   I said, "Mr. Love, you've never done this before, but creating a brand for yourself should be interesting.   Just think about your natural strengths. From my perspective, they are: 1) Your brains---you're a pretty smart guy, 2) Your physique---you are a powerhouse weight lifter and great athlete and 3) You have an extraordinary ability to communicate and coach other people."

Mr. Love was *extremely* aggressive (think NFL linebacker or defensive end!) when it came to coaching other men.   This was a talent you can't learn, and only the best coaches around, have it.   Mr. Love had the skill to be tough and aggressive to inspire performance, yet he also had the interpersonal skills needed to make sure everyone didn't get angry and reject his advice.

It is a rare talent and a fine line.   Mr. Love had it down in spades, especially when it came to weight lifting.

He was a leader among a group of men who indeed desired to lift weights, together.   Many say they might have even lifted weights in the back of the yard, even though this would have been strictly against regulations. I really can't say where they might have gone to exercise, if and when they really did lift weights. One thing was certain, however: wherever Mr. Love went, discipline and hard work followed.

Lifting weights in prison is kind of a time-honored tradition--- just like a prison softball, or football team. Since weights were against regulations at the Camp, certain men might even have considered smuggling in weights, or they might even have thought to make them out of materials they could hijack from the military base. After all, being on work detail did have its "benefits." Personally, I have no certain idea who actually might even have done such a thing, but magically, weights would show up in Camp and men would sure use them.

But, like most good things at Fort Dix, one day the BOP did a massive search of the entire back "yard," and they confiscated weights and any other contraband they could find. The men laughed it off it seemed, because if inmates are nothing else, they are ingenious when it comes to hiding things from the guards!

The very next day, men were out pressing iron (or, in their case, cement blocks) once again, in the back yard of the Camp. Everyone got a good laugh out of that one.

While we were discussing Mr. Love's plans for his gym and developing his income statement, cost-of-goods-sold calculation (he had an energy drink he wanted to market), marketing budget, etc., Ace was in his normal seat at the back of the classroom.

He suddenly lit up like a Christmas tree.

Ace had been observing everything I was teaching and he saw some real ideas coming to light, with some real potential solutions being exchanged in the classroom, between Mr. Love, myself and the other men.

He suddenly blurted out in his distinct West Virginia accent:

> "Hey Kelly! I want to create a beauty product which keeps ya' young! I'm gonna' put my face on the bottle (Ace is a handsome guy and does not look like he is in his late 40s), and fill it with vitamin E cream---along with some other sh**! ...and I'm gonna' make a fortune!"

I could have been knocked over by a feather, because Ace had never participated significantly in class before. I immediately leapt on this great opportunity and told Ace, "That's a GREAT idea! Now, what about your business plan?"

We then went through the same exercise I undertook with Mr. Love. We went through sales projections, distribution, manufacturing, costs, marketing, sales, etc.

He hadn't thought all of this quite through, yet, but I walked his brain out of his kitchen---the place he was planning on making his beauty product and Vitamin E mixture---and out into a manufacturing environment---where he would have UPC codes and a bona fide capability of selling the products into the big box stores, and/or the gift market. I taught him how NOT to think like a kitchen-based drug manufacturer---and how *to start* thinking about a legitimate business which required marketing and outsourced production. We went over a great deal, including how to attend trade shows, and meet hundreds of potential buyers and store owners, in one shot.

Ace got excited about all this, and I hope one day he executes on his plan. If he keeps his costs down and can start distribution, even slowly, he could do quite well. Margins are sky-high in the beauty business---probably about the same as what he had when he was selling illegal drugs! Competition is also intense, but you never know. Inmates can be pretty clever.

Anyway, this segue into a man's life was truly remarkable, because this particular guy was one tough cookie. He began to trust me, and we were able to talk about things outside of class, from time-to-time. Some of these, I believed, reached him in some of the most important areas of his soul.

Over the course of the next several months, into the summer of 2016, right up until I would leave Fort Dix, Ace would quietly call me over in the classroom, and have me check on certain problems he was working on in math, or in other subjects.

I was really proud of him. He was also smarter than anyone else in the class, because his answers were quietly, nearly always, correct. He didn't want anyone to know, however, so I kept my mouth shut---at least for the most part. Ace liked his privacy and protected it, as near as I could tell.

In one of our last discussions, before I was released, I turned to Ace, out in the back of the prison yard, and said:

> "You know, Ace, I'm leaving soon, but did you ever notice the kinds of guys *Jesus* chose to be his disciples? They were real men. These guys were fishermen and workers. They were also, very much like **YOU** at their core. They were **honest** men. In fact, they remind me a lot of **YOU**."

Ace looked at me, and I continued:

> "You are one of the most direct, candid and honest men in the Camp. You speak your mind, and never lie. These are the foundations on which God works, sometimes."

At this moment, I gave him a small, pocket-sized Bible. I can say I could feel his emotions running deep when he said, with incredible sincerity and graciousness:

> "Kelly...I never had no Bible before...thank you. I will read it."

He shook my hand, and he walked inside. Ace wasn't a man of a lot of words.

Ace had been sentenced and been in prison for years. He had shared with me during some of our conversations, how he would *never* sell Meth again, *ever*, as he had enough of prison. He said he NEVER wanted to go back.

It's important to remember when he spoke to me, I was just another inmate. I certainly would have nothing to do with him leaving prison anytime sooner than his sentencing end-date. As a result, his words and thoughts were the words of an honest man confiding in another man he trusted. I hope Ace does great things and he has a great life when he gets back home to his family, in West Virginia.

But even after this occurred, like most tough inmates, Ace *still* continued to put on appearances in the classroom.

After all, he would lose his entire reputation if he became known as a guy who was paying attention in class!

I had a great laugh at this, because in the very last days of my teaching at Fort Dix, immediately before my release date, and knowing he and I were friends, Ace *still* shouted, in front of the whole class to hear:

> **"Kelly, I'm just gonna' have to take you in the bafroom' and smash you in the head...that's what would happen to you in the medium for doing all this teaching sh**!"**

The "medium" is a higher-level security prison.

When I heard him shout this, I laughed 'til it hurt---Ace was smiling too, he was kidding around and doing a little "playin'."

What a difference a year makes. Prison had changed him, and he was definitely seeing something in life, other than dealing Meth. Ace would wind up with my Ryrie Study Bible, too. I gave it to him just before I left prison. He was humbled and touched to receive it, this I can promise you. This is the version of the Ryrie Study Bible I used while in prison. Ace owns it now.

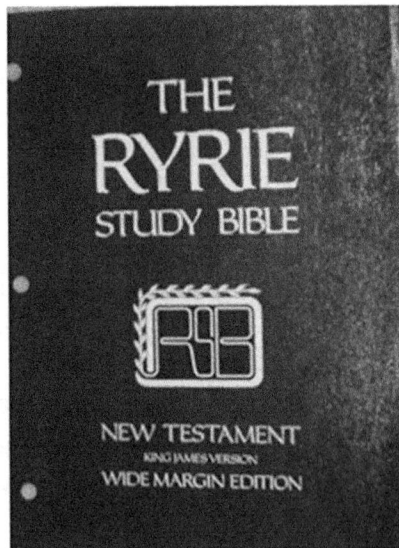

THE RYRIE STUDY BIBLE

NEW TESTAMENT
KING JAMES VERSION
WIDE MARGIN EDITION

CHAPTER 23

THE STONE WALL OF SILENCE

What am I doing now, other than writing a book about my experience, you might ask? Well, I have programmed on my compuer, the Turtle system I created and taught the inmates at Fort Dix. I've made some great improvements and enhancements to the system, as well.

As you can imagine, trying to get a job, after you have been to prison, is pretty much impossible---especially for a former CEO. Society treats you with what I call:

"The Stone Wall of Silence."

You can send hundreds of letters and resumes out, and no one wants to touch you---regardless of the circumstances you were arrested for, and/or plead guilty to.

The highly respected federal judge in New York for the Southern District of Manhattan (the same district I was sentenced in, where prosecutors tout an over 98% conviction rate under Preet Bharara's prosecutorial direction while he was the District Attorney there) wrote an interesting book titled, Why Innocent People Plead Guilty.

Since I forever have to plead "guilty," and cannot appeal my conviction pursuant to the terms of my plea bargain agreement,

I hope Judge Rakoff's words help educate the world at large, as to what has been going on between the prosecutor's office, the defendants in their cross-hares, and the judges involved with the cases---in New York City, especially. The devastation to lives, as a result of "plea-bargain" pleadings, is monumental.

Here are brief excerpts of portions of the lengthy review of Judge Rakoff's work, by the "New York Review of Books."

Source: http://www.nybooks.com/articles/2014/11/20/why-innocent-people-plead-guilty/

The New York Review of Books
Why Innocent People Plead Guilty
Jed S. Rakoff

NOVEMBER 20, 2014 ISSUE

"The criminal justice system in the United States today bears little relationship to what the Founding Fathers contemplated, what the movies and television portray, or what the average American believes...

To the Founding Fathers, the critical element in the system was the jury trial...a shield against tyranny.

...The Sixth Amendment guarantees that 'in all criminal prosecutions, the accused shall enjoy the right to a speedy and public trial, by an impartial jury.'...He may be convicted only if an impartial jury of his peers is unanimously of the view that he is guilty beyond a reasonable doubt and so states, publicly, in its verdict...

...The answer may be found in Jefferson's perception that a criminal justice system that is secret and government-dictated ultimately invites abuse and even tyranny. Specifically, I would suggest that the current system of prosecutor-determined plea bargaining invites the following objections.

First, it is one-sided...before we deprive a person of his liberty, he will have his 'day in court,'...numerous guarantees of this fair-minded approach are embodied in our Constitution...because of the Founding Fathers' experience with the rigged British system of colonial justice. Is not the plea bargain system...similarly rigged?

Second, and closely related, the system of plea bargains dictated by prosecutors is the product of largely secret negotiations behind closed doors in the prosecutor's office, and is subject to almost no review...Such a secretive system inevitably invites arbitrary results.

Third, and possibly the gravest objection of all, the prosecutor-dictated plea bargain system, by creating such inordinate pressures to enter into plea bargains, appears to have led a significant number of defendants to plead guilty to crimes they never actually committed."

As most people know, and can interpret from Judge Rakoff's words, the criminal justice system is broken. Bankers are let off scot-free, while little guys in particular, have been picked on. This was to make up for the Department of Justice's failure to prosecute *a single executive* in the banking system---even though their institutions were found guilty of criminal fraud.

This also can be laid directly at the feet of none other than--- Preet Bahrara, his pack of attorneys, and the U.S. Justice System during the nine years prior to President Trump's election.

This prompts the important question, did the plea-bargain system cause *me* to enter a guilty plea, to avoid the dangers inherent in the system?

Hmmm...that's a tough one...let me think about that for a second!

I was 58-years old when I was sentenced, and I was at the peak of my career, with at least ten great years ahead of me. I was being charged with two 20-year counts---facing up to a 40-year sentence, theoretically.

Realistically, if I went to trial, and lost in the Southern District of Manhattan, where Preet Bahrara's vicious attack dogs and unfriendly-to-CEO juries sport the 98% conviction rate in the post-Bernie-Madoff era, I would be looking at a 10-12 year sentence. I can tell you when imprisoned at Fort Dix, I knew men facing similar sentencing terms (who went to trial and LOST), and received sentences of 20+ years! I kid you not.

Joe Kerns is an example of this specifically---and I CAN comment on his case.

Joe is 100% INNOCENT! The people involved with prosecuting him and conspiratorially coming after Joe gave him, effectively, a life sentence. Joe has been in and out of the hospital while incarcerated, and was even taken out on a stretcher at Fort Dix, while I was in prison, on March 2, 2016.

To a man, everyone was concerned for Joe. Joe wound up returning to the classroom about thirty days later, after receiving an implant of a medical device/pace maker to control his now diagnosed, arrhythmia in his heart.

I wish Joe a million-million (that's a trillion!) stars in heaven. He certainly deserves them, as I see it here from the cheap seats.

Regarding my decision to enter a plea bargain agreement, my thinking was IF I went to a jury trial and LOST, I was looking at a life sentence. After seeing Joe near death, after seeing Shabaz die from cancer, while imprisoned (yes, the same Shabaz who called me, "The White Devil,"), and after seeing many other men suffer horribly due to poor medical treatment while incarcerated, I have no question, faced with my circumstances, I made the best choice I could, given the hostile-to-CEO environment found especially in New York city juries.

I remember I thought to myself at the time, *"Regardless of everything my attorneys and accountants had done to try and make sure everything was disclosed on the related-party transactions with Rymatics and WWEBNET---I don't like the odds against me in the Southern District of New York."*

By the way, if any reader wants to go on the Internet, or go in person to Companies House in London and see Direct Choice TV Communications Ltd. financial statements publicly available with complete disclosures of related-party transactions going back to 2004, they were all on file there before I went to prison. Additionally, a person could go to Edgar and see the publicly-filed Form 10 statement, with the SEC, disclosing the transactions there, as well. The Form 10 was filed when we were trying to go public on the American Stock Exchange.

These are a matter of public record, and exist even in civil litigation here in the U.S., where I actually won my cases against shareholders. I fought to the "death" in civil litigation, because I wasn't facing a life sentence in these battles---they were monetary in nature and I fought with full force and effect for my defense, as a result. And I won, using the law to defend myself.

If I was robbing people---why would I publicly disclose it and permit a private company (Direct Choice TV Communications Ltd) to be audited---when it was not a requirement to do so? Why try and go public in America, at all? Why file a Form 10? I could have brought everything public in Europe because we were originally based there!

To even the most casual observer of my situation, with respect to my prosecution, and as I noted at the end of chapter four of this book, Shakespeare's play <u>Hamlet</u> comes to mind, when Marcellus says:

"Something is rotten in the State of Denmark!"

In any event, the flip side of fighting against the state and rolling the dice in the Southern District of Manhattan was for me to enter into a plea bargain, which saves the government a lot of money, and then counts on me to throw myself on the mercy of the court. Ultimately, this is the decision I made.

As you know, I received a 27-month sentence. Because of good behavior and halfway house time, I served 21-months inside Fort Dix. Perhaps Judge Crotty looked at the disclosure information and showed mercy in the 27-month sentence, I don't know.

What I do know, is that through it all, God would be my General at the fort, and I would try and do the best job I could for Him---as I always have tried to do in my life.

I hated going to prison. I hated being separated from my family and loved ones. I hated having my life destroyed, in every conceivable way. I hated going from a highly respected CEO with a technology which had beaten Netflix, to now a Scarlett-lettered Felon.

But, I am alive---and I had an amazing opportunity to be around men who needed my help, many of whom came to appreciate it...and this was *my* payday.

There is one final note regarding my situation. On March 7, 2016, shortly after Joe had been whisked away to the hospital, I was teaching my guys during our 12:30 p.m. class, alone (Joe was in the hospital for a month). These men were great. We had some amazing discussions and we all tried to be of fairly good cheer together, despite the situation in prison and our sorrowful separation from family and loved ones. The students were men of the street---and then, there was me---teaching the class.

One of the men, Mr. Gray, a Muslim friend of mine, was sitting in the back of the room---at his favorite corner table. He owned this corner and woe be to any many who would even *think* to try and take it over at the 12:30 p.m. class!

On this day, completely unprompted, Mr. Gray stated loudly and flatly, while directing his remarks to me when I was at the white board, in front of "Ace" (the subject of Chapter 22 in this book), Mr. Brown (a classic rock star in class when it came to discussing politics!), Jeffrey Eugene (another great guy), the amazing Dillon Edwards and the rest of the GED class:

"Mr. Kelly...I don't believe you did anything wrong to be in prison..."

Mr. Gray always called me "Mr. Kelly" And I always called him, "Mr. Gray." It was a sign of mutual respect we had for each other, with him being a Muslim, and me a Christian.

Either Mr. Brown or Ace, seconded his opinion, with what seemed like a murmur of approval from the rest of the class.

I wasn't prepared, at all, for this. All I could think to do was to lower my head and I tried not to show the tears which welled up in my eyes.

These men had just paid me an honor and showed me great respect. While my head was lowered, I tried to blink the water out of my eyes.

I know Tom Hanks coined the phrase, "There is no crying in baseball!" but, there *REALLY* is no crying in prison. In a few moments, after I composed myself, I lifted my head up. I looked each and every one of them in the eyes.

The entire classroom was waiting patiently for my response, and the room had become completely silent.

I then pointed to **each** of them and said, with conviction:

> "Well...that would have been a shame, because then I wouldn't have met *YOU...YOU...YOU...YOU...YOU...YOU, YOU and YOU...!*"

I pointed to each and every man in the room. In prison, no one has to say anything nice about anyone, this is for sure, but these

330

fine men did. These fine men have great souls and I know they have huge hearts. These men helped *me* get through prison and all the rigors and difficulties prison brings upon a person who is caught in the jaws of the U.S. Justice system.

I am sincerely and ever grateful to all the men who were there for me, and every inmate I met. Some hated what I stood for, I know, but most, at least respected me.

That was something, I guess.

Today, with all my money taken from me, and no job to look forward to, I once again find myself working hard to create something from scratch, which may be valuable. Retirement is not in the cards, as there is no 401k plan, there is no IRA and there are no hidden bank accounts.

But, I continue to press forward, relentlessly, to try and help my loved ones, and those around me, into the future. At sixty years old, I am blessed with a sharp mind and I would like to use the Turtle system I created, along with my knowledge of the financial markets to find success, as we did at Fort Dix.

Obtaining capital is a real challenge when society has imprinted on your chest the scarlet letters of "P," "I," "C" and "F"--- Prisoner, Inmate, Convict and Felon.

Hopefully, the perfect partner will be sent to me, who will help launch Turtle Trading and Turtle U. "Turtle U" is a school I thought of opening, while incarcerated, for people who want to learn to trade on Wall Street.

For the men I had to leave behind and with whom the government says I can never have contact with again, I leave you all with the following old, Gaelic blessing:

MAY THE ROAD
RISE UP TO MEET YOU

May the road rise up to meet you.
May the wind be always at your back.
May the sun shine warm upon your face;
the rains fall soft upon your fields
and until we meet again,
may God hold you in the palm of His hand.

To all the men at Fort Dix, and others like you, YOU are truly the ones "Holding the Fort," and I dedicate this book's memory to all of you.

Take solace in what Jesus promised the criminal on the Cross when the criminal put his faith in Jesus on that solemn day:

"Today you will be with me in paradise," (Luke 23:43)

Good luck and God speed, men.

The End.

Author's Personal Note

Invitation to Make a Commitment

<u>Holding the Fort</u> is a work of non-fiction and is the true story of Robert Kelly during his life in America's largest federal prison.

Mr. Kelly has written five other books, three of which are also non-fiction works. They are called <u>The Federal Reserve Trilogy</u>. These books include <u>The $30 Trillion Heist---Scene Of The Crime?</u>, <u>The $30 Trillion Heist---Follow The Money!</u> and <u>D'Apocalypse™ Now!---The Doomsday Cycle</u>. Together, they prove vital to the discovery of the truth of what the bankers did to America during the credit crisis. They will also help you become prepared for the dangers heading our way---both societally and economically. The forecasts made in <u>D'Aocalypse Now!</u> were profound and eerily accurate by 2017. The predictions of this book, originally written in 2013, include the Dow Jones Industrial average reaching 22,000, the Euro collapsing from $1.36 (today it is at $1.06) and gold would drop from near $2,000 to at least below $1,200 (Gold dropped, so far to nearly $1,100/ounce, before bouncing).

Without a proper understanding of the Federal Reserve, readers will find it difficult to understand why America has changed dramatically---in seemingly dastardly ways, at all points of the compass. It is only through the process of education, can real reform be accomplished. Understanding the fact the Federal Reserve is *the problem* will be critical to the reader's ability to educate Congressmen, Senators, neighbors and friends.

It is hoped these works, together with Mr. Kelly's fiction works, Blood Moon Over D'Apocalypse™ and Black Storm: Curse on the Caliphate, will highlight important issues Americans need to pursue in their quest for justice against the elite, the banks and the Federal Reserve System in the aftermath of the great D'Apocalypse™ and The $30 Trillion Heist.

If you don't know Jesus Christ and you are led by the Holy Spirit, pray to Jesus for your salvation and watch the miracle of a changed life begin to take place. You will no longer fear for the future, but will find you are now in the army of God and are one of His confident foot soldiers who KNOWS they will be victorious in the end. It is a great retirement plan.

Depending on where you are in your life, here are three different prayers which might help you in your search for the truth in faith through our Lord and Savior Jesus Christ.

God Bless You! He is mighty, indeed!!

1) FOREVER CHANGE YOUR LIFE!

"Dear God, the sole God for all eternity, I pray in your son's name, Jesus Christ, to please forgive my sins and hear my prayer. I accept Jesus Christ as my Lord and personal savior and believe you sent Him from heaven to earth, where He was born of the Virgin Mary. I believe in His life, His teachings, His horrible death and the sacrifice He made for my sins---and all mankind's sins. I KNOW AND BELIEVE HIS RESURRECTION IS TRUE AND I KNOW AND BELIEVE HE ASCENDED INTO HEAVEN AND SITS AT THE RIGHT HAND OF THE FATHER. I accept your gift and promise of eternal life through faith in Jesus Christ, for you have promised us by your grace, the grace of the one and only eternal God, I can be saved through the gift of faith. I also know my earthly works will not get me into your heavenly kingdom because you don't want any man to boast. I know we are created in Jesus to do good works out of the love and gratefulness we have for your mercy, power and gift of eternal life through the sacrifice made for us by Jesus Christ, your son and savior. AMEN"

"**For it is by grace you have been saved, through faith—and this is not from yourselves, it is the gift of God—not by works, so that no one can boast. For we are God's handiwork, created in Christ Jesus to do good works, which God prepared in advance for us to do.**" (Source: The Bible, Ephesians 2:8-10, New International Version).

"**For God so loved the world that He gave His only begotten son, that whosoever believeth in Him should not perish, but have eternal life.**" (Source: The Bible, John 3:16, King James Version).

If you pray this prayer, or a form of prayer accepting Jesus Christ as your Lord and Savior, I urge you to find brothers and sisters in Christ to nurture your walk with God. The Holy Spirit will guide you and you will notice a difference in the way you walk and talk through life.....you will see differences in your attitudes and actions. Embrace these, read and study His Holy Word, The Bible, and REPENT of your sins. Your heart will naturally want to do good works, because you realize what an amazing *free* gift has been given to you---ETERNAL LIFE!

After all the reading, studying, successes, failures, sacrifices and opportunities in life---there is only one thing which matters.

Jesus.

To any and all backsliders who are out there—I urge you to read the Holy Scripture and take heed and warning. Pray for the strength to overcome evil with good AND DO SO!!

2) BACKSLIDER'S MAKE OR BREAK TIME!

"What good is it, my brothers and sisters, if someone claims to have faith but has no deeds? Can such faith save them? Suppose a brother or a sister is without clothes and daily food. If one of you says to them, 'Go in peace; keep warm and well fed,' but does nothing about their physical needs, what good is it? In the same way, faith by itself, if it is not accompanied by action, is dead.

But someone will say, 'You have faith; I have deeds.' Show me your faith without deeds, and I will show you my faith by my deeds. You believe that there is one God. Good! Even the demons believe that—and shudder.

You foolish person, do you want evidence that faith without deeds is useless? Was not our father Abraham considered righteous for what he did when he offered his son Isaac on the altar? You see that his faith and his actions were working together, and his faith was made complete by what he did. And the scripture was fulfilled that says, "Abraham believed God, and it was credited to him as righteousness," and he was called God's friend. You see that a person is considered righteous by what they do and not by faith alone.

In the same way, was not even Rahab the prostitute considered righteous for what she did when she gave lodging to the spies and sent them off in a different direction? As the body without the spirit is dead, so faith without deeds is dead." (Source: The Bible, James 2:14-24, New International Version).

Sadly, there are millions of souls who believe in Jesus, but go back to their old ways of sin after they have received Jesus as their savior and don't do any good works. The Holy Scripture is very clear on this topic. FAITH WITHOUT WORKS IS DEAD.

If you truly have given your heart and life to Jesus Christ, your natural desire---and your own predetermined destiny, is to do good deeds! Backsliders, one and all, you must believe in the imminence of His arrival and I implore you to make a different, real change in your life.

Remember...*"Even the demons believe...and they shudder."* (Source: The Bible, James 2:19 NIV)

It is not enough to just "believe." Make a difference in the life around you---just as Jesus and the disciples did, and "do" for other people. Help them, pray for them, feed them, cloth them, return to a simpler life (e.g., Jesus and His disciples didn't have any worldly possessions). Do not go down the slippery slope of, "Well, the Lord blessed me with this, so it is all OK...."

"It is easier for a camel to go through the eye of a needle, than for a rich man to enter into the kingdom of God." (Source: The Bible, Matthew 19:23-24, KJV)

Of course, the wealthy will go on to the next words of Jesus when the disciples asked Him who can be saved and Jesus replied all things are possible for God.

The admonition is clear, however, the wealthy shall be scrutinized very carefully by our heavenly and just God.

The disciples themselves gave up EVERYTHING THEY HAD TO FOLLOW JESUS. They all changed. They were all afraid at His death and went into hiding (fearful the Romans and the Jews would crucify them, just as they had Jesus), but they became ferocious and vociferous zealots for Christ---brandishing the helmet of salvation, the shield of faith, while swinging with all of their might, the sword of the Holy Spirit. They died martyrs' deaths, with one spared to write the Book of Revelation---the Book of the Apocalypse, who of course was the Apostle John.

It was quite a change for a small group of men---all once terrified and in hiding, yet every one of them became unafraid to die for Christ. I don't know of a single case in history where any person, let alone an entire group of people (except John, spared to write the Book of Revelation, the Book of the Apocalypse) would die for a lie when they could have just walked away.

3) THE MOST DANGEROUS ROUTE TO HELL IS BEING TOO COMFORTABLE!

"Then Peter said to Him, 'Behold, we have left everything and followed You; what then will there be for us?' And Jesus said to them, 'Truly I say to you, that you who have followed Me, in the regeneration when the Son of Man will sit on His glorious throne, you also shall sit upon twelve thrones, judging the twelve tribes of Israel. And everyone who has left houses or brothers or sisters or father or mother or children or farms for My name's sake, will receive many times as much, and will inherit eternal life. But many who are first will be last; and the last, first.'"
(Source: The Bible, Matthew 19:27-30, New American Standard Version).

The biggest miracle Jesus gives us ALL is the miraculous change He brings to those who truly give themselves to Him. This is the miracle of a changed life. If you are not saved through the blood of Christ and your absolute faith in His resurrection and teachings, pray to God as you have been led by the Holy Spirit. Ask for His forgiveness in His son's name, Jesus Christ, and commit your life to Him. SEEK other like-minded individuals who can help you learn more about your new walk and birth in Jesus. This is what Jesus meant when He said you cannot enter the Kingdom of Heaven---UNLESS YOU ARE BORN AGAIN!!

Finally, for all you backsliders out there, whether RICH or POOR, Jesus did not put a limit on how many times you can ask for, AND RECEIVE, complete forgiveness and thus eternal life in Heaven.

With your new life, you have a new beginning. Make the most of it---for His glory and not your own.

I hope and pray you always choose the side of might for right, and if my story and tale of woe touches you, then it was worth it. Sometimes God can only use us in His work, when we are stripped down to nothing.

It is only at this moment of a man's, or woman's life, when their true character shines. Please always keep the faith, just like Job did...and just like I did, no matter what!

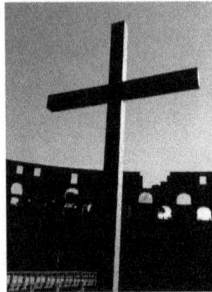

Christian Cross in the Roman Coliseum

340

www.ingramcontent.com/pod-product-compliance
Lightning Source LLC
LaVergne TN
LVHW051450080426
835509LV00017B/1725